PETER BEARDSLEY

PETER BEARDSLEY

MY LIFE STORY

CollinsWillow

An Imprint of HarperCollins*Publishers*

To Sandra, Drew and Stacey

Published in hardback in 1995
by CollinsWillow
an imprint of HarperCollins*Publishers*
London

First published in paperback in 1996

1 3 5 7 9 8 6 4 2

A CIP catalogue record for this book is
available from the British Library

ISBN 0 00 218705 1

Printed in Great Britain by
Caledonian International Book Manufacturing Ltd, Glasgow

Photographic acknowledgements
The publishers would like to thank the following for their permission to
reproduce copyright photographs (identified by page in plates section;
t: top, c: centre, b: bottom, l: left, r: right): Allsport 5c, 13b, 15bl, 16t;
Action Images 9t, 10b, 13c, 16b; Associated Sports Photography 2b, 4t,
5b, 12bl; Colorsport 3b, 4b, 5t, 6t,bl, 7b, 10t, 11, 12t, 13t,; Empics 6br,
13t, 14c,b, 15c; Ian Horrocks 15 br; Hulton Deutsch 8t; Newcastle
Chronicle 1t, 3t, 7t; News Team International 2t; Popperfoto 9b, 14c;
Professional Sport 9c, 12br, 15t; Rex Features 8b;
Syndication International 10c

CONTENTS

FOREWORD
by Kevin Keegan

It just seemed like any one of the many trips to the North-East that I had made in my two seasons as a Newcastle player between August 1982 and May 1984. I certainly did not notice the young lad sitting in the departure lounge at Heathrow Airport waiting to catch the flight to Tyneside. Had he walked up to me and said, 'Hello Kevin, I'm Peter Beardsley and I'll be playing at Newcastle with you' it still would not have registered because I hadn't even heard of him. But, of course, 'Pedro', which was the nickname I was to give him, would never have done that … being presumptuous is just not his style.

I have since learned in the time I have been associated with Peter as his team-mate and now his manager that he prefers to let his talent do his talking. He is still the same quiet, unobtrusive character as on that September evening eleven years ago. Fame – and he has had plenty of it – has left him totally unspoiled. He can do things on the field that people marvel at. What they might consider even more remarkable is that he thinks he is lucky to be a footballer in the first place. He lives every day taking nothing for granted, getting maximum enjoyment from the situation he finds himself in.

His whole life has been and still is a love affair with football.

I have never met anybody either as a player or manager who has demonstrated more enthusiasm for the game. In Yorkshire where I come from we have an expression which sums up in a couple of words the highest esteem and respect one person could have for another. I could not think of a better way to describe Peter Beardsley ... he is a reet smasher!

INTRODUCTION

I have one major regret as I progress further into the autumn of my football career. I just wish I was starting all over again! I would settle for being 25 instead of 35. There have been ups and downs, successes and failures, delights and disappointments, triumphs and tragedies. In my sixteen years as a professional, the game could not have been more generous. It has won me trophies, taken me to faraway places, given me financial security, introduced me to prime ministers and princes – and found me a wife. And all because I was blessed with a talent that set me apart from thousands of other kids; one that plucked me from the factory floor and put me on the world's great soccer stages. No wonder I see the lads just starting out and those with their feet already on the bottom few rungs of the professional ladder and feel more than a touch of envy. I look at the likes of Lee Clark, Steve Watson, Steve Howey and Keith Gillespie, my young team-mates at Newcastle, and visualize their future. For them it is only just beginning and I would love to be in their shoes. If I wished them all that has happened to me, I could not wish them any more. I wouldn't change anything I have done. The shame of it all is it cannot go on for ever and ever.

I haven't won a World Cup – but I have come within a penalty kick of a final. I have won league championship medals and known what it is like to have them snatched from my hand. I have experienced the ecstasy of FA Cup victory and devastation of Final defeat. It would be churlish, therefore, to dwell on things that might have been, like the possibility of being part of a Liverpool side which added to their four fabulous European Cup triumphs. We twice earned the right to compete while I was at Anfield but that was at a time when the door to the Continent was closed. It is more than enough consolation now to know I have played with the best for the best.

And the story has not finished. If the great Stanley Matthews played until he was fifty plus, I can surely hang in there for a few more years, and no player could have more reason to squeeze every last second out of his playing life. Things are going to happen at Newcastle over the next few years and I am determined to be part of it.

I have already extended my football perimeters since returning to St James' Park in the summer of 1993. Two seasons ago I kicked my first ball in European competition. It was an experience to savour and one I will be happy to repeat later this year. Only next time I'll make sure it lasts a little longer.

1

THIRTY SOMETHING ... AND STILL GOING STRONG

Having qualified for Europe in 1994/95 after Newcastle's magnificent first term back in big-time football, losing in the second round of the UEFA Cup was one of the major disappointments of the year. The irony of it all was, having waited with growing frustration to play in Europe, when the opportunity came around I thought I was going to miss out. In fact I regarded my chances of playing in the first game against Royal Antwerp as practically nil.

By an amazing coincidence I began my second season at Newcastle as I had the first – in hospital. History had almost repeated itself when I broke my right cheekbone in the opening game at Leicester City, the only difference being that a year earlier it was the opposite side of my face and, unlike that injury, the Filbert Street collision was a pure accident. But that was not much of a consolation as I faced the prospect of missing out again on important games. The Leicester fixture could not have started better for us. I made a goal for Andy Cole and added a second myself, shooting through the keeper's legs after side-stepping a City defender. Then Robbie Elliott came on as substitute and rattled in the third and we were cruising at 3–0.

Then the lights went out. As I have said, it was a freak accident. The ball was played to me by Marc Hottiger, our Swiss international full back, and I turned sharply but straight into Steve Thompson, the Leicester City midfielder, whose shoulder smashed into my face. I knew from experience that it was serious, a fact which was confirmed by our physio Derek Wright when he came running on to the pitch. Derek, who for my money is the top man in the game at his job, shook his head and just said , 'Sorry Peter, but it looks like you've done it again.' Steve was really upset about it. He later wrote me a letter wishing me a speedy recovery; he was particularly sympathetic because he had only just returned from a long injury lay-off himself.

I was carried into the dressing-room where Arthur Cox, my former Newcastle manager who is now on the club's coaching staff, packed ice on my face to try and keep the swelling down. Just then the City club doctor came in and, to our amazement, inquired whether I was going back on or would we be bringing on the sub. Arthur politely drew his attention to my face and mentioned that it was hardly likely I would be taking any further part in the game. I went through the familiar hospital routine of X-rays and examinations before it was decided to ferry me back to the North-East.

Now one thing we're not short of at Newcastle is style. My 'ambulance' to the Nuffield Hospital on Tyneside was nothing less than a Rolls-Royce belonging to our vice-chairman Freddie Shepherd! I was examined by a specialist and the following morning moved to a bigger hospital in the City – with a hospital dressing gown covering my football strip – where I underwent surgery to set the cheekbone. They estimated I would be out of the game for four weeks, which would certainly rule me out of our first round UEFA Cup match in Belgium against Royal Antwerp.

I couldn't believe my bad luck. Here I was missing out again on the euphoria of the start of Newcastle's season. And what a start – four successive wins, with Coventry City, Southampton and West Ham all suffering Leicester's fate, and Andy Cole in rampant form as he followed up his record-breaking first season in the FA Carling Premiership by averaging a goal a game at the start of this campaign. My concern was not only how soon I could get fit but whether I would get back into the side when I was.

That particular worry was eased somewhat as we prepared for our fifth Premiership match, against Chelsea. The gaffer, Kevin Keegan, came to me after our final training session the day before the game and asked me if I fancied playing. 'Not a problem,' I answered enthusiastically. I had been doing a lot of running and generally keeping myself in shape and I couldn't wait to get started again. Unfortunately, the club doctor expressed a few doubts and the boss had no option but to leave me out of the side. The players then made it even harder for him to change the team by walloping the Pensioners 4–2 with Andy scoring another couple – and apparently revelling in the absence of the man who was supposed to be his striking partner!

The Antwerp game was the following Tuesday. I was convinced I didn't have a prayer about playing. Why should the boss risk me in a vital game, especially after five wins on the trot? I was asking myself the same question on the plane over to Belgium when Keegan sat himself in the seat next to me and said, 'What do you think, Pedro? You're in.' I thought I was going there just to watch but I was playing after all – and I jumped at the chance. We trained on the evening before the game and I felt good afterwards, even more so when the boss

15

got us all together and announced that I would be playing. It was hard on Steve Watson who was relegated to the subs' bench after playing magnificently in the opening games of the season and scoring three goals. To his credit 'Watto' swallowed his disappointment and told me I was the only player he would have been happy to drop out for.

As it turned out the lad still played his part in a magnificent team performance. He came on for me late on and completed a five-goal hammering of Antwerp. It was a night of celebration too for Rob Lee who scored a hat-trick, taking his season's tally to eight in six games, and for Philippe Albert, our Belgian international defender, who made a happy return to his native country. The second leg a fortnight later was academic. We led 5–0 again with Coley proving anything Rob could do, he could match – his hat-trick gave him ten for the season so far. Rob and I knocked in the other two. Antwerp came back with two consolation goals that hardly seemed to matter but in hindsight were a warning which maybe we should have taken more notice of. As far as I was concerned my European delight was long overdue. I was especially proud to be captain and lead Newcastle back into Europe after an absence of nearly twenty years.

By the time it came around to our next UEFA Cup venture against Athletic Bilbao from Spain, we were really buzzing and establishing ourselves as one of the favourites to win the competition. Defeat seemed out of the question when Ruel Fox, Coley and myself catapulted us into a three-goal lead in the first leg at St James' Park. Maybe we thought it was too easy; maybe in our naivety we went chasing another hatful instead of tightening things up and settling for what would certainly have been a winning margin. We learned our lesson the hard way – Bilbao caught us twice on the break with sucker goals and suddenly the stroll had become a struggle. We played well in the return in front of the fiercely partisan Basque supporters, but not well enough to prevent them scoring the goal which got them through on the away-goals rule. We were very disappointed but at least we had given ourselves and the supporters a taste of European football – something we want a lot more of.

What made it worse was that the Bilbao setback came only three days after we lost our first league game of the season against Manchester United at Old Trafford. We had led the Premiership table from the start of the season with six successive victories and recording nine wins and two draws in our first eleven games. My first league game was at Highbury against Arsenal and it could not have gone better. We beat the Gunners 3–2 and I scored twice, the first a deflected shot and the second a penalty.

As luck would have it, the first points we dropped were against Liverpool at home. I suppose something had to go wrong that day because there was a mood of high expectancy as the club was also celebrating the 25th anniversary of its victory in the Inter Cities Fairs Cup, the forerunner to the UEFA Cup. All the Newcastle players involved in that Cup run, including my first manager Bob Moncur, were introduced to the crowd before the match. There had been suggestions that Liverpool had gone off the boil a little but they played well that day and we were a bit lucky to be goalless at half-time. The gaffer gave us a bit of a dressing-down during the break, telling us we weren't winning our tackles and we needed to be more committed. Liverpool played for the first time with three centre-backs, with Phil Babb playing his first full game alongside Neil Ruddock and John Scales. We improved in the second half and Rob Lee scored a good goal to put us ahead, but then my former scoring partner Ian Rush equalized with a shot that our keeper Pavel Srnicek was disappointed he did not save. To make matters worse, we had Albert sent off for a second bookable offence and in the end we had to settle for a 1–1 draw.

Two weeks later we faced another big challenge to our leadership of the Premiership when Blackburn Rovers came to St James' Park. Kenny Dalglish had again pushed the boat out during the summer to break the English transfer record by paying £5 million for Chris Sutton, who had struck up a great partnership up front with Alan Shearer. Sutton was a big pal of Ruel Fox at Norwich and Foxy had warned us what to expect. But it was Shearer who maintained his great scoring record against his hometown club. He knocked in a penalty which looked like ending our unbeaten record until, much to our relief, Steve Howey rocketed in an equalizer two minutes from the end. I think the boss summed up our performance that day when he told the media afterwards that we were far from our best and that we lacked real passion or urgency. There was some excuse for me because I picked up a thigh injury which forced me to pull out of the England squad for the game against Romania the following Wednesday.

By the end of October we were still on top of the pile and went to Old Trafford as the Premiership's last unbeaten side. In the end, we couldn't grumble about the result. United, champions in the two previous seasons, were clearly up for it with something to prove against a side which at the time was threatening to take their title away from them. To be fair, they played like champions, never giving us time to settle and achieving a standard of football that even they have found hard to match since. Gary Pallister put them ahead with a great header and Keith Gillespie, demonstrating the skill which later encouraged the boss to sign him for Newcastle, came off the bench and scored the second after a brilliant solo run. We were never at the races.

I have to be honest and say that we were never really a threat in the league after that, although on occasions we did show what we were capable of. We upheld our reputation for being one of the most watchable sides in the league, especially against Spurs at the beginning of May. It was acclaimed later as the best match seen at St James' Park for a long time and it was easy to understand why. It had everything. Keith Gillespie and Darren Peacock, with his first goal since arriving at the club from Queen's Park Rangers, gave us a two-goal lead early on. But Spurs came back with an astonishing burst of three goals in about five minutes. Then we had Pavel Srnicek sent off for bringing down Nicky Barmby in the box. Mike Hooper went in goal and it looked curtains when Jurgen Klinsmann strode up to take the penalty. But Mike made a great save with his feet and, even with ten men, I thought that gave us a chance of snatching a result. Colin Calderwood joined Pav for a premature bath to even up the sides and it was a special thrill for me to have the final say when I managed to equalize, chesting down a bouncing ball and shooting low to Ian Walker's left. The goal was my hundredth in a Newcastle shirt, which was a terrific milestone. Typically, the first to congratulate me was Arthur Cox. He knew it was important and how much it meant.

The Old Trafford game was the only time I felt we were really second best all season, which cannot be bad over 42 games. I believe we gave a clearer indication of what we were capable of when we played Blackburn, the team destined to be crowned champions, in our penultimate game of the season. As it turned out it was the match which eventually gave

Rovers the title but we showed we were more than their equal. In fact we camped out in their half for the second period and they were only rescued by a series of magnificent saves by their keeper Tim Flowers. Everybody later acclaimed one stop he made from a shot that I caught just right. Tim is a great keeper but on that occasion I felt he had made a meal of it. It was just the right height for him and I don't think it needed the exaggerated dive.

Alan Shearer, the player whom I believe did most to win the championship for Kenny Dalglish, had scored early on but we battered them after that without getting the equalizer we deserved. Keegan came in afterwards and told us the game was a measure of how close we were to being the best. At the end of the day it was a result that would cost us a place in Europe but even that took second place to the self-belief the game gave us. When the title was finally decided, the Blackburn fans rightly gave their team a wonderful reception at their special gala night at Ewood Park when they paraded the Carling Premiership trophy. They were worthy champions, but when it came to a contest between their supporters and the Toon Army they came a bad second. The black and white brigade are the best in the business.

The occasion could hardly have been lost on Shearer, who may have spread his football wings but is still a Geordie at heart. He has expressed a desire to wear a black and white shirt some time in his career and I believe that will happen. I don't see him moving to St James' Park to finish his career, but I do think it would have to be in the next five years when he is at his peak. He knows too much about what is important to the Newcastle fans to go to the club when he is past his best. One of my lasting memories of the trophy presentation was the picture of him gazing at his title medal. I know the feeling, but I also know if he matched that achievement as a Newcastle player his satisfaction would be even greater.

The two domestic cup competitions promised much for our supporters but in the end produced little. The players have to shoulder the responsibility for that. We got as far as the fourth round of the Coca-Cola Cup, beating Barnsley and then ousting a Manchester United side that was far from what could be considered their most formidable line-up. At the time their manager Alex Ferguson clearly had greater priorities in the European Cup and the Premiership, which he proved by turning out a much stronger side three days later when we went to Old Trafford for our league match. If United weren't too concerned about the Coca-Cola, we were happy to oblige them even though they could look back and say they won the game that mattered. Their neighbours Manchester City turned out to be less accommodating, although we did the hard part, going to Maine Road with a below strength side and earning a replay with young Mike Jeffrey's goal. We should have beaten City at home and played well enough to do so but couldn't take our chances and then got punished for defensive mistakes.

But it was the FA Cup which was the real tragedy ... another instance where we appeared to have success on the horizon only to watch it slowly disappear from view. The first hurdle could hardly have been tougher and our chances of further progress seemed doubtful when we failed to beat Blackburn at home. Rob Lee levelled Chris Sutton's opener with a great goal, but Rovers were odds-on to win the replay and I was especially frustrated at having to miss the game through injury. Not for the last time we demonstrated that we need feel no inferiority complex when matched against Dalglish's team. Marc Hottiger's unstoppable, swerving shot gave us a deserved lead and although Sutton squared the game, Lee Clark's equally superb goal gave us a memorable 2–1 victory.

I couldn't have been more pleased for Lee if I had scored myself, especially because he had been getting a lot of stick about not getting his name on the scoresheet. The goal was a fitting climax to a terrific individual performance which underlined just what a talented player he is. He almost predicted it on the morning of the game when he grabbed me and said, 'I'm hot, Pedro – I really fancy it.' I think the lad has a great future in the game. His situation at Newcastle was similar to the one I was in at Liverpool. He did nothing wrong and played well enough but the competition for first team places was so fierce that he often missed out. He found the situation difficult to accept, especially having been a regular in the side, and I for one appreciate that. He is still only 23 but until he picked up a serious foot injury towards the end of the 1993/94 season he had hardly missed a game for three years. I think the gaffer and everybody else at the club wants him to stay. I have talked to him a lot and I know the only club that matters to him is Newcastle; he is black and white through and through. But he has insisted he wants first team football and the manager told him he cannot guarantee that, as much as he would like to. I don't think there is any player at the club whose situation is as strong as that.

I have known Lee since my first spell at Newcastle when he was a 14-year-old schoolboy who came for coaching sessions in the evenings and during the holidays. I used to look after him and try and help him because I knew then he was going to be a good player. He has already represented England at Youth and Under-21 levels and I have no doubts he will one day play for the full international side. He has everything it takes to make it to the top, as he proved in the Cup victory over Blackburn.

The following Cup-tie against Swansea City was a triumph for Paul Kitson, who hasn't had the best of times since he arrived from Derby County. He showed just what an asset he is going to be at Newcastle with a brilliant hat-trick to get us into round five. Revenge could not have been sweeter when Manchester City were our next victims. Appropriately it was the game that young Keith Gillespie got his name on the scoresheet for the first time since he moved to Newcastle from Manchester United. Keith helped himself to a couple of goals and confirmed his growing reputation with another superb performance. He stole the thunder a little from John Beresford who claimed a rare goal with an effort which he swore later was intended as a shot but which myself and the rest of the lads thought looked more like a cross.

That got us into the last eight and a sixth round trip to play my old club Everton who couldn't have complained if they had been dead and buried by half-time. We murdered them in the first half and although we let them off the hook after that, I couldn't see us losing the game. Then they scored a scrappy goal through Dave Watson, a player whose competitive qualities I have always admired. Even then we wasted several chances to force at least a replay. It is always sad to go out of the FA Cup but we felt it particularly tough that day because I honestly thought we could go all the way and perhaps win the trophy. As it turned out, our conquerors made it all the way to the Final where they put on a tremendously professional performance to see off the holders and favourites, Manchester United. And who was Man of the Match? None other than Dave Watson!

In the end it was all a bit of an anti-climax. After carrying all before us, our results in the latter half of the season could have been better. We managed to finish sixth in the Premiership, but Everton's FA Cup triumph meant that they qualified for Europe in the Cup-Winners' Cup, while Manchester United took what would have been our place in the UEFA Cup by virtue of losing the FA Cup Final but finishing second in the championship.

They say you should never offer injuries as an excuse but we suffered as much as any side during the 1994/95 season from not having the strength in depth the boss would have liked. Paul Bracewell, Lee Clark, Philippe Albert, Robbie Elliott, Scott Sellars, Barry Venison, John Beresford and myself were all out for varying spells, some much longer than others. The loss of Philippe for such a long time robbed the fans of what should have been a football treat. I had remembered him from the World Cup playing for Belgium: he looked a class act then and I could never imagine that a player with such international status would join Newcastle.

He is something different in the English game. He is a defender but not as we have been accustomed to knowing them. He is more skilful than most and is not someone who goes round kicking opponents. Philippe reads the game tremendously and then eats up the ground to get to where he wants to be. He is also a superb professional and his presence at the club has clearly rubbed off on the younger lads who have seen how he applies himself in training and how much importance he attaches to physical condition. Newcastle have bought foreign players in the past but none with the reputation or value of Philippe. It was a serious setback when he damaged his knee ligaments in training early in the season. The first I knew of it was when he was carried into the treatment room where I was having a spell on the table. It was

24

a bad injury, but hopefully he will be back at the start of the season ready to show everybody what they have been missing.

The club also imported another World Cup star in Marc Hottiger, who may not have the charisma of Philippe but who has made just as much of an impact. I rate him very highly and I think, at times, he is almost too switched-on. The club paid a little over half a million pounds for Marc and made a quick profit when they sold him to Everton last season. In their first season in English football, Marc and Philippe allowed the fans a glimpse of just how good they could be. In future years clubs will look increasingly to the Continent for top players but they will not come any better than these.

The fact that Newcastle were able to attract such high quality continental stars proves the change in attitude at St James' Park. The club has a record for under-achievement which has lasted far too long. The harsh fact is we have not won the top League Championship since 1927 and that is a disgrace. Why should the likes of Nottingham Forest, Derby County, Ipswich Town – and yes – even Arsenal, Leeds, Liverpool and Manchester United have managed that while Newcastle have languished in their so-called deeply-hidden potential? Fortunately times are changing. As I have said I have already achieved most of the things I set out to do in football but winning an honour with Newcastle would just about top it off.

Only time will tell whether I am involved, but I will confidently predict that Newcastle will win the Championship within the next three years. I have absolutely no doubts about that. In many ways our disappointments in the latter half of the past season will prepare us better for what lies ahead. We finished three places lower than the previous season, and on the face of it people are entitled to think our league placing might suggest we have deteriorated as a side. That is far from the reality of the situation. The second season was all about establishing ourselves as one of the top clubs and there cannot be many who would not recognize Newcastle as being in that category. There will be no going back to the days of settling for mid-table mediocrity. The people behind the club will make sure of that.

I think the boss summed it up when he used the word 'disappointing' to describe a season which began so well for the team and ended with us failing to clinch a place in Europe. It was a serious setback which proved you cannot rely on other teams to do you favours. We went into the last game against Crystal Palace knowing we had to win and at the same time Leeds United had to lose at Tottenham to get us there. Beating Palace 3–2 sent them into the First Division but, unfortunately for us, Leeds took a point at White Hart Lane and with it our spot in the UEFA Cup. Even then we still had a chance had Manchester United beaten Everton in the FA Cup Final but that was not to be either, and the depression we felt then was nothing compared with what we felt when the European competitions got under way the following season.

I suppose our supporters must feel like those of Manchester United who were going for their second successive League-Cup double on the last day of the league season and ended up with nothing. Of course, their consolation will be a place in the UEFA Cup but even that must be regarded as something of an underachievement. They say you get what you deserve in the league and sadly that might have been the case as far as both teams were concerned. Looking back, the crucial game was the visit of Leeds which was the only league game we lost at St James's Park that season. We lost 2–1 and it was not one of our better performances. We only took five points out of a last possible 18 although we murdered both Blackburn and Spurs and managed only one point. I don't think there were many times in the season where we won points our performances did not merit, but there were several games when we perhaps deserved a little more than we got.

As I have said, injuries didn't help our situation. The gaffer mentioned a conversation he had with our physio who said that twice as many players received treatment during the season than the one before. But his priority will be to secure a big enough squad to cope if that situation occurs again in the future. From a personal point of view I would have done better than scoring 15 goals. It was not a big enough return. I certainly should have got a lot closer to the 24 I bagged in my first season back at Newcastle.

People will inevitably point to the departure of Andy Cole, who was transferred to Manchester United in January for £7 million. It was without question the biggest topic of debate throughout the season and it is easy for anybody to say that had he stayed at the club he might have scored the goals that would have secured our European place. That is all pure conjecture but, while wishing Andy the best of luck at Old Trafford, it is worth pointing out that we were only fifth in the table when he left and he had only scored once in his previous eleven games. It was a tough decision to sell Andy but it is water under the bridge now and the future is what is important.

When Liverpool sold Kevin Keegan to Hamburg they said life would never be the same at Anfield but they replaced him with Kenny Dalglish and became an even more dominant side. The Cole controversy will run and run but the gaffer has earned, by what he has achieved already at Newcastle, if not the benefit of any doubt then certainly to be allowed to use his judgement in buying and selling players. The money he has received from the Cole deal put him in a formidable position which he has exploited in some style. Newcastle topped the summer transfer league in an incredible three days' spending at the beginning of June. First we had the arrival of Warren Barton for £4 million and, as we found our later, when Warren was signed, the boss had already finalised the £6 million purchase of Les Ferdinand. I couldn't wait for the season to start. Both players will be tremendous assets at Newcastle and I looked forward to playing with them.

There were similarities in the Premiership between our situation and that of Nottingham Forest. Like us they have gone like a bomb in their first season back, with an incredible second half which carried them into the third spot and a place in Europe for the coming season. But their big test will be whether they can sustain that. I had no doubts whatsoever that would finish above them in 1995/96.

We will be even bettered prepared. There is a great psychological advantage in knowing what to expect and the Premiership holds no secrets for us now. There have been lessons which we have learned and will benefit from. We started with a bang last year but because of a lack of resources could not sustain it. That will not happen again. A side has to be something special to succeed these days in the top flight. The competition has never been tougher. Blackburn collected a massive 89 points and could still have lost the title on the last day. Their first championship for 81 years has cost the club's owner Jack Walker £60 million but he has proved money talks and he will not stop there. Manchester United will not take the runners-up spot lying down. They too have a capacity to spend big to improve what is already a quality side. I also expect my two former Merseyside clubs Liverpool and Everton to be in challenging mode and I would not rule out Spurs or Arsenal trying to muscle in on what has been an almost total domination of the game by the North.

One club I would like to see do well is Middlesbrough, for whom Bryan Robson has done a magnificent job in his first season in management. Boro' came out on top in a keenly fought conclusion to the First Division promotion race. 'Robbo' has clearly taken a leaf out of Kevin Keegan's book and I could see them following the example set by ourselves and Forest in their first season back at the top. That could mean a battle between up to ten teams for a place in Europe. Manchester United, with two titles and two runners-up spots in the last four years, are clearly the team of the Nineties so far but I cannot see them being allowed to dominate the Premiership in the way that Liverpool did ten years ago. There is far too much competition around for that. But there is a great divide developing between the teams who can sustain a heavy spending programme and the teams who cannot. You may get the odd one flirting on the fringe but that is as close as they will get. It may be sad for the low budget clubs who can only hope they may have their day in one-off situations like cup matches. But when it comes down to the league they will just become fodder for the big spenders.

I welcome the fact that the Premiership will be reduced to twenty teams. I think the reduction of fixtures will be of enormous benefit when it comes to accommodating the international and European programme. It will also mean a fairer spread of league matches with teams better equipped to make a challenge for all the honours. Even a club as powerful as Manchester United who, with a fully fit squad, could probably turn out two teams to compete in the Premiership, found it difficult to cope with a four-pronged bid for the European Cup, League Championship, FA and Coca-Cola Cups. In the end they finished up with a bare cupboard. The extra time for rest, recuperation and concentration on skills and technique can only improve the game as a spectacle and increase our chances of succeeding both internationally and in European competition.

I certainly believe my legs can stand up to two or three more years at the top. As I have said, that should encompass at least another championship medal to go with the two I won at Liverpool, but if I was to make a choice, I would plump for an FA Cup Final winner's medal. The thought of taking the Toon Army to Wembley thrills me no end. I could just picture the occasion, walking out of that tunnel and gazing around at a sea of black and white. If it happened I don't think there is a team in the country who could spoil the occasion by beating us. The league is one thing. It opens up a route to Europe that is paved with pound notes. But for sheer one-off enjoyment and excitement, there is nothing like that day in May.

I'll know when it is time to quit but my plans at the moment are to keep playing as long as possible. Then I want to stay in the game either in a coaching or management capacity. I hope I could reap the benefit of the lessons taught by the many talented men for whom I have worked. Ideally you would want to pick up on what you thought were the strengths and discard any possible weaknesses, but one thing I have learned is that being a football club manager takes a special kind of person. The job can take you from the heights of ecstasy to the depths of despair in successive matches. I suppose, if offered the opportunity one day, I would have to give it a go. I would want somebody alongside me who I could rely on and trust – someone to be there for support and advice when I needed it.

Even now there are people I would always listen to because even at my age and knowing what I do, I am still learning. I respect and take notice of what Kevin Keegan says. But Arthur Cox, my former Newcastle manager has been even more of an influence and is the man I would look to for guidance even more than the boss. I have spoken to Arthur at least once a week ever since the days he was in charge at St James' Park. He has always been on the end of a telephone, and I have valued his conversation and encouragement. I remember when I got into the World Cup squad in 1986 he wrote me a letter congratulating me on getting there. It was a simple gesture which meant a lot.

I look at Kevin Keegan sometimes and wonder how he has the capacity to handle all the different situations which occur in the everyday running of a Premiership team. There is certainly a lot more to the job than buying players and picking a team. A boss has to be on call 24 hours of the day to deal with the problems of his players. Sometimes I wonder what drives people to take on clubs in the lower divisions. More often than not, for not very much money, they are buying themselves a lot of heartache. The rewards are few and the pitfalls many. And it counts double at the top. What prospects were there for the likes of Colin Todd at Bolton whose anxiety was obvious for all to see in the last few crucial matches of last season? They are trying to emulate the achievements of their other more financially endowed colleagues with a fraction of the resources. Being in their shoes cannot be easy and yet they are the lifeblood of the game.

The difference between staying up and going down, in financial terms, amounts to millions. That means pressure from chairmen and directors. There can only be a few winners and the wages of failure are inevitable redundancy season. Any manager will tell you the only certainty about the job is the sack, and yet there is always a queue of possible successors. Football really is a funny old game ... only a lot of the time nobody is laughing.

Being honest, I think I am probably better suited to being a coach and one of my priorities at the end of my playing career will be to obtain the necessary qualifications. I hold the FA preliminary badge but I have never been available to take the full badge at the end of the season as I wouldn't exchange my international commitments to go on the course. Football has taken enormous strides forward since I signed my first professional contract and will continue to progress at a pace. I want very much to be part of what is going to happen to the game which has been both my love and my life.

2

WORKING HARD FOR A BREAK

To say I got into professional football by the back door would be an understatement comparable to suggesting Pavarotti is not a bad singer. It would be to simplify the struggle I had before somebody finally gave me the opportunity I had been hoping for ever since I was a schoolboy in short pants and the scourge of the neighbours in Longbenton, Newcastle.

My football education was normal for any kid from my background which was somewhere on the poor side of working class. I was born on 18 January 1961, one of a family of four children of parents Sammy and Catherine. I had two elder brothers, George and Ronnie, and a younger sister, Sandra. When I arrived in the world we lived in a block of council flats. They have since been knocked down to make way for more habitable dwellings – which shows the kind of neighbourhood I was brought up in.

My dad was a long-distance lorry driver who spent a lot of time on the road for just enough money to make sure we were all well fed and decently dressed, but there was never a penny to spare. One of the luxuries we could never afford was a holiday. On the odd occasion we went for a day trip to the seaside at nearby Whitley Bay or Tynemouth and once an aunt and uncle took me up to Seahouses on the Northumberland coast where we stayed in a caravan for a few days. That was it as far as holidays were concerned. They were something we either read about or watched on television. But it was still a happy upbringing despite the hardships and as a family we were very close. We still found plenty to amuse ourselves and what we never had we never missed.

While I was growing up there was a great sense of friend-ship and fellowship among everybody. You knew the score and just got on with life. Nobody made a song and dance about not having a lot of money because you knew there were a lot of people even worse off than yourself. When I look back, I have to wonder how my dad and mam managed to bring up a family of three boys and a girl on the money which came in. It did get better when my two brothers left school and started work but the luxuries of life were still well out of our financial reach. I'm lucky that football has enabled me to do things differently for my two children. Even so, they will always be taught the true values of life, for I wouldn't like them to stray too far away from their roots.

All the kids played football simply because it cost nothing but with me it was an uncontrollable addiction. Every available second I had was spent kicking a ball around in the street or on any waste patch of ground I could find. We used to play a game between lamp-posts, much to the annoyance of people who lived in the street as we were forever asking them if we could have our ball out of their gardens. My prize possession was the first football I ever owned. It was light and made of plastic and used to fly all over the place, especially when it was windy, but keeping that ball under control helped me to develop the skills which later took me right to the very pinnacle of the game I love.

With my dad away a lot, we were all given jobs to do. One of mine was going to the shops for my mam. I didn't mind – just as long as I took my precious ball with me. I used to kick it all the way there and back, working out little tricks and targets en route. I would play one-twos against garden gates and garage doors or try and keep it up either with my head or feet for the distance between each gate. Then I would stand in the queue at the shops with the ball tucked under my arm like some pet animal. I must have been a comical sight to the rest of the shoppers: small and scrawny, trousers flapping around my knees, the ball as much a part of me as my hands or feet. Everybody got so used to seeing me that on the rare occasions I went out without the ball, people would stop me every couple of yards and enquire after my health. 'Are you all right, Peter? Where's your ball today?' I sometimes wonder if they remember those days as much as I do.

I played a lot of football at school, firstly in the juniors at Somervyl School and later when I went to Longbenton High. I was sports mad and loved to join in with everything. I was scrum-half at rugby and wicketkeeper at cricket, although to be fair my limitations as a batsman were well known; enough for me never to be any higher than eleventh man in! I remember my first sports teacher was Mr Woodcock. He was an elderly chap with a young mind and we got on really well. I wish I could say I pleased the rest of my teachers. It wasn't that I was ever any trouble, for I never got into any mischief or anything like that. It was just that I wasn't the brightest pupil in the class. I was good at maths and perhaps if I had set my mind to it I could have been better at other subjects, but academically I never reached the level I should have done and I think the teachers resigned themselves to the fact. I just became known as 'Football-daft Peter' and they just basically left me alone. I certainly would not encourage my own kids to have the same attitude as I had.

I wouldn't say that I was particularly successful in school football. None of the teams I played in either at Somervyl or Longbenton High won any cups or trophies. The closest I came to winning a medal was when I was at Longbenton when I was 15 and just before I left school. We played Benfield School, whose team was captained by Steve Bruce, in the final of the Newcastle Schools Cup and drew 1–1. In those days when you drew a cup final you shared the trophy for six months each. There were no replays. It was a terrific performance because we had no reputation for being a football school and Benfield were, at the time, the top school in the city. We were definitely the underdogs.

I didn't really have any close pals, none that I could name anyway. Basically I kept myself to myself. I suppose I was a loner but never felt lonely. Football was my best friend. There was a group of six or seven of us who would always have the ball out but I couldn't pick out any who was more of a chum than any other.

Of course Newcastle were my team but I had to support them from outside St James' Park. It was a case of pressing my nose against the shop window. We hadn't the price of a ticket so I hardly saw them play. Once my brothers started work they would take me to the odd match but not very often. In fact I used to watch the reserves more than the first team because it only cost a few pence to get in. Nowadays clubs get a lot of bad publicity for the way they keeping bringing out new strips and, remembering how I was, I can understand why parents complain about having to pay for a different outfit every time a new one comes on to the market. After he started earning, my brother Ronnie bought me a football strip every Christmas. One I remember in particular was Coventry's with stripes down the front of the shirt and shorts. I was the proudest kid on the field wearing that. I didn't support the Sky Blues but I thought their strip was really something.

Strangely enough, one club I did develop a passion for, apart from Newcastle, happened to be north of the border. When I was about 14 years old I started taking a healthy interest in Celtic. Why? For no other reason than I became a big fan of their ace striker, Kenny Dalglish. In fact he was my boyhood idol. I just loved the way he played. It was strange I suppose because there were many possible football heroes nearer home, but as far as I was concerned, nobody could touch Dalglish. I used to nip into the paper shop and have a sly read through the football magazines whenever there was an article about him. And I was glued to the television whenever they showed him playing for either Celtic or Scotland.

Then in May 1975 I had the greatest thrill of my young life when I actually got the chance to see Dalglish in the flesh. The team I was playing for, Cramlington Juniors, went to Scotland to play a friendly against a youth side in East Kilbride. We all stayed with the families of the lads in their team. I had never been as far away from home before and it was all a bit of a novelty. But the highlight of the trip as far as I was concerned was going to Hampden Park to watch the Scottish Cup Final between Celtic and Airdrie. It was my first taste of a big match atmosphere and it is a memory that will live with me for the rest of my life. Celtic won 3–1 and Dalglish was everything I thought he would be. He was the example I wanted to follow. At the time it was just a wild boyhood dream. I could never have envisaged that not only would I get the opportunity to experience many times the kind of passion generated on the day by 80,000 fanatical Scotsmen, but I would actually come to know and play for the man who had such an early influence on my football career. Watching him in action only made me more determined than ever to fulfil my ambition to be a professional footballer.

I played a lot of football in those days for my school and in local junior leagues. But the games I really used to look forward to were the Sunday league matches when I eventually played in the same pub team as my brothers. Ronnie was a useful player; in fact later in life he had the chance to sign as a professional with Hartlepool but he was settled in the job he had since leaving school and it wouldn't have been worth it for him. But he and George turned out regularly for The Fusilier, our local pub in Longbenton. At first I used to turn up just to watch, but all the time I was itching to get out there and show them what I could do. I did get a few opportunities when somebody failed to turn up. I remember they used to stick me out on the right wing just for a laugh. But later when I reached 16, I started playing on a regular basis. The Beardsleys were some trio and we played in a few local cup finals together. In fact The Fusilier was a team to be feared. We won promotion three years in succession.

I had two spells with Wallsend Boys' Club. Every aspiring young player like me knew that, if you wanted to be spotted by one of the army of scouts who saturated the Tyneside area, you either had to play for Wallsend, Cramlington Juniors or Montague and North Fenham Boys' Club. They were akin to enrolling in a top drama school if you were a budding actor. Ironically my first experience of Wallsend was all too brief. I played in one game against another local boys' club and we won 17–2. To be honest, it was a waste of time. The other lads in the team told me it was always like that because they were so superior to all the other sides. Just to make the games interesting they used to do things like switch the defence and attack at half-time to get everybody involved. I got little pleasure or benefit out of games like that; I preferred a situation where the teams were more evenly matched instead of camping out in the opposition's half all the time. So I made my excuses and left, joining Longbenton Youth Club which was in the area where I lived. The games were harder but I was playing with my mates and it was a lot more fun.

Wallsend came back for me when I was 16 and this time I found the teams more evenly matched. It was the start of the most crucial time of my young life; a make or break period which was to shape my destiny. And the two men I have to thank for eventually pointing me in the direction I was desperate to go were both involved with that famous club which launched the careers of players like Steve Bruce, Alan Shearer and a good many others. Peter Kirkley ran the football side at Wallsend and his good friend Brian Watson, who did a bit of scouting for Carlisle United, was always around to offer advice. Everybody loved Brian. He was a great character, always laughing and joking but behind that cheerful exterior was a shrewd, extremely knowledgeable football brain.

I don't believe that I played too much football as a schoolboy. I know the authorities these days are aiming to cut down on the number of games kids play because they feel it could cause problems later on in life, but I had a kick-about every day and played in at least two games a week and it hasn't affected me. I never had any coaching. In fact, I think the young lads these days get too much coaching. Obviously I think they can be shown certain things. Take Johnny Carver and John Murray for instance, who run the School of Excellence at Newcastle – they're brilliant with the kids. The secret is to let lads develop in their own time; demonstrate skills and ideas but try not to put too much pressure on them. The big danger is when rigid coaching begins to stifle individual flair. I believe that until they are 15 or 16, kids should be allowed to do their own thing. Later, of course, they will be taught different things like team formation and tactics, but this aspect of their football education should be a million miles away from their natural development.

I had a few doors slammed in my face which I will talk about, but when I look back, maybe the fact that I was not taken on by a club at an early age was a blessing in disguise. All the time I was involved in schoolboy and youth club sides I was just doing what came naturally to me without being distracted by people telling me to play the game their way. I am not convinced that it is a good idea for young boys to be attached to football clubs from an early age. They are very vulnerable, open to suggestion and easily influenced. Only a certain number get hauled in by the net and rejection can be a traumatic experience for a lad with ambition. It isn't plain sailing for those who are taken on either. For every one who goes on to become a fully-fledged professional there are ten who fall by the wayside. But try telling that to a young lad who thinks he has got it made because a manager has shaken his hand and given him and his parents the red carpet treatment. The big danger comes when a boy allows himself to think 'I'm going to be a footballer, who cares about school?' Neglecting your education could be a lot more costly nowadays than it was when I was a lad.

I was extremely fortunate that, in the end, everything worked out the way I hoped. But supposing it hadn't and I had never made it as a footballer. I was marked down to work in a factory for life. That is no disrespect to the people who do that. It's just that for me it would have been a poor substitute for the career I had playing the game which meant so much to me. Not that factory work was an option open to me when I left school at the age of 15. All the teachers knew how I felt. They were never critical or nasty even though they probably sensed I hadn't been all that I should have been academically. They patted me on the head, wished me luck and sent me out into the real world. My job prospects were somewhat less than non-existent. I had no qualifications at all. I had my mind set on becoming a footballer but apart from that I had no idea, whatsoever, about what I was going to do.

The first requirement was to sign on the dole. Having experienced that dubious pleasure, my heart goes out to all those for whom it is one of life's necessities. To have little prospect of a job must be soul-destroying. I know there are many thousands of unemployed supporters of the teams for whom I have played and I just hope that football can provide them with an escape from all their problems. I'll never forget the Tuesdays I used to walk to the job centre near Killingworth and give them my signature on the dotted line. Four or five of my mates were in the same boat as I was, living blissfully from Thursday to Thursday. That was the day the giro cheque – all £16.50 of it – dropped through the letter box. I handed a fiver to my mother and the rest was usually gone by Saturday night, leaving me four days when I hadn't two pennies to rub together. Most of my money went on buying drinks and sweets and paying for my football at the youth club and the five-a-side indoor league we joined in Newcastle's Eldon Square shopping centre. I also played a bit of golf at the Bridle Path course in Newcastle where my brother George was a greenkeeper for a short spell after leaving school. I remember having to borrow his clubs in order to have a bit of a knock. They were hard but happy times, tolerated by my conviction that my football opportunity was about to come.

I went for two or three job interviews without success. One I remember was with a firm called Palmers Scaffolding. They were just labouring jobs, but for every one that came up there were about twenty applicants and you had to be very lucky to get taken on. I spent six months on the dole before I was sent on one of those Government Youth Training Schemes that were designed not only to get lads like me off the streets but, supposedly, teach us a trade and then, in theory, provide us with a job at the end of the twelve weeks of training. I was one of a group who were directed to a school in Dudley, one of the suburbs of Newcastle, where our task was to clean graffiti off the desks and chairs. We were shown how to sand them down and then varnish them to try and make them as good as new. We didn't earn any more money than we picked up from the dole but it was something to do and life was made bearable by the humour and attitude of everybody doing the work. There was a tremendous bond of friendship between us all and I have often wondered if the lads remember me and the days we cleaned up after the vandals.

It used to annoy me to see so much wanton damage. My background was certainly no less difficult than these kids but happily I never felt the urge to act like a hooligan. I could never accept deprivation as an excuse for vandalism and law-breaking. Still, the job provided a welcome relief but when it was over most of us were back where we started, existing on our handouts from the state. I was out of work for a few months but then, thanks to my dad, I managed to join the ranks of the employed. He asked a friend who worked at a factory in Killingworth called Young and Cunningham if there was any chance of fixing me up with a job. About ten days later I went to see his boss and he agreed to give me a start. To be honest, I was little more than a dogsbody – a 'gopher' – going here, there and everywhere. But I used to enjoy the morning walk with my brother George who worked nearby.

The factory manufactured valves for the shipping industry and one of my tasks was to clean all the machines down with a wire brush and then sweep up all the metal turnings. I also had to brush metallic paint on the valves in a little back room on my own. Every working day between nine and ten, I would be sent to the shops to buy the sandwiches, drinks and cigarettes for the workers' ten o'clock break. Then around eleven o'clock I would go around everyone again and take the orders for lunch before taking the ten-minute walk to the fish and chip shop in South Gosforth. It wasn't brilliant but the money was good. I picked up around £30 a week, which was a lot more than I'd ever had. It enabled me to develop a dress sense. Every couple of weeks I would splash out on a T-shirt or a pair of trousers and all in all it felt great to have a few quid in my pocket.

My football was getting better all the time. Everybody at the factory knew what I wanted and I am certain they wished me well. I used to enjoy joining in with the lads for a daily ten-minute session with a ball after lunch at the back of the factory. They were forever pulling my leg – 'Football? You must be joking! Stick to sweeping the factory, Pete,' they used to tell me. Years later, after I signed for Newcastle, I used to pop in to see them and the same people would say, 'Well done son, we always knew you would make it.' Looking back, as determined as I was to succeed, I don't think I would have done had it not been for the help and moral support of the few people who believed in me as much as I did in myself. There was my dad, who used to call me 'golden feet', my brothers and of course Peter Kirkley, who used to ferry me to all the Boys' Club matches.

There were plenty of others who did not share their opinion, such as those responsible for choosing the county team. More often than not whenever I was picked for South Northumberland Boys, it was only as substitute. But here again I found myself in the role of messenger boy. At half-time, if it was decided the subs were not going to be needed, we would be sent to fetch the pies for the end of match snack. On the rare occasions I did play, I would be stuck out on the right wing where they thought I wouldn't get in harm's way. I suppose they thought that in view of my size, they needed to protect me. These were the kind of setbacks I just had to put up with. There were others, like hearing of lads who played junior football with me getting signed up by professional clubs. Nobody knocked on my door, but I never gave up hoping they would.

Ironically the first hint of any interest in me came from abroad. That was after Wallsend took a team to Holland for a youth tournament. The fact I was there at all was down to my mam and dad who scraped around and went into debt to come up with the money to pay for the trip. I ended up winning the Player of the Tournament award which I was very proud of. Amid all the congratulations Peter Kirkley took me aside and told me that both Sparta Rotterdam and PSV Eindhoven wanted to give me a trial. I was absolutely dumbstruck.

Having to go Dutch to get started was something I had never contemplated. Apart from the trip to Scotland, this was

44

the first time I had visited another country. All I could gasp to Peter was, 'What shall I do?' His advice was to sit tight and be patient. 'Don't worry son, you'll get fixed up back in England,' he reassured me. Years later, after I signed for Carlisle, Brian Watson took me to Goodison Park to watch Everton play Sparta in a pre-season friendly. I couldn't help thinking, if I had taken them up on their offer of a trial, I might have been out there playing. But Peter was right to tell me to turn them down – and, as time would show, he was as good as his word. But a few million gallons of the murky Tyne flowed under Newcastle's famous arched bridge before that happened.

Time was passing and I was getting no further in my chosen career. I had reached the age of 18 and deep down I was beginning to think my life as a footballer was just a pipe dream. As the days went by I felt I would be at the factory for life, doing the messages, sweeping up and painting the valves. I was also still playing for Wallsend and for The Fusilier with my brothers on a Sunday morning. Then, out of the blue, Peter gave me the message that made my heart miss more than a couple of beats. 'I've got you a trial with Gillingham. They want you to go down there for a week,' he said. I couldn't have felt happier or more hopeful. A couple of years earlier Gillingham had taken on another Wallsend product in Steve Bruce and I was told he was doing really well. All I wanted was to follow in his footsteps and show what I could do. It was a long way to go, but it might be worth it.

I went down with another lad called Steve Redhead. We caught the train together full of excited anticipation and eventually arrived in Kent where our accommodation had been arranged with a family down there. For the first time in my life, I really felt I had arrived in football. I loved every minute I was involved. There was a group of us together all hoping for the big break. I was completely overawed by everything that was going on around me. Of course, you mingled with the senior professionals but they kept you at arm's length and you were terrified about saying a word out of place in case you upset anybody. The last thing I wanted was for anything to go wrong. I saw Steve a few times but we didn't spend much time together. He had his own things to do and I got on with doing what I was told.

The first three or four days were spent training and doing work with the ball. Then I played in a friendly at Brentford. It was not a brilliant game but I enjoyed it and I didn't think I did too badly. I was just revelling in the whole experience and my head was in the clouds. That proved to be my first big mistake.

There have been times in my career during which setbacks have occurred when I have least expected them. I have learned, painfully sometimes, that in football you never know where the next kick in the teeth is coming from. The game can pick you up and then dash you to the ground within a minute. But the starry-eyed kid who walked into the office of Gillingham manager Gerry Summers at the end of that week knew little of that. He was soon to discover that there is a hard and ruthless world out there. That feelings count for nothing when decisions have to be made. 'I'm sorry to have to tell you that we won't be taking you on.' Summers delivered his verdict with a hint of sympathy but it didn't lessen the impact of what he said as I stood before him. 'Unfortunately we don't think you are any better than what we've got and we don't believe you have what it takes to make it.'

I was absolutely devastated. To be honest I didn't expect it. I felt, looking at what I'd seen at the club, I was as good as anybody there – certainly no worse. At the very least, I had done enough to earn another chance, maybe go back again for a further trial. I just muttered my disappointment but there wasn't much else I could say. He was the boss – no doubt he was acting on the advice of his backroom staff – and I had no alternative but to accept the situation. I thanked him anyway and walked out of the office with my heart somewhere down near the soles of my shoes. Poor Steve was given the same 'don't call us' verdict. We went back to our digs, packed our boots and caught the train back to Newcastle.

My main preoccupation on the journey was what I was going to say to my dad; my brothers, mates and the chaps at the factory. It was my first big knockback and I did not enjoy the experience one little bit. But it's a long ride from King's Cross to Newcastle Central. We tried to look on the bright side; we cheered ourselves up with a few laughs and by the time I got off the train I was ready to take the world on again. 'Right, Mr Summers,' I remember thinking to myself. 'So you think I haven't got what it takes. Well, I think you're wrong. I know I'm good enough and I'm going to prove it.'

Of course I didn't have to look far for moral support. My dad was brilliant. Far from telling me I was living in cloud cuckoo land and that I should be directing my mind to doing a proper job, he put his arm around my shoulder and said, 'Never mind, son. I know you'll make it. Just keep on trying. You'll show them.' My brother Ronnie was just as encouraging. 'Cheer up, Peter. You still have a great chance. You're good enough and still young enough. Something is bound to happen for you,' were his comforting words. Outwardly I stayed cheerful but inside I was really depressed and down-hearted. I don't know what I would have done without their support and that of Peter Kirkley at the Boys' Club. He was as enthusiastic and optimistic as the rest. They kept me going when otherwise I might have thrown in the towel. After all, it wasn't as if I had been rejected by the most glamorous club in the country. Gillingham were no Manchester United or Liverpool. The one consolation was I felt it could not get any worse. But like I said, you never know what is around the corner in football, and worse it certainly did get.

Two months after my Gillingham experience, the long-suffering Peter Kirkley arranged with Lou Nainsby, the North-East scout of Cambridge United, for me to go down to the Abbey Stadium for another week's trial. This time I made the journey alone but instead of the eager optimism I felt on the way to Kent, this time it was grim determination that shrouded me like a cloak as I watched the countryside fly by my carriage window. By the time the week was out I was sure I'd be taking a giant step towards that football career I had been promising myself since I was ten. Chance would have been a fine thing as I didn't even last the week I had been promised! Four days later I was heading back to Geordieland with another dream broken into little pieces.

It had been arranged that I stayed with Peter Graham, the Cambridge player-coach and his wife. At first things could not have gone better. They were a really nice couple who made me feel very welcome. Also in digs with them was a young apprentice called Frank Cassidy and he helped to break the ice. It was the usual thing – training, demonstrations, one and two-touch football, five-a-sides – all highly enjoyable and again a wonderful experience. Then, on the Tuesday night, we all got on a bus for the short trip to play a match against Newmarket Town. The game ended in a 1–1 draw. I played well, perhaps well enough to impress the Cambridge manager John Docherty. I was happy with the way things were going and I had the rest of the week to really give it a go. But little did I know that fate had already taken a hand to ruin that plan.

While I was staying with the Grahams, they had the misfortune to suffer a family bereavement and were travelling to York on the Wednesday of that week for the funeral. I realized the significance of that after the game at Newmarket the previous evening. We got back to the Abbey Stadium and I was preparing to go back to my digs when suddenly, without any prior warning, Docherty came up to me and rasped out, 'You're not what we are looking for, son. You are not good enough.' He went on to mention that Peter Graham was driving to York the following day and he thought it would be a good idea if I got a lift with him and caught the train the rest of the way to Newcastle. Diplomacy was hardly Docherty's strong point. At least at Gillingham I had been shown the door in a decent, honourable fashion. But the Cambridge manager demonstrated a level of insensitivity which I have rarely come across since. All right, he did not fancy me as a player but at least he could have given me the benefit of the full week's trial rather than leave me suspecting he only wanted to save on expenses by getting me a lift most of the way home. I had hoped to complete my promised seven days and then maybe get a game on the Saturday. I just wanted a fair chance to show what I could do. Docherty, in his wisdom, would not even grant me that.

I have never been a vindictive person. It is enough for me that eventually I did prove Messrs Summers and Docherty to be bad judges. I leave them to think of what might have been. I can put the honours I have picked up in the game on the table and rest my case. But I would have expected at clubs like theirs where talent is discovered rather than bought in, a little more attention and time could be spent in making a proper assessment of a player. I have since played a couple of times against sides managed by Docherty. In fact he brought

Millwall to Anfield and gave us a really good game. He obviously has excellent managerial qualities. I hope, if he is in the same position in the future, he doesn't make any other lad as miserable as he did me.

Peter Graham did his best to cheer me up on the drive back but it was hardly a happy day for him either. It seemed we were both on the way to a funeral – in my case it was to bury any thoughts I had of playing football for a living. I felt a lot worse than I did after my first rejection. Standing on York station waiting for the train, I felt the loneliest teenager in the world. I had never really travelled on my own before and that hour and a half it took to get to Newcastle seemed like an eternity.

I was also wondering about how I was going to face everybody again. Were they just trying to be nice by telling me not to give up? What could I say to the lads back at work and at the Boys' Club? I felt uncomfortable and embarrassed, repeating over and over again: 'It didn't work out.' In the end I just didn't want to talk about it. Peter was typically upbeat about the whole thing. 'If I say you are a player, I mean it. There will be other days, other clubs,' he bellowed at me. My dad was just the same. 'You know what they say son ... third time lucky,' he laughed. But there was one other thought that kept me going as I pulled on my overalls the next day before marching to Young and Cunningham's ready to run more messages, sweep more floors, and paint more valves. I had been to two clubs and although they both turned me down, I hadn't come across anyone whom I believed was better than me.

If the lads I had seen at Gillingham and Cambridge had what it took to become footballers, surely there was hope for me yet.

3

RECOGNITION AT LAST

One story I will always remember from my school days will be the tale about Robert The Bruce. While I hardly needed to draw inspiration from the antics of a spider to push my claims to become a footballer, I had to wonder where the opportunity to try, and maybe try again, was going to come from. I should have realized who would be responsible but when at last my luck began to change it happened so fast I was almost swept off my feet by the speed of it all.

Good old reliable Mr Kirkley collared me one night at the Boys' Club and told me he had arranged for me to play in a youth match at Burnley. 'It isn't a week's trial or anything like that, Peter,' he said. 'But it will give you the chance to have a game and show them what you can do.' Peter did in fact do a bit of scouting for Burnley but I hadn't gone there earlier because he had sent so many lads from the area that they were overloaded and it was difficult to get them accepted. So my boots went in my bag and off I went across the Pennines to Burnley, thinking I would give it a go. But I didn't have a great deal of faith in anything coming out of playing in one youth team match.

Again I discovered that football teaches you to expect the

51

unexpected. The Burnley manager Harry Potts was suffi-
ciently impressed with my performance to approach me
immediately after the game and invite me back for a longer
trial. 'Come for two weeks and we'll have a good look at you,'
he said. It was the first hint of any professional recognition
and I was knocked out by it. After my other experiences I was
ecstatic that there was somebody in the game who had a bit of
faith in me. Mr Potts seemed a warm, genuine man who said
he enjoyed the way I played and told me he thought I had a bit
of ability. I couldn't help thinking that, at last, my chance had
come and containing my excitement was my biggest problem
on the way home. I pictured myself going back to Burnley,
sailing through the trial, and joining the list of many North-
East born players who had gone before me to play with
distinction for the Turf Moor club. I was on a football roller-
coaster. I had been down and now I was on the up and it felt
great. What I was certainly not prepared for were the
dramatic twists and turns that were to change the location of
my career launch-pad to somewhere a little further to the
north of that famous Lancashire cotton town.

When I went back to the Boys' Club, Brian Watson was
waiting for me. He asked me if I wanted to go across to
Carlisle to play in a game over there. But that was only the half
of it. Newcastle, of all teams, had also suddenly expressed an
interest. God knows what had kept them. I had only been
kicking a ball around in their backyard for as long as I could
remember. Geoff Allen, a terrific player for Newcastle until an
injury put him out of the game, had been given the job of
looking after the kids at St James' Park and he invited me to
spend a week training with them. After the famine, this was
undoubtedly the football feast.

After speaking to my dad and brothers, I thought I would

try my luck with Newcastle. The chance of joining my hometown club was too good to miss and I was told to report to the training ground at Benwell on the Monday. It was just as I was about to leave home that morning, my nerves stretched to the limit, that Brian came round with a message from the Carlisle manager Bob Moncur. 'The boss wants you to play for the reserves in a friendly against Blue Star on Thursday night,' he told me. That threw me into even more confusion. In the end I decided to train at Newcastle for three days with the intention of meeting up with Carlisle and playing against Blue Star, a good local side whose ground just happened to be conveniently at Newcastle Airport.

Everything went well at Newcastle. We didn't do a lot apart from working on skills and technique and the usual training routine. I was with a group of lads who must have been around 16 years old. There were no senior players around, they were on a pre-season tour of the West Country. Thursday came along and I knew Geoff would be round to pick me up like he had on the first three days. I was as nervous as a kitten. I didn't want to put him off because I hoped to keep the Newcastle option open, but at the same time I didn't feel an energetic training session was the ideal preparation for a match in which I was anxious not to let myself down. I persuaded my mam to tell Geoff a little white lie when he knocked on the door. 'I am afraid he isn't feeling well and he's staying in bed,' I heard her say as I waited, heart pounding, at the top of the stairs. Geoff said he hoped I felt better soon and maybe he would see me the next day.

The stage was set for the game that was to change my life. Bob Moncur actually played against Blue Star. We beat them 3–2 and, what made it even better, I managed to score one of the goals. Afterwards we were all ferried to a local pub called the Diamond in Ponteland, a village just west of Newcastle. We had an upstairs room booked for after-match refreshments and I was sitting there enjoying a coke and a few sandwiches when Bob and Brian walked over to me. 'How do you fancy signing for Carlisle?' asked Bob, smiling. I honestly thought he was pulling my leg. 'I think you could do a good job for us and it would be the right move for you,' he went on.

It was what I had been praying for since I was in short pants. I tried to stay cool and clear-headed. Maybe I should have said I wanted to think about it, but I was in no mood to throw away this golden opportunity. I found myself spluttering an answer which came out something like, 'That would be great, thank you very much', and we shook hands on it. It was arranged that Brian would pick me up the following afternoon and drive me to Darlington where the Carlisle first team were due to play a pre-season friendly, and where Bob would have the forms for me to sign.

Bob seemed happy, while Brian patted me on the back so hard I thought he was going to damage my spine, and I was jumping inside like a kid who had just discovered Christmas. That pleasure and happiness and maybe more than a little relief was shared by everybody at home. It meant as much to my mam and dad and brothers and sister as it did to me. It was only a start but at least I had been able to justify, albeit in a small way, their belief and support. My dad couldn't resist a chuckle. 'Didn't I tell you it would be third time lucky?' he laughed.

Friday dawned but I was awake and ready for it. Geoff came to pick me up but I had to tell him that I had been offered a professional contract at Carlisle which I was going to accept. He was obviously disappointed and indicated that he thought Newcastle would have taken me on. But by that time

I had given my word to Bob Moncur and had no intention of going back on it. In any case there was no guarantee about Newcastle. At the time Bill McGarry, the United manager, was away with the team and hadn't seen me play. I was also starting to realize that Newcastle in those days were more inclined to buy in players rather than produce their own. But one man I was anxious about was Harry Potts and I told Peter about that. He said he would fix things. 'This is the chance you have been waiting for. You have got to grab it with both hands.'

The time dragged before Brian arrived at the door and off we went to Darlington. Billy Elliott, who was manager at Feethams, had kindly allowed Bob the use of his office for the great signing. The date was 9 August 1979. My first contract was for two years at £60 a week. The wages happened to be double what I had been earning at the factory only a week earlier but the money was not important. I had my foot on the ladder. I was getting the opportunity to prove myself and not within the confines of a week or a few days. I had two years. If I didn't make it in that time, at least I would have the satisfaction of knowing I had given it a real go.

As it was, I thought if I did well at Carlisle, I might have a chance of playing in the first team. Maybe that indicated a slightly dangerous ambition on my part – after all, a few weeks earlier I would have been happy just to sign for any professional club. But I was now in first gear and anxious to put my foot on the accelerator. I was desperate to make up for lost time, for all the years of waiting. I had been patient for long enough and now I was thinking that I didn't want to settle for playing in the reserves. I felt that at Carlisle I would get the chance to play first team football quicker than I would at a bigger club. What I did not anticipate was that within a month of becoming a professional footballer, within six weeks of saying goodbye to the boys at the factory, I would be sharing a football field with the likes of Howard Kendall, Duncan McKenzie, and a man who was later to coach me at Newcastle, Derek Fazakerley.

My first few weeks as a professional were spent riding a mad, magnificent football merry-go-round. The involvement in that first pre-season preparation was simply magnificent. It was as if my fairy godmother had waved her magic wand and I had been plucked from the life to which I had become accustomed and dropped into a dream world. It was hard, a lot harder than I had ever been used to. There were endless cross-country runs which Bob always led from the front; shuttles, exercises to build up muscles and long sessions with the ball, which for me was the best part. But it was a great time for me, just being part of the build-up. I have known it many times since but you never forget the first. It was all a terrific, unbelievable thrill.

I quickly made a lot of friends in the dressing-room. The closest was a player called Graham Winstanley, or 'Tot' as he was always known. He was one of the senior pros who was in his second spell at Carlisle, having started his career at Newcastle with also a spell at Brighton. When you are young and as green as grass like I was, you appreciate any help you can get and Tot was always there when I needed advice or reassurance. He took me under his wing, especially when we played together in the reserve team in the pre-season games. I remember after a couple of games he came to me and said, 'Stick at it Peter, you have a great chance of becoming a top player.' It was great to hear that coming from somebody who had been around and knew the game as much as he did. With compliments like that and what I felt were useful performances on the field, I could not have had a better introduction, especially when I celebrated the first day of my first season in football with a hat-trick.

The first team started that 1979/80 season with a visit to Southend United. I was picked for the reserves to play Wrexham in a Lancashire League game at Brunton Park. I remember it well because the club had started to bring out a new line in leisure wear and Alan Ross, the former goalkeeper, who held the club record for appearances at Carlisle and was now looking after the reserves, promised me before the game, 'Score a hat-trick and I'll get you a club jumper.' So I did and Alan was as good as his word. But he did give me short shrift when I had the cheek to ask for the match ball. His reply was short and two-worded. Apparently balls were too expensive to waste on mere reserve team players. But the Wrexham game was significant for two other reasons. It had memorable consequences for me – and it also taught me a lot about pre-match diets!

I joined Carlisle with another lad called Stan Gate who signed as the club's only apprentice professional. For the first six months we were there we actually stayed with Bob Moncur and his wife Camille. In those days I knew nothing about food such as pasta and steak so when Camille asked me what I liked to eat, I just said fish and chips. She laughed and ended up compromising on the chips and made me fish and roast potatoes for lunch instead. It was hardly the sort of meal the purists these days would recommend. Anyway, it did the trick although I never tried it again. And roast potatoes were certainly not on the menu when I played my next game in a Carlisle shirt – a dream debut against Blackburn Rovers three days later.

My head was filled with the memory of my three goals that

weekend. Along with the rest of the second team we had been given the Monday off. I spent my Sunday at home as usual and popped out for a couple of hours in the evening to see a couple of mates. When I got back my dad was waiting for me, brandishing a brown envelope in his hand. 'You have a telegram,' he said anxiously. It must have been a bit unnerving for him and mam. They were sitting at home when the lad delivered the telegram. When something like that arrived on a Sunday evening, it usually meant bad news. My hands were shaking as I tore open the envelope. Inside it was the old-style telegram with the words stuck across a sheet of telegraph paper. My eyes scanned the terse message ... 'REPORT FOR TRAINING MONDAY MORNING'.

I had little sleep that night wondering what it was about. I was up early enough to catch a bus to the Central station to board the quarter past seven train to Carlisle. It stopped at every station on the way and eventually arrived at ten past nine. Camille was waiting to take me to their house and then the boss drove me to the ground. I still did not have a clue what was going on apart from the fact that I was in to do some training. But after the session Bob called me into his office and put me out of my misery: 'How do you fancy playing against Blackburn tomorrow night? I am going to throw you in,' he said. I just stood there, open-mouthed and completely speechless. He said he was giving me plenty of notice so that I could get the family across for the game. I found myself in demand by the local press, giving my first interviews. I tried to stay cool but it took all of my self-control to prevent me from screaming with excitement. That evening my name was plastered all over the back page of the local paper.

The next 24 hours or so before the game on 21 August 1979 seemed like an eternity. Then came the dressing-room buzz with all the chatter and good wishes. Bob came over and tried to get me to relax. 'Just go out there and enjoy it. You'll be all right,' he told me. Then we ran out in front of nearly 6,000 spectators, easily the biggest crowd I had ever played in front of, and I knew most of them would be there to pass judgement. I just prayed I would not let anybody down.

As it turned out I didn't do too badly. The highlight for me was when I 'nutmegged' Howard Kendall, who was Rovers' player-manager at the time. It was in the first ten minutes of the match and I could take anybody to the spot on the Brunton Park pitch where it happened. I remember the reaction of the man who was later to pay £1 million to take me to Everton. 'Hey, you cheeky little sod, you can cut that out,' he said, at the same time chuckling at my sheer audacity. We drew the game 1–1 and Paul Bannon scored our goal.

Strangely enough I found it easier than I thought it would be because I was like a little kid and I went out to play my natural game. I have noticed a similar reaction since with other young lads who have come into a side. Without meaning to be, you feel cocky and slightly arrogant. I just tried to do what I thought I was best at. But I still wondered whether I had done enough to be kept in the side. The manager must have thought so because I played the following Saturday against Bury at home and we won 1–0. By this time I was full of myself and looking forward to the visit to Millwall seven days later. Imagine my disappointment when Bob took me aside and brought me down to earth with a bump. 'You won't be playing at Millwall. I don't think the game will be suitable for you,' he explained. But he reassured me that I would be back in, although he did not say when. In fact we lost at Millwall by the odd goal and I was recalled for the following match at Gillingham and hardly missed another for the rest of the season. I made 37 first team appearances and scored nine goals including one in the FA Cup.

There was a bit of doubt about the first goal I ever scored in league football. I tried to claim one in a game against Rotherham which we won 3–2. I reckon my header was going in anyway but it struck an opposing defender who was later 'credited' with an own goal. But there were no such doubts when the next one came along just when I was beginning to wonder if I was ever going to score. We were playing Chester and the ball came to me about ten yards out. I really could not miss and I just tucked the ball into the corner. I wouldn't say it was a cracker but I had my name on the scoresheet at last and that's all I cared about.

Things happened fast for me in that first season at Carlisle. I became a first team regular, was awarded a new contract, got my first car – and I met the girl who was later to become my wife. The new deal, which took my wages to over £100 a week, came as a pleasant surprise. I had been at Carlisle about five months when the manager called me in and told me the club were reviewing my situation. 'We have decided to offer you a four-year contract at £103 a week,' he said. Of course I was absolutely delighted. It was more money than I had ever dreamed of. But what I was even more pleased about was the club was now doubling the period in which I had to prove myself.

There were not many happier 18-year-olds and I couldn't wait to tell Tot and the other lads like first team skipper Bobby Parker and Jimmy Hamilton who I got on well with. I expected them to be pleased for me … I certainly was not prepared for the reaction I got. Tot looked at me in disbelief. 'You must be bloody daft,' he snapped. 'The club has got you on the cheap. They obviously think you have a great chance of making it and this is their way of covering themselves. Now if anybody comes in for you, they are in a great position to bump up the transfer fee.' I was aghast. I must confess talk of transfers, even the thought of playing anywhere else, had not occurred to me. But Tot meant well and he taught me a lesson I have not forgotten. I have never had a problem agreeing contracts wherever I have been but I have always made sure I have looked at what has been on the table from every angle.

But my new affluence allowed me to indulge myself with my first car, although even that brought more than a few problems. It was Carlisle's policy to award first team players new cars. Usually they were arranged through a sponsor who paid to have his name painted on the car along with that of the player and the club logo. Because I could not drive, my sponsor forked out £100 to rush me through a course of lessons at a fiver a time. I would be out two or three times a day and finished the course in a little over a week. Then I got a shock when the sponsor suddenly decided to pull out, leaving me high and dry without wheels. Fortunately the club arranged for me to have more lessons which cost me £10 a week and I soon passed my test. I'll never forget that first car, a white Fiat 131, if only because on the first day I drove it, I crashed it! I dented the side trying to get through a gap between two parked cars. It was very embarrassing because my car locked bumpers with one of the others and I had to get some help to physically lift it clear. Fortunately there was only minor damage.

The incident had happened while I was on my way to show off the car to my girlfriend Sandra Devlin. Not only do I have to thank Carlisle United for launching my football career, I owe them an even bigger debt from bringing Sandra and I together. She worked in the club offices and we first met when

I used to hang around after training waiting for Stan Gate, who shared a flat with me after we moved out of the Moncurs' house. I had a lot of free time so I would sit in reception at Brunton Park and eventually started chatting with Sandra. The problem was I was too shy to take it any further and really she was the same. I wanted to take her out on a date but was terrified of asking. In the end I persuaded one of my team-mates, Mike McCartney, to pop the question for me. I remember I was sitting on a skip in the boot-room and he brought her along. That gave me the courage to invite her out and I was relieved when she said yes.

Our first date was a foursome with Mike and his wife. We went to a local pub for a bar meal – I had scampi and chips! – and that was the start of our courtship. We were together a lot after that. I met and got on really well with her mam and dad. In fact I spent most of my free evenings at their home and had my meals with them. It was perfect for me because I was away from home and, by then, looking after myself. I became part of their family and their hospitality meant I was not hanging around, getting bored with a lot of wasted time on my hands. It certainly prevented any homesickness that I might have otherwise suffered. I owe Sandra and her parents a lot. I am sure that without the kind of stability they provided, I would have spent my money as I earned it without realizing its true value. Sandra made me the happiest man in the world when later she agreed to be my wife. But a lot happened at Carlisle before then.

Bob Moncur departed to take over as manager of Hearts in Scotland. It was a sad day for me. I don't know where I would have been without his help. Before he left we wished each other the best of luck. Ironically the consequences of his departure were to have an enormously beneficial effect on my career. Bob's former assistant Martin Harvey was appointed manager and he brought in John Pickering as first team coach. I have worked with many of the top back-room staff in the game both at club and international level but for me there have been none better than John. In fact the only one I could put on a similar level is Derek Fazakerley, my former coach at Newcastle who is now at Blackburn. There are extraordinary similarities between the pair in their attitudes and ideas. 'Pick' was a major influence on my career. He was unknown to me when he came to Brunton Park but he soon became somebody for whom I had the utmost admiration and respect.

Martin gave him a completely free rein with the coaching and I remember his training ideas; they had so much variety and were highly enjoyable and often very amusing. His technical knowledge was also excellent. I was basically free every afternoon and he would come back in his own time and help me work at my game. We would go through every aspect, practising control, shooting and other skills. One significant improvement I made as a result of working with Pick was in the use of my left foot. As a kid I used it only to stand on. But I worked long hours trying to improve my striking of the ball and now I don't think there is a lot of difference between the two. I certainly feel equally confident with either foot.

Pick is now working with Bryan Robson at Middlesbrough. As a matter of fact he was indirectly the cause of me putting my foot in it after Bryan joined the England set-up as a member of Terry Venables' back-room staff. I remarked to him, 'You have the best coach I have ever worked with at Middlesbrough with you.' On reflection it was hardly the most diplomatic thing to say to a new England coach. But Robbo saw the funny side of it. 'That's nice, isn't it. So what's wrong with me?' he laughed.

After Pick and I left Carlisle, our careers crossed again later when I joined Newcastle for the first time. I am happy to say I played a small part in him getting a job. Willie McFaul was manager and he asked me if I knew any decent coaches. I had no hesitation in recommending Pick. He was appointed to handle the youth team but he was so good that the senior players used to come back in the afternoons in their own time just to work with him. In fairness Colin Suggett, who was first team coach at the time, noticed that and volunteered to swap responsibilities and Pick was promoted to first team duties. The ironical conclusion to all that was when McFaul was sacked, Pick got the boot too and Colin stayed. By that time I had moved on to Liverpool but I remember saying at the time that Newcastle should have given Pick a run in the job. I thought the club acted too hastily in parting with somebody who has enormous talent as a coach. It was a joy to work with him, both as a kid and later when my game had matured, because of his ideas, enthusiasm and dedication to the job.

I mentioned that I would now put Derek Fazakerley on a par. Maybe that's because they were once at Blackburn together, and now Derek has returned to Ewood Park. 'Faz' was a bit of an unsung hero at Newcastle but all the lads were aware of and respected his contribution at the club. He deserves a lot of credit for the entertaining football we like to play and the results we have achieved. The boss Kevin Keegan joins in as a player and says his piece when it is needed. But in terms of what we did in day-to-day training sessions, like playing keep-ball, five-a-sides or concentration on control skills, that's all down to Faz. I have been lucky to come across these two men at times when I needed them most. Any success I have had in an individual sense has had a lot to do with them.

Thanks in no small way to Pick's unselfish assistance,

things really took off for me in my second season at Carlisle. I scored 15 goals and suddenly the papers were full of speculation about me being sold to one of the big clubs. If it was not Manchester United, it was Liverpool or Everton – three clubs I was eventually going to join. But I learned not to believe what I read in the papers. As far as I was aware, the only concrete bid that came in was from Sunderland who offered £150,000 plus a player called Tim Gilbert, but that was turned down. I was devastated to hear that Tim had died suddenly while coaching a team of youngsters. He was only 36 – no age at all. I was content with the way things were going at Carlisle but I knew where there was smoke there had to be fire and I felt, as long as I kept doing my stuff, the club would be happy and at the same time I could not be harming my own prospects. When my first transfer eventually did come along, I could never in my wildest imagination have envisaged either the circumstances or who would be my next club. If somebody had told me I would be spending the next three summers playing for a team in Canada, I would have suggested that some sort of certificate of lunacy would have been appropriate.

I knew that for some time many footballers, mainly those reaching the end of their careers, had seen an opportunity to take part in the great American soccer revolution. But I never contemplated being one of them. As far as I was concerned the United States was as far away as the Moon. After all I had never even been on a plane in my life before! But fate was beckoning again and I followed its fickle finger in the truest pioneering traditions. Although I was not heading west to discover gold, there was certainly enough money to make it worthwhile.

The seeds of my move to Vancouver Whitecaps in April

1981 were sown on a foggy night at Brunton Park where I helped Carlisle to an FA Cup third round replay victory over Mansfield Town with a nicely-chipped goal. Unknown to me, in the crowd that night, with the set purpose of checking on a Mansfield player, was the former Leeds United and Scotland forward Peter Lorimer who was now player-coach at Vancouver. Lorimer was impressed enough by my performance to give a glowing report to the Whitecaps manager, no less a person than Johnny Giles. At the first opportunity, when the Whitecaps came over to England on what was for them a pre-season tour, Giles decided to watch me himself. He saw me play at Brentford and I did enough for the machinery of what was a record sale for Carlisle to whirr into action.

Bob Stokoe had returned for a second spell in charge at Brunton Park and a few days later he called me into his office and, in his typically forthright manner, announced that Vancouver wanted to sign me. 'They have made what I think is a good offer and they want to know if you will talk to them,' Stokoe declared. To be honest I just did not know what to say. I didn't even know where Vancouver was. I asked the manager for time to consider my situation and the first thing I did was talk to Sandra. I also sought advice from Pop Robson, who was player-coach at United. He was brilliant. He worked out the financial side of it and came to the conclusion it would be a great experience for me.

I could hardly blame Carlisle for allowing me to leave. Vancouver had offered £275,000, which was a lot of money for a club that was not too well-off and they would also benefit from the rather complicated three-year deal which meant I would play for Vancouver for the six months of their season, which coincided with our summer, and then they would loan me back to play for Carlisle for the other six months. My wages would be the equivalent of £400 a week which was almost four times what I was earning at Carlisle. It was all very tempting, especially as Sandra and I were engaged and due to be married the following year. She was as unsure as I was but her parents urged us to grab the opportunity to begin our lives together by enjoying this wonderful adventure. So after hours of talking and careful thought, we decided to take the plunge. We brought the wedding day forward and were married at the Church of Our Lady and St Joseph, in Carlisle, on 22 April 1981. Four days later we packed our bags, boarded our first airplane and headed for Canada.

Pop Robson was right, as it turned out to be a wonderful experience and one I have never regretted. Maybe I was a little disappointed that only one English club had come in for me and I know there was a lot of criticism at the time from people who accused me of taking an easy football option. There was talk of me lacking ambition and that I would go soft playing in the North American Soccer League. Many well-meaning folk were genuinely concerned that I was doing the wrong thing. I respected their opinions but I disagreed with them. After all, I felt, it wouldn't be the first time people had been wrong about me.

4

BIG RON,
LITTLE KEV

It would be fair to say the prior impression I had of football Yankee-style as I prepared for that first season for Vancouver in the summer of 1981 could not have been further from reality. I imagined that a lot of the older players who had crossed the pond to play in the NASL had gone there to pick up some easy money in the twilight of their careers. Maybe there were a few foreigners who came into that category but the majority, especially those who had played in the Football League, took it just as seriously as if they were playing for the big prizes at home. One thing is quite certain, our boss at the Whitecaps, Johnny Giles, would never have tolerated anybody he felt was there just for fun and frolics. Fortunately, in all of the three seasons I spent in Canada I didn't see him put to the test. He had his reputation to think about and so did the rest of us. And I am certain the Vancouver supporters, many of whom were expatriates who loved their football, would have spotted any phoneys a mile away.

Up until that time I had never played in front of such big crowds as those who came to watch the Whitecaps. We had regular attendances of 25,000 plus for our home matches, with only the New York Cosmos attracting more. The crowds were as loyal to the team as any English fan is to his favourites. The players were equally committed. As a young player I found myself a wide-eyed extra on a football stage packed with celebrities. Alongside me in the Whitecaps side at various times were Peter Lorimer, Dave Watson, Terry Yorath, David Thomas, Frans Thijssen, David Cross, Roger Kenyon, Ray Hankin and David O'Leary's brother Pierce.

I'll never forget the day I appeared on the same pitch as George Best. Not only because I'll be able to tell my grandchildren that I had as an opponent one of the greatest players the game has ever produced but also because I marked the occasion by scoring my first NASL hat-trick. We had a comfortable victory against Best's team San Jose Earthquakes and afterwards, when I was presented with the ball, the great man himself came over to congratulate me. He has had a lot of nice things to say about me since which I have always appreciated. Our lifestyles may be different but the only judgement I would offer on Best was that I wish I could have been half as good as he was. It was a privilege to pass the time of day with him. Another great opponent over there was the 'Kaiser' himself, Franz Beckenbauer, who still looked a class apart even in his late thirties. He and Best came from a generation of all-time greats and I was fortunate that the end of their careers overlapped a little with the beginning of mine.

Giles was up there among them too and, having played for him, it is a mystery to me why he has not become one of the game's top managers. His ideas on the game were brilliant and he had a great relationship with his players. Nowadays, it seems he prefers the role of a media observer which to me is a waste of his managerial talent. Maybe he is not into the everyday hassle of buying and selling players and the problems that often go with that; or he thinks life is too short to have to bother with the pressures of management; or that he is doing well enough without it.

Anyway, I found him terrific to work with. I had never met Giles until I arrived at Vancouver because all the nuts and bolts of my transfer were handled by Tony Waiters, the club's general manager, and a chap called Peter Bridgewater, who was vice-president. Giles and I got on well. As well as having a vast football knowledge, he had a tremendous sense of humour – qualities which he combined one day in Seattle when he substituted me before half-time. I have to admit I was having a stinker. I trudged off the pitch and Giles beckoned me to sit next to him on the bench. 'I had to bring you off,' he said. 'You're trying your best, I can see that. But the truth is you are having a bloody nightmare.' He was right, and I respected his straightforward honesty.

We established ourselves as one of the top teams in the NASL. In the three years I was there, we qualified every time for the end of season 'Soccer-bowl' play-off jamboree. The honours system was typically American. The priority was to qualify for the play-offs by finishing in the top eight. What followed then was a best of three knock-out to decide the champions. We did the hard bit but unfortunately we never got further than the first round of the play-offs which was very frustrating.

When I first went to Vancouver there were twenty-four teams in the NASL. By the time I left the number was down to nine. It was a shame it did not take off because it was well organized and reached a very high standard. If I had to give a reason why, I would have to say it was because many of the clubs tried to go too big too soon. They tried to run before they could walk. An awful lot of money was thrown into the game and in a lot of cases the return was a long way from matching the outlay. At Vancouver we were lucky because we were very well supported but other teams had a nucleus which they never seemed to be able to improve upon. Mistakes were made and the American public passed the death sentence on the game as we knew it, but I still believe there is a big future for football in the United States.

Surely the 1994 World Cup proved that. The failure of England to qualify took a lot of the impact out of the tournament as far as we were concerned but it would be difficult to argue against the fact that it was a wonderful spectacle and a triumph for brilliant organization. The aftermath has been a boost for the game in the USA at grassroots level. I understand more American kids are playing soccer than any other sport, and that includes the traditional homebred sports such as baseball, basketball and American football. And the standard is improving – you only have to look at the number of players who have come over to Europe and are operating at the very top. If any further evidence is needed, there is of course the sober reminder that the United States beat England in the World Cup warm-up tournament in 1993.

I must admit to more than a little bias. I received a great football education over there and playing six months there and six months in Britain worked really well. The year-round football helped to give me strength and maturity. I never felt stale because the changeover was always as good as a rest. I came back to Carlisle and played a part in their promotion in 1983. I was pleased to score against Swindon in my last ever game in a blue shirt. Not that I imagined it to be my last at the time. There was no reason to suppose I would not be back after that summer, helping United in the Second Division.

But it was towards a different United that my career was

diverted – the one whose headquarters are at one of England's best known stadiums ... Old Trafford. Of course, like most players chasing a dream, I jumped at the chance of a move to Manchester United. The dream did not become a nightmare exactly but it would hardly be correct to say my time as a player under manager Ron Atkinson was sweet. It was certainly short ...

It was at the start of my second summer in Vancouver that we played against United who were themselves on an end of season tour. It was a big game for us and our supporters turned up in force. United are a big draw wherever in the world they play. But we hammered them. I scored after 13 seconds – and that was after a United kick-off! Later in the game I managed to grab another goal and we ended up beating Atkinson's team 3–0. After the match Giles took me to one side and told me big Ron had been talking about me and that I should not be surprised if he came in for me. I thought to myself I would believe that when it happened and it didn't – well not for another two months anyway.

Sure enough, as our season was coming to an end, Giles called me in again to tell me that the United manager was definitely interested in signing me. Before I knew it, I was on my way to Old Trafford. The deal was struck on 9 September 1982 and again was somewhat complicated. I was going to Manchester on what was virtually an extended trial, the proviso being that, if I didn't make the grade, I would go back to Canada the following summer. The Whitecaps were paid £250,000 which would be returnable but, if I did join United on a permanent basis, they would double that, topping up the transfer fee to half a million pounds. I must say it was not the sort of arrangement that would encourage anybody to put down any roots but I went there full of optimism and eagerness. I was joining the most famous club in the land and I was going to give it my best. What is more I had enough confidence in my ability to believe, even considering I would be competing for a first team place with top internationals, that I could be at United for years to come. As it turned out, I was barely there six months.

Although I got on well with big Ron and have nothing but respect for him both as a bloke and a manager, I will never believe he gave me a fair crack of the whip. I was forever knocking on his door, pleading for an opportunity. He was always considerate, approachable and understanding of my situation, but that was as far as it went. The break I was looking for did not come. I spent most of the time with United playing for the 'stiffs'. Even then you had to marvel at the reserves of strength they had at the time. I shared a dressing-room with the likes of Paul McGrath, Mark Hughes, Scott McGarvey, Ashley Grimes, Steven Pears and Alan Davies, to mention just a few. The football was enjoyable but after being used to regular first team duty at Vancouver, it was hard to take. I appreciated Ron's predicament. It was difficult trying to cram a pint of talent into a gill pot. He had an embarrassment of riches.

But at long last he did give me the opening I was hoping for. He might just have been persuaded by the hat-trick I scored in the reserves against Stoke City on the Saturday before United were due to play Bournemouth in the home leg of a League Cup second round tie. For the first and, as it turned out, only time I saw my name on the teamsheet to start a game. I suppose playing against a team from a lower division should have presented an ideal opportunity to show what I could do. But, as is often the case, Bournemouth, with nothing to lose, were no pushovers.

I have to be honest and admit that I did not play well. But I was certainly no worse than a few others I could have named and I was staggered when Ron brought me off with twelve minutes to go and put Norman Whiteside on instead. It was a poor game but we won 2–0. Frank Stapleton scored one goal and I was actually only inches away from scoring the other. I was perfectly positioned to side-foot an Ashley Grimes cross but the ball hit Bournemouth winger Harry Redknapp first and was deflected into his own net. That was just my luck.

I was hurt and angry about not being allowed to finish the game. Twelve minutes is a long time in football. Who was to say I would not have scored in that time? I didn't really see the need to exchange a striker for a striker. If Ron was looking to score more goals, I would have thought he would have been better taking off a midfielder or a defender, especially as Bournemouth were not causing us any problems at the back.

Ron knew I was upset. His assistant Mick Brown, who is now with him at Coventry City, tried to cheer me up, telling me there would be other days. But I knew deep down that my United dream was over. In fact Ron did put me on the bench for a home game against Stoke City the following Saturday and again when we played Coventry around Christmas time but that was as close as I got to the playing surface on both occasions. In the end Ron took me into his office overlooking the pitch at the Cliffe training ground and gave me the news I had been expecting. He was not prepared to make it a permanent move. He was kind enough to explain the situation fully to me ... that he did not feel inclined to pay £500,000 when he already had what he believed were ample playing resources at the club. I understood his point of view – but I still think I deserved more than one unfinished game in a United first team shirt.

In spite of the way things turned out, I will always be glad of the time I had at Manchester United. I know it may sound strange coming from me but I loved Ron's style of management. He had an infectious personality. He is very enthusiastic and, in spite of his flash public persona, he is deeply committed to his profession. The odd time I was involved in his team meetings, I was impressed by his manner and the way he put his ideas across. And he was always great to the kids at the club which says more than anything about the kind of person he is. He talked to them as if they mattered.

There was never a dull moment on the training ground. I have to say that Ron thought he was better than Best, Law and Charlton rolled into one. He'd run with the ball at his feet muttering to himself ... 'It's Best, he passes to Law, on to Charlton and there's a brilliant cross,' and he would bang the ball over to where we were, standing in the middle like spare tyres. You couldn't help but like him. I just happen to think he made a mistake with me. After I left he bought Laurie Cunningham which seemed to indicate he was looking for somebody ... I just did not happen to be that player.

It was a different kind of rejection to those I had as a teenager at Gillingham and Cambridge. At the time United had probably the best team since the glory days of the sixties, bettered maybe only by the one they have now. They finished third in the league, won the FA Cup and were beaten in the final of the Milk Cup. In the end I went back to Vancouver two weeks early because we both knew we were wasting each other's time. As a matter of fact, Sandra and I were able to go to Florida for a fortnight and enjoy the only holiday I had in three years. I lay in the sun nursing my wounded pride but after a few weeks I was into another season in Vancouver and that helped to get it out of my system. And, if there were any lingering regrets, they were certainly dispelled the next time Giles called me into his office to tell me an English club was interested in signing me.

Six months earlier, as I was preparing to join Manchester United, I was out shopping with Sandra in Vancouver in one of the vast malls on which our Newcastle chairman Sir John Hall had based his concept for the magnificent MetroCentre on Tyneside. I just happened to be listening to the news on the radio and suddenly it came over that Newcastle had signed Kevin Keegan. I couldn't wait to tell Sandra when she came back. Even from a few thousand miles away I sensed the excitement and anticipation that Keegan's arrival would bring to Tyneside. Later, while I was languishing in United's reserves, I must admit to a tinge of envy at what was happening in Keegan's first season with Newcastle. Little did I know the following year I would be jumping on the great football bandwagon which was careering all over Geordieland.

It all started with that message to go and see Giles. 'Newcastle would like to sign you,' he told me without realizing the delirium his words instantly triggered off inside me. He had arranged for their manager Arthur Cox to ring me from the other side of the Atlantic. The phone call came that evening and my answer was an immediate and emphatic, 'yes'. In fact we never even got around to discussing money! I just told Arthur I was coming and would leave all the details to him. As it was I did not get much more than I was earning with the Whitecaps but what did it matter? The ironic thing about it all was that the transfer fee was a mere £150,000 which was a lot less than what Manchester United had been asked to pay a few months earlier. But circumstances had changed. The NASL was on its last legs and the Whitecaps officials probably felt they had to cash in before the league folded or they might not get anything.

Sandra and I were absolutely buzzing on that flight back to England. I had negotiated a few detours from my home in Longbenton to get to St James' Park. What is now a 15-minute ride on the Metro had taken me four years and a round trip of a few thousand miles via Carlisle, Vancouver and Manchester. It was worth the wait and I felt I was going to Newcastle at the right time. I was ready to do myself justice but I could appreciate there must have been a few niggling doubts. I was coming from so-called 'Mickey Mouse' football in Canada, having apparently failed dismally at Manchester United.

But there were no such negative thoughts occupying my mind. I was bursting with eager hope; determined to prove wrong those who lacked faith in my ability and, most of all, itching to share a dressing-room with the great Kevin Keegan. Here was a man from whom I could learn things that could only improve me as a footballer. I was looking forward to making his acquaintance. I did not have to wait long. As chance would have it as Sandra and I waited in the departure lounge at Heathrow before catching the shuttle to Newcastle, we caught sight of Keegan. He was on the same flight going up to begin training the following day.

We had never met before and he did not know who I was. I did not feel it was my place to bother him so I left it at that. But somebody must have told him who I was because he came up to me at Newcastle and introduced himself. He told me I had done the right thing in signing for the Magpies and that he was looking forward to playing in the same side. He was so natural and unaffected and I was bowled over that he should take the trouble to make my acquaintance. It was the start of what to me has been a very special football relationship – first as a team-mate and now as manager and player.

And I have to say that playing for Newcastle was everything he said it would be – and a lot more. We had some terrific players. As well as Keegan there was Terry McDermott, Chris Waddle, Jeff Clarke, David McCreery and later Glenn Roeder arrived from Queen's Park Rangers. It was also my first experience of playing for another man who has been a great influence on my life both on and off the field, the United manager Arthur Cox. Keegan has likened Arthur to the great Bill Shankly – nobody could bestow higher praise than that. But I soon found out why. You could not come across anybody with a greater depth of feeling either for the game or for the players around him.

To him football is a 25 hours a day profession. He is still totally immersed in what he does and nobody was more pleased than I was when Kevin brought him back to Newcastle to reunite the group which had such a marvellous time together in the mid-eighties. But he was a hard taskmaster when he was in charge. Training was tough and tiring. He would have us running up hill and down dale. He put a tremendous reliance on physical fitness.

I remember one day, not long after I signed, we were back at the club training ground for an afternoon session. We assembled in the sports hall ready to start but when we looked around there was no sign of either Keegan or McDermott. It was not like them to be late and we began to wonder if they had forgotten we were due back. Suddenly we saw these two bodies, dressed entirely like army commandos, crawling around on elbows and knees outside the sports hall. They were wearing the full works – steel helmets complete with twigs sticking out, dungarees, boots, everything. It was the terrible twins all right. They had gone to a fancy dress hire shop during the lunchtime break and picked up the gear. It was a hilarious leg-pull. If Arthur wanted to treat us like soldiers, the message was that they might as well dress like them. Everybody fell about and nobody laughed louder or longer than the boss himself. In a way it was a compliment. It certainly did not persuade him to ease up one little bit.

But there was a ruthless side to him as well as Waddle once discovered. We were playing at home and were leading 4–1 with two goals from Chris ... when the boss suddenly pulled him off! 'You weren't hungry enough for your hat-trick,' he told him curtly afterwards. In spite of incidents like that, all the players had a high regard for Arthur. It was only after he left without warning at the end of our promotion season that we all realized how much we respected him. The supporters loved his style of football and how could we play any other way with so many exciting and positive players in the side? It was entertaining, it was successful and it was highly enjoyable. Arthur's idea of the perfect game would be a 5–4 victory. That was how he geared the training. No warm-ups, just straight into it, and he supervised everything.

I signed for Newcastle on Tuesday 20 September 1983 and immediately went into action in the reserves at Leeds the following night. Three days later I was on the bench for the first team at Barnsley and came on after Jeff Clarke picked up a bad knee injury. We drew 1–1 thanks to a Waddle equalizer and I was never out of the side again that first season, apart from missing one game through injury. There was celebration after celebration, culminating in the biggest one of all when we won promotion to the First Division. I played up front alongside Keegan who scored 27 league goals during that campaign. I was happy with 20, the most I had ever scored in a season.

The first one in a black and white shirt will be one of my

most cherished memories. It was in a game at Cardiff City. Keegan headed us in front and then early in the second half I put Waddle away down the left. He returned the ball perfectly for me to hit a left-footer past Andy Dibble. Ten days later I had three more reasons to believe life was really worth living with my first Newcastle hat-trick. St James' Park was packed to the rafters for the visit of Manchester City – always a big occasion, especially since they fancied their promotion chances as well. After eight minutes Waddle was through on goal but was hampered by City keeper Alex Williams. Fortunately the ball broke kindly for me and I dummied Williams before side-footing it into the net. Keegan made it two before half-time and the manager's interval pep talk was all about 'giving the Geordies a day to remember.'

Well, this particular Geordie won't forget it in a hurry. On the hour, I cut in from the left and played it across to Terry Mac whose shot was parried by the keeper. But I had continued the run and again the ball dropped nicely for me to knock it in. Ten minutes from the end Waddle played me in with a tremendous pass inside the full-back and all I had to do was slide the ball past Williams. Two minutes from the end Chris put the icing on the cake with goal number five. Unlike at Carlisle, at Newcastle match balls were not in short supply so they could afford to present me with that one after it had been autographed by the United team. It was Keegan who threw it over saying, 'There you are Peter, that's yours and you deserve it.' I still regard it as one of my prized possessions along with the seven others I have accumulated throughout my career – but there is still plenty of room in the cupboard for a few more.

Afterwards Keegan was impressed enough to suggest in a newspaper article that Bobby Robson pick me for the England team. When Bobby eventually took that advice over two years later, I owed my selection in no small way to the football education I received playing alongside the man whose own international career had been curtailed by the England manager. Keegan was a magic partner. He set a great example with his dedication, supreme fitness and attitude. He would always say that what he achieved in the game was the result of hard work and application. But he could play as well. He would make a killer pass you hadn't even spotted. Nine times out of ten he would do the easiest thing because, as he still preaches today, that is often the best thing. But he had a habit of making the difficult ball look easy. And he would always try to protect me by insisting on taking the difficult high balls. His excuse was, 'I'll go for them because I'm coming to the end of my career … yours is just getting started.'

I think Chris benefited from him playing in the same team as much as I did. He gave us both the confidence to realize what we could do. There might have been occasions early on when, through being overawed by him, we gave him the ball too much. All he would say was, 'Look, I'm here as an option. If you think you could do something else with the ball, do it. Don't look for me all the time.' In the end we developed the freedom to think for ourselves a lot more.

In spite of his vast knowledge, experience and personal success – Footballer of the Year and twice European Player of the Year – all Keegan wanted was to be treated as one of the boys. He would never attempt to belittle the boss by going against what Arthur said. He always listened, offering a contribution only when asked.

It was a major personal disappointment when he announced his impending retirement on his 33rd birthday – St Valentine's Day 1984. Apparently he said he made up his mind to quit at the end of that season after Mark Lawrenson ran past him in a disastrous FA Cup game at Anfield which we lost 4–0. With all due respect, being outpaced by 'Lawro' was no reason to turn it in. In those days the Anfield defender could run away from the quickest opponent. If I dare to question my Newcastle manager's judgement, it would be to say he finished too early. He could have played at the top for at least two more seasons. But you had to give him credit for doing what he thought was best.

His bequest to Tyneside was First Division football, which is exactly what he went to Newcastle for. His legacy to me was self-assurance, knowledge, maturity ... and a nickname! He called me 'Pedro' on my first day's training at Newcastle; the rest of the lads picked it up, and it has stuck ever since.

Keegan's finale at Newcastle was something to be seen but a prouder moment for me personally had come a couple of weeks earlier when we clinched promotion by drawing 2–2 at Huddersfield. Ironically, for the first and only time that season, Kevin was missing through injury. But his absence, tragic though it was on the very day the team was to achieve what had been our top priority for the season, had memorable consequences for me. On the way down, Arthur sat beside me on the team bus. 'How would you like to wear Kevin's number seven shirt at Huddersfield?' he asked. Of course, he didn't have to say it twice. I just said, 'Thanks boss. That would be a great honour.' There really was a special tingle as I pulled it over my head but that was nothing to the elation I felt when I scored one of our two goals. Years later that situation was mirrored at Liverpool when Kenny Dalglish also handed me a number seven, the one he had worn with so much distinction at Anfield.

As far as Arthur was concerned, it was a one-off. Like the rest of us, we could not wait to have Kevin back for the football fiesta that marked our last match of the season. Appropriately our skipper brought the curtain down on a fabulous career with his 500th league appearance. He really did have a sense of the occasion, didn't he? Brighton were the visitors but they were mere incidentals on an afternoon of pure fiction. They made up the cast but nobody noticed them. Keegan led us out to the accompaniment of a deafening roar from a 36,000 strong St James' Park crowd. You could almost feel the desire from the supporters for us to sign off with a victory. You could grasp their desperation for Keegan to score.

Nobody let anybody down that afternoon. In fact the crowd's patience was hardly tested. After 20 minutes a Waddle effort came back off a post and who was there just to tap it in? Keegan, of course. Brighton attempted to spoil the party with an equalizer but there was no room for gatecrashers. KK dropped a centre on Waddle's head and we were back in front, and five minutes from the end he set me up for a goal which I still regard as one of the best of my career. We linked up in a crisp one-two passing move and when the ball came back I chipped it over Joe Corrigan, one of football's goalkeeping giants, into the net. It was the perfect end to what had almost been a perfect season. I wanted the goal to be seen all over England, especially Gillingham, Cambridge and Manchester!

Grown men cried that afternoon. And Keegan, unashamedly, cried with them. It was an occasion that underlined the football passion that has long been part of Geordie culture. I have often wondered if, had my football career not lifted off, I would have been one of the thousands of factory workers who filled the terraces and stands at the Park. And the tear-shedding was far from over either. Five days later the ground was full again, this time for Keegan's farewell match, a friendly against who else but Liverpool. The game did not really matter, I don't think anybody was keeping score. It was an honour and a privilege to be a participant on that incredible evening, when two of the biggest clubs in the land came together to pay homage to one of football's great careers. Then at the end of the match came the grand farewell, a *piece de resistance* that would have put any Hollywood epic to shame. Out of the evening sky dropped a helicopter to land in the middle of the pitch before whisking Keegan away. I watched his departure with mixed feelings – delight and despondency – mainly because before he jumped into the helicopter, he whipped off his number seven shirt and passed it to a nearby policeman with the request, 'Give it to Peter Beardsley.' That was the last either of us saw of the shirt!

There was a farewell banquet in the Gosforth Park Hotel later that evening. I thought it would be the last professional connection I would have with Keegan. Fortunately I was wrong about that. I also thought when, a few weeks later, Arthur Cox dramatically resigned following what could only be termed as irreconcilable differences with the Newcastle board, that might be the last professional contact I would have with him. I was wrong about that too. Professional footballers have to get on with life even after managers they know and trust move on as Arthur did to take over at Derby County. I put my signature to a three-year contract when I arrived at Newcastle and the boss told me he would look after me. Now I wondered who would be coming to see me through the other two. But when Arthur's successor was named as Jack Charlton, I rubbed my hands with anticipation. Now he was the sort of bloke I could really have a terrific working relationship with.

Oh yes ... I was very wrong about that too!

5

ALL WRONG, JACK

I have had a wonderful England career with well over fifty appearances. But I just wonder how many international caps I would have managed if I had been Irish and had to rely on Jack Charlton for my selection. Or even if, as was once widely speculated, big Jack had ever been given the job as England manager. My apprehension stems quite naturally from my experiences as a player under Charlton after he took over at Newcastle following Arthur Cox's shock resignation in May of 1984. Like I said, nobody was more pleased than I was about the appointment. He was a Geordie, like myself. He had a great playing career with Leeds United and England followed by a tremendous track record as a manager, first at Middlesbrough and later Sheffield Wednesday. He also had a reputation as one of the game's most innovative coaches.

I remember talking to the late legendary Jackie Milburn after we heard big Jack was coming to St James'. 'Take it from me, Peter,' said Wor Jackie. 'He'll be the best thing that's happened to this club.' And he was not saying that because he was Jack's uncle. If he was looking for an argument, he didn't get one from me. Although we had just won promotion there was bound to be something of a hangover from the previous season. Kevin Keegan was gone; so was Arthur Cox. There were holes to fill but there seemed nobody more capable of filling them than Big Jack.

The first few months of his reign at Newcastle did nothing to change that opinion. Pre-season training was lively, hectic, enjoyable and at times highly amusing. Jack's habit of forgetting names is well known, and at times it had us in stitches. There was also plenty of variety to keep the players on their toes. I remember one session where he coded various exercises by giving them names of colours. He would shout out the colour and we did the appropriate routine. We did a red, a blue and a green and were well into the swing of it when suddenly he called out: 'Puce'. We all stopped dead in our tracks and looked at each other in amazement. 'Puce, Jack? What the hell sort of a colour is that?' somebody asked. 'I just said it to test your sense of improvisation,' he retorted. Everybody just fell about laughing.

I soon discovered that Jack was an absolute one-off. When he was created they definitely threw away the mould. He spent a lot of time working on my skills which I was grateful for. What was different about his coaching was that he often did it wearing a checked sports jacket and flannels! Under his watchful eye I would practise curving balls from the left-hand side of the semi-circle on the edge of the penalty area to the farthest post. If I was not doing it to his satisfaction he would march on to the pitch, take off his shoe and start bending balls almost to perfection with his stockinged foot! I am not joking when I say he would hit the post five times out of ten. 'That's the way to do it,' he would say. Then he would calmly put his shoe back on his foot, which by then was coated in mud, and walk off with a grin as wide as the Tyne Bridge.

Initially we had a great relationship. And a one hundred

per cent record after the first three games of the season, which saw Newcastle at the top of the First Division table for the first time in 34 years, only seemed to cement what seemed a wonderful team spirit. We thought it a bit strange when the manager did not travel down with us on the day before our opening fixture at Leicester. But he showed up before the game and although he did not waste much breath on pre-match instructions, we still went out and won 3–2 with Waddle scoring the winner. In the next seven days we beat Jack's former Sheffield Wednesday team 2–1 and then trounced Aston Villa 3–0, thanks to an awesome individual performance by Waddle, who scored two goals and almost destroyed the Villa single-handed. Jack had Chris and myself playing through the middle in the early matches and everything went really well.

Chris's form, especially in that first three months back in the First Division, was inspirational. It won him an England call-up, but unfortunately for Newcastle supporters, it also led eventually to his departure to Tottenham Hotspur in the summer of 1985 for £590,000. To be fair, I don't think Jack broke his back to keep him. By that time the honeymoon had been well and truly over for some time. We began to experience another side of the manager after we followed our opening three wins with a hat-trick of defeats, including a 5–0 hammering against Manchester United at Old Trafford.

Then came an extraordinary match at Queen's Park Rangers when we appeared at first to have arrested the slide in some style with Waddle scoring a great hat-trick and then making a fourth for Neil McDonald – and that was before half-time! But the wheels came off disastrously in the second half with Rangers coming back to square the match at 5–5. I thought Jack was going to burst a blood vessel after the match. Kevin Carr, our goalkeeper, was the main target of his anger. The consolation, at least as far as Chris was concerned, was that Bobby Robson was at the game and it was only a matter of time before he was awarded his first England cap.

Chris's international career took off but both his fortunes and my own at club level took a decided turn for the worse. Jack decided to change his tactics and tried without success to buy George Reilly, a towering six-feet-plus centre-forward, from Watford. He went out and signed Tony Cunningham, another giant, from Manchester City instead. But then, two matches later, Watford changed their minds about parting with Reilly so Jack finished up getting them both. With two big men up front it did not need a master tactician to realize what our main attacking ploy would be. I was despatched to the right wing, Chris to the opposite flank, both of us with explicit instructions to gallop up and down like demented dervishes and try and get on the end of any knockdowns from the big men.

The full-backs John Anderson and Malcolm Brown were ordered to launch balls forward over our heads; passing to us was definitely not one of their options. They used to knock in plenty of good balls and the tactics were mildly successful because we finished in 14th place. But I certainly didn't enjoy the way we played; neither did Waddle, and I am quite certain the supporters didn't like it much either. To be fair to Chris, he coped with his left-side role a lot better than I did with mine. He had played as a winger under Arthur and knew a lot more about what was required of him. But I got bored playing the way I did because it was just not my game. I needed to be more involved with the play. Jack could have got anybody to do my job. I did my best but I was not happy and the boss knew how I felt.

There followed two major rows which strained our relationship almost to snapping point. Whatever the situation, I have always felt, as a professional footballer, that any manager is entitled to loyalty and one hundred per cent effort. Nevertheless, I have to say my respect for Jack dwindled after what I felt were astonishing incidents in successive home games. The first was against Luton Town. We were leading 1–0 with about a minute to go when I picked up the ball in the inside-right position with only Mal Donaghy, Luton's talented Northern Ireland international defender, standing between me and a clear run on goal. I decided to take him on and tried to jink the ball around him. I felt it was worth having a go because if I had succeeded in getting past Mal I would have had only the goalkeeper to beat. Anyway, he stuck out a foot and stopped the ball, and the the final whistle went.

We shook hands and started walking off, me feeling satisfied at our team having won the game. Suddenly I was aware of Jack bearing down on me from the dugout. I was still about 15 yards from the touchline when he came up, grabbed my arm and, in front of an audience of nearly 24,000 people, bellowed, 'Don't *ever* do that again!'

I just stood there transfixed with amazement as he continued to slag me off. 'He could have taken that ball off you, booted it upfield, they could have grabbed an equalizer and the score would have been 1–1.' It was such an incredible outburst that I thought for a brief moment he might have been taking the mickey. But then I saw he was deadly serious. I just pulled my arm away and walked off without saying a word to him.

The time it took to get into the dressing-room had little affect on his mood. He was still going on about it. That didn't bother me so much. He could rant and rave at me as much as he felt entitled to in private – or even in front of the other players – but he had made a fool of me out on the pitch. I felt it was time to say my piece. 'Fine, have a go at me in here if you like,' I said, 'but don't come on the field and do it. It's just not on.' It was left at that for the moment but it was no surprise later that the press wanted to know what had happened and they gathered in force outside the players' lounge waiting for me. As it happened my wife Sandra was standing there too.

As soon as I approached them, one of the reporters asked me what had happened. At the same moment, out of the corner of my eye, I saw Jack coming down the stairs behind me. I nodded towards the boss and replied, 'You'd better ask him.' Jack, clearly unrepentant, dived straight in again.

'I'll tell you what happened,' he blurted out. 'You'd better not do that again,' mixing his sentences with a few expletives. I asked him to watch his language a bit because Sandra and everybody there could hear quite plainly what was being said. He then just stormed off, muttering something along the lines of 'To hell with the lot of you!' as his parting shot. It was a simply unbelievable episode.

I thought I had heard the last of it, but far from it. The following Saturday we had another set-to, and this was even more incredible than the incident a week earlier. It came after something I did in a game against Watford. Time was running out and we went into the last minute leading 2–1 when we were awarded a free-kick on the corner of our opponents' 18-yard box. I picked up the ball and took the kick quickly, floating the ball into the middle where Reilly glanced a lovely header into the net to make it 3–1. We were all pleased that big George had managed to score against his former club – apart from Jack. We got back into the dressing-room after the game feeling quite pleased with ourselves when Jack suddenly turned on me again.

'What did I tell you last week?' he shouted. 'When you took that free-kick, their keeper could have caught the ball. He could have thrown it down the field to one of their players and there could have been an equalizer.'

I felt embarrassed – but not for me, for him. I believed he would end his tirade by saying something like, 'You shouldn't have done it, but it worked out well in the end.' But he didn't and I just thought this bloke is not for real. There were certain basic things on which Jack and I clearly did not see eye to eye but, in spite of everything, I did not feel I wanted to leave Newcastle. In fact I signed a new contract during the following close-season. I still had a year to run on my old deal but after quite a lot of discussion I agreed to sign an extension which committed me to the club for a further two years. Jack had driven a hard bargain. At first he came up with a package which entitled me to about a fiver a week more. I managed to squeeze a little extra out of him but not much.

Anyway we prepared optimistically for the new season, in spite of losing Waddle to Spurs. Chris's move was the worst kept secret of the season. Newcastle wanted £750,000 for him but an independent tribunal fixed the fee at £590,000 which was a record deal at the time for the club. He must have been one of the best bargains for years. He has given tremendous service wherever he has played and it was a real treat having him as a team-mate. But the show had to go on. Before the start of the 1985/86 season, we took part in a tournament on the Isle of Man and a week before the big kick-off Jack arranged a home friendly against Sheffield United. I thought that was slightly unusual. In the three years I had been at the club this was the first pre-season game we had played at St

James' Park. In any case not many people set a great store by these non-competitive matches. But nobody could have been prepared for the drama that was to follow the game. I certainly could not have guessed that the respective football paths of Big Jack and myself would take completely different directions even before a ball was kicked in anger.

It must be said that United gave us a bit of a going-over. I don't know whether they had had a longer pre-season than us and were that bit sharper for it but they played really well and took an inevitable lead. Fortunately we hung on and five minutes from the end Tony Cunningham managed to score an equalizer. I was pleased for Tony, who had not had a happy relationship with the supporters ever since he arrived at the club. He was as game and genuine as they come but it seemed he was just not what the fans had been used to or even wanted. I felt so sorry for him because being black he also used to take a lot of stick about his colour. Some of the abuse he received was disgusting and there were times when I was ashamed that it came from followers of Newcastle United. I am happy to say that it has died down since those days. Andy Cole and Ruel Fox became just as big favourites with the crowd as any other player at the club. Racial chanting is a curse that has no place on football grounds.

Anyway, to get back to the Sheffield game, there had been rumblings of discontent from the crowd for most of the match. There were only about 6,000 in the ground but the final whistle was the signal for a crescendo of booing and concerted criticism of Jack. They absolutely slaughtered him. It had to be something of a carry-over from the previous season. The fans never really took to Jack's style of direct football and our performance that day did little to comfort or appease them. Still it would have been difficult to predict the manner in which Jack reacted. He marched into the dressing-room after the game and suddenly announced to the astonishment of everybody, 'That's it. I don't need this. I'm off', and promptly turned on his heels and walked out. He had been in the job a mere 14 months. I never saw him at the club as manager again. Later, when we came out of the dressing-room, we found out he had resigned and gone home.

Of course his walk-out made all the Sunday morning headlines but the players kept out of it. My feelings about the whole thing were quite clear. Like many of the lads he had inherited, I thought – good riddance! Jack had done all right in terms of results but I shed no tears when he left. He did me no favours and he knows that. He has great ideas and, what he has achieved since as manager of the Republic of Ireland team, proves he is a top-class coach. Nobody can take away his record of two World Cup finals appearances by a country which had never qualified before he took over. The variety of formations he has used while he has been in charge has worked with the players he has had at his disposal and its success cannot be disputed. Big Jack has earned the hero worship he receives in the Republic. It was an ideal arrangement and the job suited him down to the ground. He must have been fed up with all the day to day hassle of club management. He could combine a job he loves with the leisure activities he enjoys. He could do his fishing and his shooting and still involve himself in the considerable behind the scenes work that the job of Irish team manager entailed.

But I would be hypocritical and dishonest if I said anything other than it did not happen for me while he was at Newcastle. He tried to programme me into becoming a right-winger and it did not suit my game at all. His coach Willie McFaul took over as caretaker manager and I was happy with that. He had

93

worked with Arthur Cox and tried to change things back to how they used to be. That was more to my liking than life under Jack.

It was a traumatic year of ups and downs but, in many ways, it was one I could have well done without. By the time Jack left, another star was beginning to emerge on the Newcastle horizon, a cheeky, chubby lad who I had first come across when he used to come to training sessions as a 14-year-old schoolboy. Nothing that Paul Gascoigne has ever achieved since has come as a surprise to anybody who was at the club to witness his precocious young talent. Arthur Cox, who was manager at the time, used to allow Gazza to join in with the first team's training sessions. That's how good he was. There was a cocky arrogance about the lad but he had so much ability it was simply phenomenal for somebody so young. At the time every top club in the country was clamouring to sign him. His parents were offered fortunes to try and persuade them to allow him to sign. But all he wanted to do was play for Newcastle. He was black and white daft.

It was Charlton who first gave Gazza his chance. He was not afraid to put him on the subs' bench a couple of times before his 18th birthday and I know one of the things he had been looking forward to was to see him blossom in the first team. Jack was top class with the lad. I would have to give him a pat on the back for that. He really looked after him, taking him under his wing and spending a lot of time with him. Gazza was a bit like me in his eating habits. We both had a tendency to eat the wrong things. Maybe we hadn't been used to the finer diets, but he was worse than I was and Jack took steps to put that right. He made an arrangement with a restaurant in Newcastle where Gazza used to go for lunch every day and get proper food like steak and salads.

It was no surprise when Willie picked him to start his first senior game on the opening day of the 1985/86 season at Southampton. I scored from the penalty spot to give us a 1–1 draw but I remember Gazza almost beating Peter Shilton with a brilliant header. He quickly became a local hero and it was clear over the two campaigns we had together that he was heading for mega-stardom. You could also sense there were possible problems ahead because of his 'sod it, let's live for today' attitude. He was happy-go-lucky even as a kid, someone who loved a laugh and a giggle and playing practical jokes. It was impossible to try and get him to be serious. He even took that swashbuckling attitude with him on the field. He was great to watch and unpredictable to play alongside but his sheer talent got him out of so many scrapes on the field. Off it he was, and still is, a bubbly, good-hearted lad who would do anything for you. He would give you his last penny. When he was a teenager and not earning much, he would sometimes borrow a few quid until he got paid. But his debts were always settled on time, even though paying up nearly always left him close to being skint again.

These days it is almost as if he is living on another planet. But from what I know of Gazza, he is a much maligned and misunderstood person. He has courted some bad publicity and it has given people the wrong impression of the sort of chap he really is. They do not know about the help he gives to people or what he does for the various charities and other groups he supports financially. I might be biased because I love the lad. He sometimes goes over the top with the press and media. I think it's a bit of a game he plays with them. They want him to be a certain kind of person so he becomes what they want. In effect he is winding them up but unfortunately he has been the loser on too many occasions. Deep down he would prefer a life out of the limelight. That's why he likes coming home to Newcastle and having a quiet night with his mates in the working men's club, having a lager and a game of snooker. This is a side of Gazza that the world doesn't see and he doesn't want the world to see. Knowing what he is really like, how he copes with the constant limelight is beyond me.

There had been talk at the end of the season and during that summer of Gazza coming back to Newcastle. Although I would have loved to have shared a dressing room at St James' Park with him again, I am glad it didn't happen. I would have thought he would have been forced to live in London and travel up for matches because the hassle he would get from the media would have been impossible. He has chosen, slightly surprisingly in my view, to join Glasgow Rangers – a move which is bound to make him an even bigger fish in an even smaller pool. We all have to live in the public eye but the spotlight on him is unrelenting. He cannot even get lost in London or Rome where he is under constant siege from reporters and photographers, so there will be no place for him to hide up there.

My main hope is that he can come back and dispel any worries about his fitness. One thing I do know is that football has missed seeing Gazza treating us to what he is good at. After battling back from the kind of serious knee injury which has finished other careers, he deserved better than to break his leg in an innocuous training accident at Lazio. It has been a long haul back but at least at Rangers he will start with a clean slate and I think the whole of football wants him to do well.

We played together a lot in that season at Newcastle which went better than a few forecasters had predicted. As I have said, it was very satisfying witnessing first hand the emergence of one of the finest talents to have been nurtured on Tyneside.

Above: New faces at Carlisle, 1979 ... That's Ian McDonald (No 2); Neil McDonald (second left) and Gordon Staniforth (No 11) – and me waiting for a kick.

Below: Who cares about superstition? Wearing the number 13 shirt at Vancouver Whitecaps. It turned out to be a lucky move.

September '82 and a seat at Old Trafford with Sandra and Big Ron. I did a lot of sitting down at United.

The inspirational Ray Wilkins was club captain when I arrived at Manchester United.

A year later and my first meeting with Arthur Cox at Newcastle airport. He made me welcome and gave me my big chance.

Race you Kev ... its Beardsley and Keegan in front and the rest nowhere against Brighton in December 1983.

Big Jack Charlton walks tall … he became a hero in Ireland but could not stand the heat on his native Tyneside.

Jocky Hansen and I on opposing sides for Newcastle and Liverpool but later title-winning team-mates at Anfield.

A star in stripes … Chris Waddle scoring another goal for Newcastle but we went our different ways.

A World Cup first … the Paraguayan keeper is left floundering as I score England's second goal in our 3–0 victory in Mexico 1986.

Celebrations in Mexico … the goal twins Gary Lineker and I all smiles after the Paraguayan defeat kept us in the Cup.

More England joy, this time sharing the goal pleasure with Bryan Robson, Gary Lineker and Chris Waddle against Brazil in May 1987.

I had travelled halfway around the world to get back home but wearing the black and white shirt was worth it ... with Newcastle in 1984.

Brian Clough in typical full voice ... he praised my performance but my regret was not playing under his managership.

Anfield new boy ... all smiles with Kenny Dalglish and chairman Sir John Smith on the day I joined Liverpool in July 1987.

Title honours at last in 1988 as I celebrate my first championship medal with a non-alcoholic can. For the others there was bubbly.

Kenny, pictured with wife Marina and family, receives the OBE in February 1985. We were always great friends and neighbours.

Move over Faldo ... the grip is not perfect and the follow through could be better but you cannot be good at everything.

I was pleased too with my own consistency. I had a one hundred per cent First Division appearance record and finished the club's top scorer with 19 goals. The players were happy for Willie when he was given the job permanently in recognition of the good start we made, taking eleven points out of our first five games. The difficult days under Jack were a thing of the past and I was happy that we were competing well with the top teams in the league. Willie changed things a bit. He bought Billy Whitehurst to partner me up front and sold George Reilly on to West Brom. There were hiccups of course – not the least of which was when we were slaughtered 8–1 in our third from last game by West Ham, who went on to have the best league placing in their history when they finished third, only four points behind the champions Liverpool. It was easily the heaviest defeat I have suffered in professional football but that wasn't its only significance. We played with three goalkeepers in that eventful match on a black Monday night at Upton Park – and I was one of them! Our problems had started the previous Saturday when we came away from a 1–1 draw at Chelsea with our recognized keepers Martin Thomas and Dave McKellar both suffering injury problems. It was touch and go whether either would be fit for the West Ham game but in the end it was decided that Martin was in slightly better shape and was worth risking. But we could tell straight away that he was struggling with his shoulder injury. At half-time, by which stage we were already 4–0 down, it was obvious he was in too much pain to continue. Straight away I volunteered to take over but Willie said, 'Forget it', and told Chris Hedworth, who normally plays full-back, he was going in goal. But even worse disaster was to follow before the game was much older. Chris flung himself across his goal in an unsuccessful attempt to stop an

Alvin Martin header, collided with a the goalpost and smashed his collar-bone.

This gave me my big chance. Before Willie could come on to the pitch and intervene, I grabbed the keeper's jersey and pulled it over my head. And I thought I did well – at least for ten minutes. In fact, one save I made from George Parris when he was clean through brought chants of 'England's Number One' from the highly knowledgeable Upton Park crowd. But it wasn't long after that save that I discovered a keeper's life is not all that it's cracked up to be. Paul Goddard and Frank McAvennie scored one apiece and then big Alvin strode up and made his day by sending me the wrong way from the spot. It was some way to treat a chap who had been your England room-mate but Alvin didn't care one bit. The penalty gave him the unique distinction of scoring a hat-trick against three different keepers. Such is the manner in which quiz questions are born. It was a painful experience that one and only time I played in goal. My respect for the lads who do it week in week out increased a thousandfold.

Still things weren't all that bad. I managed to score four goals in a run of five successive wins between February and March which lifted us into the top half of the table and there we stayed until the end of the season. Later in the summer I was pleased to sign yet another new contract which gave me a nice rise and extended my commitment to the club for another two years. I always felt I had a great relationship with Newcastle supporters but, during the following season, I began to share with them increasing misgivings about the club's ambitions. We had a poor season in the league although we had a mildly successful FA Cup, reaching the fifth round at which stage we lost 1–0 to a Chris Waddle-inspired Tottenham at White Hart Lane.

I have to say, for the first time since I joined Newcastle, I was beginning to feel envious about the players and teams who were almost guaranteed to win the game's top honours. It has been proved since that success does not come by accident; it has to be bought and paid for. Even back in the mid-eighties there were teams who were more likely to do well than others because they were prepared to speculate in the transfer market. Time was passing for me and I did not seem any nearer my ambition to win something. I wanted desperately to do that at Newcastle but I felt that the club was not as hungry as I was. The likes of Liverpool, Spurs and Manchester United were spending big money but it seemed we were missing the boat. A few players had been signed but, with no disrespect to the lads who came, they were not the big names the fans and myself had been hoping for. On the other hand it seemed quite clear to me that Newcastle would always snatch the opportunity to cash in if they received a decent offer for any of their better players. That had been proved with the sale of Waddle and they were about to do it again with myself and after me, Gascoigne. I certainly felt less inclined towards another new contract when Willie approached me to discuss a deal. There had already been a lot of speculation about my future in the papers with some top clubs supposedly watching the situation. I decided to sit tight and await developments.

Early in July 1987 Willie asked me to meet him for what I thought was another attempt to persuade me to sign a new contract. We got together in a setting that would surprise anybody who imagines the North-East to be a land of slag-heaps and smoking chimneys. The George Hotel at Chollerford on the banks of the upper Tyne is a picturesque out of the way place not more than half an hour's drive from

St James' Park. Willie wanted to chat without the possible distraction of interference from the press. As I anticipated, he put the question of a contract to me. I declined politely. My attitude had not changed.

Then he altered his tack. 'Well, if you don't want to make a longer commitment,' he said, 'I have to tell you we have had an offer from Liverpool for you which, in the circumstances, the directors have decided to accept.' The figure turned out to be an incredible £1.9 million, at that time a record figure for a transfer between two British clubs. Willie informed me that the Liverpool manager Kenny Dalglish, my idol from my days as a kid with Cramlington Juniors, wanted to talk to me about the move. I had watched him; I had played against him; and now I was going to meet him and possibly play alongside him. It was thrilling news.

The rendezvous was fixed for a hotel in Standish, near Wigan, but the venue was quickly switched to the Prince of Wales Hotel at Southport when we found out the original meeting place was crawling with reporters. Sandra came with me and we were introduced to Kenny, his wife Marina, the Liverpool chairman, John Smith and secretary Peter Robinson. At an appropriate time the two ladies slipped away for a chat, leaving me to talk to the Liverpool threesome.

It was hardly like going for a job at Palmers Scaffolding but I was just as terrified. I had arranged for somebody to talk to Liverpool on my behalf, an agent named Jon Smith who did a lot of deals for the England team, but he was not arriving until the following day. This initial meeting was an opportunity for Liverpool to make me a preliminary offer. They mentioned a figure which was strictly wages only, with no suggestions of lump sum persuaders or anything like that. Liverpool play it by the book. To be honest, I was quite happy with what was on the table but they did not expect me to give them an answer until I had spoken to Sandra. In the meantime I had a quiet word with Kenny who marked my card about how Liverpool handle contract negotiations.

'Their first offer will probably not be their best,' revealed Dalglish. 'Whatever they say, it will be up to you to try to get a little more. But I'll give you one piece of advice. You will only get what they think you are worth.' Kenny knew that my agent would be getting involved but he warned me it was unlikely Jon would do any better than me. He advised me to come to some arrangement whereby Jon and I agreed on a flat fee for representing me plus a percentage of any improvement he could get on top of what I was finally offered. All that remained was for me to pluck up enough courage to do the Oliver Twist bit and ask the Anfield chairman and secretary for more.

With trembling lips I ventured, 'I think what you are ready to give me is fair enough but I just thought it might have been a little better.' I didn't say how much better and I waited, heart pumping, for their reaction. Kenny was spot on, of course. He was right when he said I would get a little more, and again about the agent not squeezing another penny out of them. I paid around £1,000 for his trouble. I know other players set great store by using agents whenever they move, but I have never used one in any transfer deal since. Later when I moved to Everton I handled the negotiations myself and the Professional Footballers' Association, the players' union, acted for me when I returned to Newcastle. There are some very good agents who act honourably with the best interests of clients as their priority, but there are also others who are more interested in lining their own pockets. There are times when you need them to negotiate commercial ventures such as kit sponsorship and personal appearances. Reputable agents with experience in dealing with foreign clubs are also useful for transfers abroad. But generally speaking, if I was a younger lad, or even like me, one who felt mature enough to assess his own value, my advice would be to use the PFA. Their representatives know the ropes; they know what a club could be reasonably expected to pay and, by the same token, they know what a player is worth in wages. And in the long run they could save a lad quite a bit of money.

Anyway, the double whammy of playing for Kenny Dalglish and getting paid considerably more than I had ever earned in my life for the privilege, was a temptation I could not resist. Not that I wanted to. In fact I was desperate to sign for Liverpool before they changed their minds. The deal was for five years at more than double what I was picking up at Newcastle. But I still left Tyneside with a heavy heart. It was a pity I had to move away to realize the ambitions which were fulfilled handsomely on Merseyside. Newcastle did eventually get the cheque book out to buy players like Andy Thorn, Dave Beasant and John Hendrie after I left. My contention was why wait until then? Players should have been bought to supplement what was already at the club, not to replace them.

Such thoughts had to become part of my past. My priorities now lay in helping to restore Liverpool to their former title-winning greatness. I was 26 years old and really excited at joining such a famous club. In fact I would have gone anywhere to play for Kenny. I was moved by his gesture at our meeting which took me back a few years to that conversation I had with Arthur Cox on the journey to Huddersfield. 'I want you to wear my number seven shirt,' he told me. 'You could become as big a favourite here as I have been.'

I never was, of course, but it was nice of him to say it anyway. Kenny could not have imagined a bigger compliment than handing me the shirt he wore with such success. My career was decidedly upwardly mobile and I prepared for the first season at Anfield confident that I had finally arrived in the theatre of dreams.

6

LIVERPOOL HONOUR

I thought I saw stars in Vancouver but that was like comparing a bang on the head to the Milky Way when I first caught sight of the faces that greeted me on my arrival at Melwood for my first day's training with Liverpool. My England team-mate John Barnes had beaten me to Anfield by a month – and how much I was going to be grateful for that. We were the newcomers joining established favourites such as Mark Lawrenson, Alan Hansen, Stevie Nicol, Steve McMahon, Jan Molby and others. John Aldridge had arrived from Oxford United the previous season, and I was happy to cross paths again with Bruce Grobbelaar, a goalkeeper I had just missed playing with in Canada. I first came across Bruce when both of us were new to professional football. He played for Crewe in a reserve team at Carlisle and his performance that night has always stuck in the memory. We absolutely paralysed the opposition but, thanks to his brilliant goalkeeping, we ended up losing 3–0. It was no great surprise to me that he went on to a long and distinguished career at Liverpool. He also preceded me by a couple of seasons with the Whitecaps. So I was particularly pleased to catch up with him at long last.

When you go to a new club there is always a certain time needed to settle and, inevitably, a lot of mickey-taking goes on. It happens at every club. Players test a new boy out; they want to see what makes him tick, what sort of personality he has. It can be quite a traumatic time and I know of a few players who have found difficulty in adjusting. But there were no such problems for me. Of course, there was leg-pulling and an awful lot of pressure but there was also a lot of help and understanding and I did not have to look further than Bruce Grobbelaar and Mark Lawrenson for advice. As well as being a great goalkeeper Bruce is one of the kindest men I have ever met. He is always so nice to people, a real gentleman. Liverpool's success may be founded on an all-round contribution from everybody in the team, but while I was there I could look back on countless number of games where Bruce was the main man as far as winning points were concerned. I thought he was in a different class. He was superb and so reliable. He really was the best goalkeeper in the Football League. There were times when he must have been as anxious as the rest of us but he never showed it. There were also his antics to keep everybody on their toes. He has this zany sense of humour which often surfaced to destroy the most serious moment.

Lawrenson was every inch the perfect senior pro. When I arrived he was still recuperating from a serious Achilles tendon injury he suffered a few months earlier. Consequently he did not play very often, which was a sad blow for the club, but he was still important to have around and his assurances did a lot to get me through an important early crisis at the club. 'Don't be so anxious. Just go out and play your normal game,' he used to tell me. 'You have nothing to prove. Everybody knows you can play. The club would not have paid out all that money if you couldn't. We'll help you through it.'

I needed their help too because for the first four and a half months after my move to Liverpool I had a nightmare. I must have been a big let-down. Judged on my own and anybody else's standards for that matter, I was simply atrocious. I could not blame the settling in, although for all of the period I was struggling and a little more after that, I was living in hotel accommodation. Dalglish had arranged a 17-day pre-season European tour during which Barnesy and I really got to know everybody. We crammed in matches practically every other day, although we did not get off to the best of starts, having to endure a 5–1 hammering at Bayern Munich but there were excuses for that and we weren't too concerned. We had only been back in training a fortnight whereas the Germans had already played a few games.

By the time we got back home everybody was primed and ready for the big kick-off. Drainage problems at Anfield forced us to play the first three games away from home but that made no difference to our breathtaking opening spell. There was a crowd of 54,703 – the biggest for a league match on any ground that season – for our first game at Arsenal. The atmosphere was unbelievable and I could not have been more satisfied with my start. I linked up with Barnesy to set up the first goal for John Aldridge, and away we went. Paul Davis equalized but then I had to go off injured. Steve Williams had been kicking hell out of me all afternoon and I finished up with a dead leg. Paul Walsh came on and did well, and Stevie Nicol headed a great winner near the end.

I wished I could have played the whole match but I didn't let that disappointment spoil my day. As far as I was concerned, it was the first step towards the kind of success I hoped would come my way at Liverpool. To come away from

Highbury with a win convinced me I had done exactly the right thing. It was also the beginning of an incredible run which saw us equal the First Division's best-ever start, the 29-match unbeaten record which Leeds had set up fourteen years earlier.

I would like to have done more towards it. Try as I did, prepare as much as I did, I just could not do a thing right and it really got me down. How I envied Barnesy. As much as I was bad, he was brilliant. He was out of the traps like a Greyhound Derby winner. Thank goodness, because no one knew more than I, it was only his good form and the fact we never lost a league match which eased what could have been considerable personal anxiety. John and I had become good friends when I was picked for England. He became my room-mate for three years while I was at Liverpool and must have got fed up with listening to me pouring out all my problems and anxieties about my form but he was patient, under-standing and supportive. He gave me a lot of encouragement, but I just wish he could have lent me a little of his magic.

For two years he played better than I have ever seen him. He was the complete artist, demonstrating skill, passing, movement, tormenting opponents almost at will, making goals, and scoring goals. It was just a pleasure to be in the same side. It was tragic that his later career at Liverpool should be blighted by a succession of serious injuries. It started with an Achilles which maybe, in hindsight, he tried to come back from too quickly. After that he was out of action for several months because of calf trouble. I think that encouraged some people to write him off too early but he has certainly answered that criticism with a little interest. He has been back to something like his best the last couple of seasons. Not only did he force his way back into the England side but he also showed that if he stays clear of injury trouble he has two or three good years left at the very top as the midfield playmaker for Liverpool.

So Barnesy's form cushioned the blow of my own disastrous start. I could not put my finger on the reason for my problems. I did manage a few goals. In fact I didn't have to wait long for my first in a Liverpool shirt. It came in a 4–1 win in our second game at Coventry. Gary Gillespie knocked a ball through the middle; Brian Borrows played me onside and I dummied Steve Ogrizovic before side-footing it into the net. I also had the satisfaction of a successful first return to Newcastle. We won 4–1 with Steve Nicol scoring a great hat-trick. I helped by delivering the final pass for one of them. I felt the game underlined my new horizons as well as the yawning gap between what I had left behind and what I had to look forward to. But even that reassurance provided only small comfort for the dip in my own form. Everybody was sympathetic and very helpful, not least the manager who kept me in the side, even when at times I played absolute rubbish. Kenny was great after I missed a game at Spurs through injury. Walsh came in and scored in a 2–0 win that took us back to the top of the league, a lead we were not to relinquish again that season. But Kenny brought me straight back when I was fit enough to play in the next game. I would have loved to have justified his confidence but things did not get any better. I think I reached my lowest ebb after playing badly in a League Cup game at Blackburn Rovers which ended in a 1–1 draw. I took some almighty stick in the papers the next day. One particular tabloid plastered a headline across its pages which screamed out 'PETER THE PLONKER'. The story beneath it was all about my poor form and that I wasn't good enough to wear a Liverpool shirt. It had one lasting effect – I have never bought a national newspaper since!

I appreciate that football writers have a right to criticize and it was true that I had a bad game but I did not see the need for that kind of headline. I was disgusted by it. You try not to let things like that get you down, but footballers are only human and I was bothered. I was just pleased I had no children at the time. I would not have liked a kid of mine to read something like that about me. It could have had the same detrimental effect on him as it had on me. Even when my form was at its worst, I still went out and did my best. It isn't your day every day, but then is that not the same for doctors, teachers, politicians – and even journalists? I just wish at times they would colour their opinions with a little understanding.

My personal purgatory continued until Christmas but I managed to console myself with the fact that we were racing away at the top of the league. We went to Oxford United on Boxing Day and our 3–0 win took us ten points clear. Then, and not before time, as suddenly and mysteriously as my best form had deserted me, it came back and all I can say is, thank goodness for Coventry! My first Liverpool goal had been against the Sky Blues and they were also the opposition when I played what I thought was my first decent game since I went to Anfield. Mind you, it had taken me until New Year's Day, by which time even my own patience and morale were becoming decidedly tatty. I scored twice in a 4–0 victory. Our lead was extended to 13 points and I never looked back.

Life at Liverpool was all about milestones and we reached our next one on 16 March when we went to Derby County needing to avoid defeat to equal that Leeds record. Craig Johnston's goal helped us to a 1–1 draw. Then, four days later, it was Everton who stood between us and another place in posterity. It gave our rivals something to look forward to because they were not having the best of times. The celebrations after winning the championship the previous season had fallen flat but they were clearly up for the game because Wayne Clarke, who played up front, had made noises about preserving the record for his brother Allan who had played in the Leeds team. And he was as good as his word. He put them ahead and, although we battered them after that, we just could not get the equalizer. At least it gave the Everton supporters something to cheer about, especially as they must have known by then that the title was about to make the short journey back across Stanley Park. We were disappointed but philosophical. Good things come to an end, but I was now well enough immersed in the passion of Merseyside to appreciate that they didn't have to end at Goodison Park.

Still, at the end of the day, to begin my Anfield career by virtually clinching my first championship medal by the end of March was pure fantasy. In fact Liverpool only lost once more in the league. That was 2–1 at Nottingham Forest and I did not start that game. The boss rested Ray Houghton and myself because we were due to meet Forest in the semi-final of the FA Cup a week later and he did not feel inclined to show his hand to their manager Brian Clough. And revenge was sweet when we met at Hillsborough. Aldo came up with two goals but we played well and Forest could not complain about their 2–1 defeat. It was a great moment for me personally when the referee blew the final whistle. All right, we looked odds-on for the title but getting to the FA Cup final at Wembley was something else as far as I was concerned. It was what I had dreamed about when I was a kid. Now it was reality and, feeling as delighted as I was, it would have been slightly hypocritical to feel too sorry that Cloughie had been denied his first FA Cup final. I am afraid we rubbed it in somewhat in the week following the semi-final when we played Forest again in the league at Anfield and simply annihilated them 5–0. I have been part of few better team performances than that one. People rated it among the best by any Liverpool side in living memory, even better than when the boss, Kevin Keegan helped them win the European Cup against Borussia Moenchengladbach.

My whole outlook had changed dramatically for the better from the way I felt during the first half of the season. At least I was playing a part in the team's success instead of feeling like an expensive passenger. That was never underlined more than when I scored the goal against Spurs that actually clinched the championship when the season still had a fortnight and four more games to go. Ray Houghton played the ball across to me on the corner of the 18-yard box. I cut inside Gary Mabbutt and bent the ball inside the far post past Bobby Mimms. Anfield erupted in a mass of red and white after the whistle. The fact that the supporters were used to success did not make it any less sweet but, if they had seen it all before, it was a new experience for me and I lapped it up. This was my first honour and I was particularly pleased to share it with Barnesy because it was his first winner's medal as well. He had been in awesome shape all season and was picking up his just reward. The celebrations continued in the dressing-room afterwards and I treasure a photograph which shows Steve McMahon pouring champagne over the two new boys' heads as we sat with glasses in our hands. Barnesy had a drop of bubbly but I was just as happy drinking lucozade. 'Come on Pedro, get some champagne down you. This is Liverpool – this is what you came here for.' The lads tried to tempt me but I wasn't going to be persuaded to break the habit of a lifetime.

The fact is I have never been a drinker. I don't like the taste of lager or beer and, quite frankly, the smell makes me feel sick. I don't even have the odd glass of wine with a meal. I honestly just can't fathom the fascination for alcohol. Don't get me wrong, I don't object to other people enjoying a pint. My dad likes nothing better than a bottle of Newcastle Brown Ale; my mam used to love a glass of amber and my two brothers appreciate a lager or a beer. Although Sandra is no drinker either, she has been known to partake of the odd dry martini or glass of bubbly on special occasions. Me? I would sooner not bother. I remember in the days when I supported my brothers in The Fusilier team and later when I played for them myself, we would all go back to the pub afterwards and either celebrate or drown our sorrows. But I did it with a glass of orange. That did not stop me being a regular in The Fusilier where I also used to run the pub goals buster competition. I rarely missed a Saturday from six o'clock until maybe ten, chatting and having a few games of pool before going home to watch 'Match Of The Day'.

I have always been around people who like a drink. If I am out for a social evening I'll have a coke, lime and lemonade or orange squash, and be perfectly happy watching my friends and relations getting tipsy. It was not a pre-ordained plan to maintain a decent physical condition but it has certainly helped. I know I am an exception as far as footballers are concerned but it takes all kinds. I'm no do-gooder; the only thing I would say is I think it is a shame when some players throw away their God-given talent too early. There is no doubt that a few brilliant careers have been shortened by overdoing it.

Some managers insist that social drinking is good for dressing-room morale and I wouldn't argue with that. I remember when I signed for Everton, their manager Howard Kendall winked at me and said, 'I know you don't drink Peter but you soon will here.' To be fair, he tried a few times but then gave up. It was enough for him that, if we were on a trip together to somewhere like Ireland, I would be out with the rest of the lads, joining in the fun. It's true I have been accused of being a boring sod but I can take all that. I'll keep anybody company in the evening but the next morning I don't wake up with a hangover and I can remember everything that happened the night before. I think there's a lot to be said for that!

Well, if I couldn't be tempted to hit the bottle after winning my first honour, I never will. But there was not a player at Liverpool who relished the moment more than I did. Later, I discovered how success was received at Anfield and I must admit I got a bit of a shock. There was an official presentation of medals on the pitch with the chairman handing them to the players. Then we all passed them over to Ronnie Moran, the first team coach, who collected them before the pre-match warm-up. Maybe I thought we would get them back at a private club ceremony or something like that. How wrong I was. After the match, Ronnie brought a cardboard box into the dressing-room and dumped it on the table. 'There you go,' he announced. 'If you have earned a medal, take one.' And that was as far as ceremonies go at Liverpool. One by one we walked over and picked one out of the box and put it in our pockets before we left. Talk about being brought back down to earth with a bump!

That was not only typical of Liverpool, it was par for the course as far as Ronnie was concerned. He is certainly not a man to stand on ceremony. Before I went there I heard stories about the no-nonsense attitude of the back-room staff but you have to experience it to know what it is really like. The Anfield dressing-room might have been filled with household names but try to act like a star and you are soon taken down a peg or two. Not that anybody tries that too often. You were just not allowed to be a prima donna, or have any edge, with blokes like Ronnie Moran around. He has a tremendous rapport with Roy Evans. Of course, Roy has since taken over as manager but these two are essentially a team. When I was there, Ronnie was the hard man – he would be the one doing the shouting and he didn't mince words. If he thought you were a pillock, he said so in the kind of colourful language you became used to. But you respected him for that. Roy was the one who would pat you on the back and try to cheer you up, especially after one of Ronnie's tirades. It was an ideal link in what it takes to make a successful partnership and it is no surprise at all that the pair of them, with Roy in charge now, have turned things around at Liverpool. What they demand is one hundred per cent effort. They want to win. If you did your best and had a bad day they accepted that, but woe betide any player they thought hadn't put everything in during a game. Life would not be worth living for that person – no matter who he was.

Ronnie was the main man as far as the training and coaching were concerned. He used to do the lot. It was never too complicated a programme. In fact, it hardly changed much from day to day. A typical session would start with a jog round for about six or seven minutes with Ronnie and Roy at the front dictating the pace we should go. Then we would form a circle and do a few muscle stretches. Those would be followed by some more running and walking before we joined in an eight-a-side match across the training pitch. Ronnie would constantly change the rules of the game from keeping the ball below hip height for one or two touches, to below head height. That would normally last for twenty minutes and afterwards there would be a few shuttles. Then it was another eight-a-side with varying rules for another twenty minutes. We always finished with another match. At different intervals we would practise crossing and shooting with the goalkeepers. It was all so simple. All they ever preached was pass and move.

The practice matches got a bit tasty at times. The teams were usually the same – the staff team included Kenny, Ronnie and Roy supplemented by senior players like Jocky Hansen, Steve McMahon, Ronnie Whelan and Stevie Nicol. They would also try and pinch Barnesy but that was always under protest. The one unchangeable rule was that the staff team must never lose. In fact they would keep playing until they won! If they were behind or it was level, Kenny would say, 'Let's have another five minutes' which would always last until the score was in their favour. The trick was, if the lads didn't fancy a long session because they might have had a heavy night, you let them win. It was all deadly serious in a light-hearted sort of way. The main thing at Liverpool was that you were expected to behave responsibly and that was how you were treated. Nobody worried if the players had a few beers in the evening. They were just expected to do a bit more running the next day.

If I could sum up the whole Liverpool gospel from administration down to match preparation, the word I would use would be – professional. As soon as one match was over, it was all about the next one. There was no question of being allowed to rest on our laurels after winning the title for a record 17th time. We were expected to finish our league programme in the style of champions. Then of course, there was still the FA Cup Final against Wimbledon and the prospect of landing the League and Cup double for the second time in three years. I was looking forward to the build-up to Wembley but again I discovered that the Liverpool way is more about the match and less about the occasion. We didn't indulge ourselves in a week-long preparation in some fancy training quarters. The team left on the Thursday, stayed at High Wycombe and trained at Bisham Abbey. But I loved all the Cup Final trappings which even Liverpool involved themselves with – new track suits, specially-made strips, and smart club suits for the big day. And then the drive down Wembley Way. It was all just as I imagined it would be.

It was just a pity Wimbledon spoiled the script. We fancied our chances after taking four points off them in the league. I'll always remember the Anfield game. We were leading 2–0 when Kenny, who had named himself as sub, decided to make a rare appearance. Wimbledon promptly pulled a goal back and at the end we were hanging on to the points. The boss got some almighty stick from Ronnie and the lads afterwards, 'Well, we can say one thing about that substitution gaffer, it certainly changed the game,' they told him. That was funny – and so was Vinnie Jones in the tunnel before the Final, the difference was that Jones didn't mean to be. He was ranting on to us before we went out, bawling and shouting things like, 'We're going to give you a good stuffing. You're no great shakes, Liverpool.'

I only wish we could have proved him wrong but in fact the team had a bit of a stinker at Wembley. Looking back, the boss might have bent over backwards to be too fair to Gary Gillespie and Nigel Spackman. Five days before the Final we had a game against Luton Town and there was a terrible clash of heads between the two players which resulted in both of them needing almost 20 stitches in bad gashes. They were both in a bad way and it was touch and go whether they would be fit for the Final. In the end they both played and wore headbands. Having said that, it was not down to them, we all played poorly. It might have been different if the referee had allowed a 'goal' I scored early on. There was a long ball played forward and although Andy Thorn fouled me, I managed to get away from him and was in on goal and just lifted the ball over Dave Beasant as he dived. He made out later that he knew the whistle had gone but I wasn't sure whether I believed him. I certainly didn't hear the referee Brian Hill blow for a foul. I was celebrating the goal but turned round to see Mr Hill pointing to the place where he wanted the free-kick taken from. I was disappointed he hadn't played the advantage rule and the crowd were a bit upset as well. I thought he was too far from the incident.

Anyway, what made it worse was that Wimbledon scored when Lawrie Sanchez nipped in following a free-kick and then we compounded our poor performance when John Aldridge became the first player to miss an FA Cup Final penalty at Wembley. To be fair, I thought it was a doubtful penalty because Clive Goodyear was harshly judged to have fouled Aldo. But I still fancied him to score. He's rarely missed one before and he hasn't missed many since. But he was disappointed with his effort and Beasant made a good save. The lad was devastated after the game and it took him a while to get over it. Still, I don't think we could grumble at the result. Wimbledon probably deserved it. It was just a shame we missed out on the Double and the chance to play in the European Cup the following season because of the ban following the Heysel Stadium disaster.

But there was still plenty of room for optimism, especially with the squad strengthened by the return after one season in Italy of Ian Rush. I was really looking forward to playing with him although it was obvious his arrival would step up the competition for first team places with Aldo still looking as sharp as ever. He was on fire from the first kick, starting with the Charity Shield at Wembley when he achieved some compensation for his penalty miss three months earlier by scoring the two goals that beat Wimbledon 2–1. Then he bettered that in some style with an opening-day hat-trick against Charlton Athletic. The boss had warned the three of us he would be doing a bit of swapping around and that, on occasions, somebody was going to be disappointed. I got the picture when he took me off and brought Rushie on in that first game. Then it was my turn to be substitute in a game against Aston Villa. It was the first time it had happened in a league game for Liverpool and, although I understood Kenny was making the best of his resources and accepted the situation, I was still disappointed to be left out.

I couldn't complain about the run I had after that. I was never out of the side until early in February when he decided to stick me on the bench at Newcastle of all places. I had been looking forward to going back and I did get on eventually but that again was disappointing. My dad had gone to the game and I would have liked to have been on from the start. A succession of injuries, especially in the run-up to Christmas, meant we weren't able to put out a settled side and losing at home to Norwich City dropped us to sixth place in the league, something like 19 points behind the leaders Arsenal with apparently little chance of retaining the title. Then we were beaten 3–1 at Manchester United on New Year's Day, by which time most 'experts' had completely written off our prospects. So much for an opinion which, incidentally, was never shared within the walls of the Liverpool dressing-room. That Old Trafford defeat turned out to be our last until the final game of the season when, as everybody will remember, we had the Championship whipped from under our noses in the most dramatic finale there has ever been. I enjoyed most of that unbeaten run while it lasted, particularly a sequence of nine successive league wins between March and April which, ironically, coincided exactly with the enforced absence through injury of Rushie. Aldo and I shared the striking role and managed 13 goals between us. Even more satisfying was the fact that the last of those victories, at Millwall, took us to the top of the league for the first time that season on goal difference.

So the stage was set for the showdown to end all showdowns. But 26 May 1989 was an unforgettable day for other, personal, reasons which far outweighed the destiny of the league title and made the eventual outcome of the evening's drama easier to accept. Sandra was about to give birth to our first child and that very day, she went into hospital to be induced. Her well-being and that of our baby were unquestionably my main concern anyway but other events that morning made the Arsenal match even less of a priority.

We had played a league match against West Ham on the Tuesday of that week. Before that, on the previous Saturday, we had put ourselves in line for the League-FA Cup Double which had narrowly escaped us a year earlier by beating Everton after extra-time at Wembley. Because I had played the whole of the 120 minutes in the Final, Kenny came to me before the Hammers' game and told me he was putting me on the bench. I understood and accepted his decision without a problem. With the title balanced on a knife-edge, a win against West Ham was important but there was also goal difference to think about, as it seemed extremely likely the Championship would go right to the wire.

I sat and watched as the team reached a situation where we were leading 2–1 with about 15 minutes to go. That's when the boss turned to me and said, 'Get your track-suit off Peter, you're going on.' And on I went for the final quarter of an hour during which time I made three goals for Houghton, Rush and Barnes and we finished up winning 5–1. The scoreline meant that when Arsenal came to Anfield the following Friday in the Championship shoot-out, we needed only to draw but the Gunners had to beat us by two clear goals. Come Friday I had plenty of things on my mind but I felt my contribution against West Ham was sure to win me a place in the starting line-up against Arsenal and I was really ready for it.

I was anxious when Kenny took me aside after our morning warm-up. Then he delivered his team decision. 'I want to play the side that started at West Ham, Peter. You will be on the bench again.' To be honest, I was really gutted. I had played in most of the matches and felt I had earned the chance to be in at the kill. As it turned out, I did get on just before half-time when Rushie went off with an injury but I still felt let down and because of that, and with everything else going on that day, I was probably less affected by the result than the rest.

As it happened, I thought Arsenal deserved the victory that won them the title. Their first goal after 52 minutes may have been a bit dubious because there was an element of doubt about whether Alan Smith got a touch to an indirect free-kick. We still looked odds-on as the game headed towards injury-time. I remember Steve McMahon going round with one finger up, indicating there was a minute to go. But nothing is ever certain in football, as we found out. John Lukic threw the ball out to Lee Dixon. It got knocked up the line and then crossed to where Michael Thomas had made a great run through the middle. Thomas finished it magnificently, just flicking the ball over Bruce into the net. It really was a goal good enough to win a title.

The Liverpool supporters had demonstrated a week earlier at Wembley how much they enjoyed a triumph but this night they also showed they could be magnificent in defeat. They gave the Arsenal players a standing ovation at the end. I went into their dressing-room afterwards and congratulated them and then headed straight to the hospital to see Sandra, who had watched the game on television. The following day our son Drew was born and by that time the disappointment of losing the title was almost forgotten.

The birth had been arranged for a time when I could be there and yet I almost missed it. I left the hospital in Liverpool after midnight the evening before and made the 30 minute drive to our home in Southport, leaving behind a request for them to let me know of any developments. I got a call the next morning at seven o'clock from the nurse who told me Sandra had gone into labour. For some reason I thought it was nine o'clock which is why the caller must have been a little surprised to hear me say – 'I'll be there at ten.' She went back to Sandra and told her – 'Your husband seems to be taking the birth of his baby in his stride.' Privately she must have thought I was a right pillock. Of course I realized my mistake and arrived at the hospital in good time to be there when it happened. It was the most wonderful experience anybody could ever have.

Maybe I should have felt more sorry about missing out on the Double for the second successive season, but because of all that had happened – getting left out, and then the baby being born – I was not too upset. Arthur Cox had always preached that family comes before football. Remembering that helped to put things into their proper perspective.

Anyway, my personal happiness was even less of a reason why the game and its glittering prizes took second place that season. We had brought a new life into the world but, a few weeks earlier, just because they wanted to watch a football match, 96 lives had been extinguished. For everybody who went to Hillsborough on 15 April 1989, nothing would ever be quite the same.

7

TRAGEDY THEN TRIUMPH

The mood of the Liverpool players and staff as we boarded the team coach the Thursday afternoon before the semi-final was one of quiet but buoyant confidence. We were on a high. Two days earlier we had gone to Millwall and beaten them 2–1 to make it nine league wins on the trot. Not only that, the victory had taken us to the top of the First Division table for the first time that season. Now we were on our way to play Nottingham Forest in an FA Cup semi-final at Hillsborough, the home of Sheffield Wednesday, a team incidentally we had trounced 5–1 the previous Saturday.

The trip across to Yorkshire was uneventful. Some of the lads played cards while others read books. We eventually arrived at the Hallam Tower Hotel relaxed and ready for final preparation for the game. After training on Friday, some of the players went for a walk around the shops; the rest either retired early or got the cards out again. The following morning we had a leisurely amble around the car park just to loosen up and get some fresh air before the pre-match meal. I skipped the food because I had settled for bacon and eggs for breakfast. Then we had a team chat where we discussed the match and talked about the opposition, before we got on to the bus for the short trip to the ground.

We arrived at Hillsborough around quarter to two, an hour and a quarter before the kick-off, and immediately went to look at the pitch, which looked great. There were cheers for us from Liverpool supporters and, as we expected, a few boos from the Forest fans who were mainly gathered in the huge Kop to the right of the tunnel. Then we got stripped, put on our tracksuit tops and, at half past two, went out for a pre-match warm-up. We took the Leppings Lane End where the Liverpool followers were gathering and I started kicking in against Bruce Grobbelaar. Even at that time I remember Bruce voicing concern at the way some of the fans seemed to be pushing up against the wire fence. Whenever one of my shots went wide and he went to retrieve the ball, Bruce urged them not to press forward so much. He came back to tell me there were kids at the front who didn't look too comfortable.

It was worrying but we assumed everything would be all right. We returned to the dressing-room and by the time we came back out for the match, the crowd was packing in and the atmosphere was really beginning to build. That sort of thing gets to a player. It was a big game and the only thing on my mind was beating Forest and getting to the FA Cup Final for the second successive year.

The game started and after four or five minutes we won a corner. The ball came to me and I rattled in a shot which clipped the top of the bar and went over. It was a reasonable chance and I was disappointed to have missed it. Better luck next time. The game went on for barely another minute when suddenly I saw the referee Ray Lewis tap Ronnie Whelan and say, 'Come on, we're going off.' I turned around to look back behind our goal to witness scenes of chaos with spectators climbing over the fence and into the upper areas of the stand

and spilling over on to the pitch. The players trotted off down the tunnel, thinking at the time that whatever problems there were, they would all be sorted out very quickly and we would be back on.

Nothing that occurred in the dressing room indicated anything to the contrary. We were completely cut off from the tragedy that was unfolding outside. Ronnie Moran and Roy Evans came in and instructed us to try and keep warm before we went out again. 'Keep on the move, rub your leg muscles,' they urged. The time passed slowly. We chatted about this and that and about different aspects of the game. Then we began to hear ambulance and police car sirens. Something serious was obviously going on but we did not know what and, as far as we knew, when it got sorted out we would still be going out to play a football match. We put on our tracksuits and continued our warming-up exercises. That went on for well over an hour until Ronnie came back in and told us it was all over; that the game had been abandoned. We dressed in a complete daze, totally bemused by the situation and still totally ignorant of everything that had gone on out on the pitch while we sat cocooned in the bowels of the main stand.

It was only after we left the dressing room that the real horror became known to us. We went upstairs into the players' lounge and joined our wives who were watching in silent anguish as television cameras, which had gone to cover a Cup semi-final, portrayed instead scenes of utter devastation. People were running here, there and everywhere, with some carrying advertising hoardings which had been converted into stretchers to carry the dead and injured. And the more I looked, the more I could not comprehend what I was witnessing. Nothing was said; it was all too terrible to be true. The number of dead kept mounting and each new

125

horrific bulletin brought its gasps of disbelief. Everybody felt so helpless. Then the time came for us to leave. All the players and their wives got on the bus and we all just looked out of the windows as it eased its way through the avenues of ambulances and police cars and vans that were still at the scene. We left what looked more like a battlefield than a football field – and headed back to a grieving Merseyside.

The following days were just an unreal haze. The impact of the tragedy grew more terrible as you read and heard the individual stories of heartbreak and sorrow. The worse part about it all was there was not a thing that could be done to take away all the pain. As players all we could do was await further instructions about what to do. Three days after the disaster the whole team returned together to Sheffield to visit the injured in hospital. We tried to comfort them the best way we could.

Dalglish was incredible. What he went through and what he did for the people of Liverpool had to be seen to be appreciated. And his wife Marina was just the same. It was almost as if she was a trained counsellor. They talked to the families and friends of the bereaved and injured, providing comfort and staying in control of their emotions when they must have been breaking-up inside. They went to every funeral they could physically attend, as did some of the players. John Barnes must have gone to about thirty himself. I am sorry to say I went to only one in Bury. It was just too much for me. I could not handle the grief of the relatives; it was all so heart-breaking. They were crying on your shoulder and I felt so helpless, trying to comfort them when it was practically impossible.

We had a few days when families of the dead supporters came to Anfield. Everybody on the staff – Kenny, Ronnie, Roy, the rest of the coaches and all the players – mingled and talked; anything to try and help them through their distress and despair. Everybody was inspired by the way Kenny conducted himself. He was a credit to himself, the club and to football. I kept thinking how doubly difficult it must have been for him and the others still at the club who had also to deal with the aftermath of the Heysel stadium tragedy.

Blame has been apportioned since; there have been recriminations and I don't think it serves any useful purpose. We had played the same fixture twelve months earlier on the same ground against the same opposition without a hitch. It was just a terrible act of fate. Later I heard that it was the roar which greeted my shot against the bar which might have sparked off the tragic crowd thrust through the tunnel behind the Leppings Lane goal; I have often wondered whether the surge might have been greater with even worse consequences had the ball gone in. But it was a day when you could not help thoughts of what could have been done to prevent the worst tragedy ever to hit English football.

It was two weeks before Liverpool played another game. We beat Celtic 4–0 at Parkhead in a match for the Hillsborough Disaster Fund. I was substitute, accepting that it was appropriate that Kenny played himself against his former club. Decisions were made to continue with the football programme as normal, especially the FA Cup because it was felt it was what the bereaved families wanted. We had a two-day break in Blackpool to prepare for our first league match since the disaster, appropriately at Goodison Park. I thought the fixture was well-timed because of the extraordinary rapport between the supporters of both clubs. The Everton fans shared in the tragedy which had befallen their rivals and the atmosphere that night was something special, far more emotional than in any Mersey derby I had ever played in.

Our FA Cup Final meeting three weeks later was also a memorable occasion, but Wembley finals usually are. This was different, red and blue linking arms more than they ever had before and probably ever will again. The message from Goodison Park that night was that the football show must go on. It was almost incidental that we were attempting to win our tenth successive league game. It was not the best of matches – rather low key with none of the aggression that is normally a feature of a derby confrontation – and a goalless draw was perhaps the most fitting outcome.

Inevitably there were further echoes of Hillsborough when we got round to replaying the semi-final against Forest at Old Trafford. I remember the occasion of course. It seemed fated we should win it and we did, by a comfortable 3–1 margin. But I also won't forget the little personal tribute I received from Brian Clough. There was a lot of clamour at the time for his son Nigel to take my place in the England team. But Cloughie senior came up to me as I stood in the tunnel before the game in my normal position at the back of the line. He just looked at me and said, 'Son, they talk about my lad Nigel but I'll tell you now, he couldn't tie your bootlaces.' Then he just walked off. It might have been psychology or even kidology. Who knows, he might have meant it, but he made me feel ten feet tall and I like to think I justified his opinion during the game. Later he came into the dressing room, shook my hand and congratulated me. 'Well done Peter, enjoy your day at Wembley.' That after we had destroyed his FA Cup ambition for the second successive year.

I have always admired Brian Clough. If I have one big regret from my career, it is not playing in a side he has managed. I would have loved even just one game for him to experience his style of management. He is a bit different, isn't he? I remember one game against Forest when I was at Newcastle and I picked up a rare booking for a tackle on Johnny Metgod. I thought the Dutchman had made a meal of it and so apparently did the Forest manager. He stormed up to the touchline and bawled at Metgod: 'Get up, you cheating sod!' How many bosses would have the courage to do that, especially to somebody of the reputation and calibre of Metgod? But it was typical of Cloughie. Whatever anybody says about him now, they cannot take away what he achieved in the game.

And so we were back at Wembley but this time when we faced Everton, the gloves were off. Having missed out the previous year, I badly wanted a Cup-winners medal and I was geared mentally and physically for the match. And what a final it was! We held the lead three times, starting when Aldo scored after four minutes. Stuart McCall equalized late on to send the game into extra-time which was when Rushie came on to win the game for us with two superb efforts to cancel out one from McCall. I suppose after all that happened, we were destined to win the Cup, but from a purely personal point of view the moment of victory at Wembley was something I had always hoped for.

My only disappointment was when the Liverpool supporters, naturally carried away by a wave of emotion, invaded the pitch after the whistle which forced us to abandon the traditional lap of honour with the trophy. I had always wanted to run around Wembley with the Cup. It was also a pity we missed out on the double again, but as I have said, that pain was eased by the arrival of my baby son. Anyway, a league championship and FA Cup winner's medal were not a bad haul from my first two seasons at Liverpool.

As things turned out it was the halfway point of my time at

Anfield. However, had I chosen otherwise, I could have been on my way out of the club that summer. The chance of a shock move arose when Kenny called me and dropped what could only be described as a transfer bombshell. It was about three weeks after the Arsenal match that he rang me at home and announced, 'Marseilles want to buy you.' He went on to tell me that Bernard Tapie, the famous French club president, was prepared to fly over in a private jet to talk to me. They had offered £3.6 million and I got the distinct impression Liverpool wanted to take the money.

I was astounded and not a little flattered. But a move to the Continent was not in my immediate plans. Drew had just been born and we were very settled as a family. I told Kenny I was not interested in moving to France. He just said, 'Fair enough' and that was the end of it, though I sensed he was a bit upset about not being able to do the deal. About three weeks later, Marseilles paid Tottenham £4.25 million for my former Newcastle team-mate Chris Waddle. I wondered at the time whether Chris would have had the chance of what turned out to be a dream move if I had decided to meet Monsieur Tapie.

I have no regrets about staying at Liverpool. At first I was unsure as to what it would be like the following season, especially after the Marseilles business, but to be fair Kenny never mentioned it. It was almost as if it had never happened and that suited me. It certainly did not affect my relationship with the manager. I felt just as much a part of the Liverpool set-up as I always had. We kicked off the season with the Charity Shield at Wembley where I scored the winner against Arsenal. The goal ensured my place against Manchester City for the opening game of the season and I managed to break the habit of a lifetime by scoring for the first time in the curtain-raising league game. I felt really chuffed about it, not only because of what had happened at the end of the season and during the summer, but also because I anticipated that competition for places was going to be really fierce with so many good players at the club.

I was in the side all the time and the team had a good start, topping off our early performances with a tremendous 9–0 hammering of Crystal Palace at the beginning of September. The result wasn't the only significant factor in the game. I remember scoring the fifth goal after about an hour and then a few minutes later we were awarded a penalty. I was a bit surprised to see Roy Evans holding up the number seven as we were waiting for the penalty to be taken. John Aldridge took my place on the field and, with his first touch, cracked the ball in the net from the spot. Nobody realized it at the time but it was Liverpool's way of saying thank you and goodbye to Aldo, who was transferred to Spanish club Real Sociedad the following day for £1.1 million.

It was another tremendous season for Liverpool. For the third successive year we came close to the Double, winning the championship but losing to Crystal Palace – yes, the same Palace we had hammered earlier in the season – 4–3 after extra-time in an epic FA Cup semi-final after we led 3–2 with a minute to go. My second championship medal was something of an anti-climax simply because I missed the end-of-season matches with a stress fracture of the knee which had been diagnosed after the semi-final. Apparently it had been building up for weeks, but I really felt some serious twinges in that game.

Nobody should ever take the game's triumphs for granted. I had been lucky enough to achieve a top honour in each of the three seasons I had been at Anfield but, I have to confess, that second title success did not carry the same impact as the first, two years earlier. We hadn't demonstrated the same consistency as we had then. We were beaten by the likes of Southampton, Coventry, Queen's Park Rangers and Sheffield Wednesday although it must be said that the team finished in some style, winning seven and drawing two of our last nine league games. There were rumblings in some quarters that our success reflected the falling standards of English football at the highest level. Everybody felt acutely disappointed that there weren't the rewards of European competition awaiting the successful teams. I felt that until we could put ourselves to the test against the top Continental sides, the English First Division was fair game for criticism.

Kenny was considerate about my injury and insisted I took my time to make sure my knee healed properly. He also kept me involved with the first team. I travelled on the team coach to Coventry for the last game of the season and sat in the dug-out as Liverpool finished their programme with a flourish, beating City 6–1. By this time Ronnie Moran had already performed the usual honours 'ceremony' – 'There's your medals, just take one if you've won one' – and I duly lifted mine out of the cardboard box. But my knee was still giving me a lot of concern. I badly wanted to be fit to be involved with England, especially with the World Cup coming up that summer.

The manager's attitude was superb. Whenever I had a problem, whether it be personal or professional, he was always there to listen and give advice. A typical situation was when my mam died suddenly in the summer of 1988. We were in Spain at the time for a pre-season tournament and based in La Corunna. We had just finished training on the Sunday morning when Ronnie told me the gaffer wanted to see me. Kenny sat me down and told me he had some bad news – that my mam had passed away during the night. She had been poorly with chest problems but nobody expected her to go so soon. She was only sixty and her death hit me pretty hard because although I had been away from home virtually since I was 18, we were still very close as a family. The only time I had been touched by the death of someone close before my mam was when my good friend and mentor Brian Watson died very suddenly soon after I joined Liverpool. It took me a while to get over that. Kenny left me alone and told me to use his phone to call anybody I chose. I rang Sandra and my dad. It was very distressing, especially being away from home when it happened.

We had a game that night against Real Sociedad. The boss said he would put me on the bench and give me twenty minutes if I was up to it. I sat there and then told him I wanted to go on. I just felt my mam would have approved. Nobody was more supportive than she was when, as a kid, my heart was set on becoming a footballer. It was her little white lie to Geoff Allen of Newcastle that helped to get me started. That twenty minutes was for her and I don't think I let her down. In fact, I think it was the best little spell I have ever played anywhere.

As I said, I could have no complaints about the way I was treated off the field but at the start of the 1990/91 season, one or two of Dalglish's team decisions left me mystified and not a little disappointed, to say the least. I played in the pre-season showpiece, the FA Charity Shield against the FA Cup-holders Manchester United at Wembley. We drew 1–1 and I thought I performed well enough to be in the side for the opening game at Sheffield United. I certainly didn't expect to learn at around two o'clock on the afternoon of the Bramall Lane game that I wasn't even substitute. There were no explanations although the manager had declared at a team meeting a few days earlier that he intended to make full use of a pool of 15 or 16 players. In my place he picked Ronnie Rosenthal, the Israeli international who had arrived towards the end of the previous season. You couldn't argue with Ronnie's goals record. He had earned his nickname of 'Rocket Ronnie' in the short time he had been at Anfield. In fact, in his first full game for the club at Charlton, a game I missed through injury, he scored a great hat-trick. He was never the world's best trainer, but he had a tremendous left foot – Southampton supporters had cause to endorse that in the FA Cup replay two seasons ago when he destroyed the Saints with a hat-trick for Spurs at The Dell. Ronnie's gain at Sheffield was my loss and I was upset at missing out. I remember my former Newcastle team-mate Billy Whitehurst, who by then had gone on to play for the Blades, trying to persuade me to go for a drink before the game. I certainly felt like drowning my sorrows.

On the day you couldn't argue with Ronnie's selection. He made both goals as the lads won a difficult game 3–1. But it might have been a different story had United not lost their goalkeeper Simon Tracey through injury. In those days you did not have the advantage of another keeper on the bench. The next fixture three days later was against Nottingham Forest, a match that was to bring me further bewilderment. I was back in all right and celebrated by scoring a goal in the 83rd minute. My team-mates surrounded me in delight; the supporters were happy, standing and applauding. Kenny celebrated – by pulling me off! I couldn't believe it. In the middle of all the cheers and back-slapping I spied Roy brandishing the number seven. My final contribution to the game was to stick the ball in the net. I wasn't even on the field when the game restarted. The only reason I could offer myself, since I didn't get one from the boss, was that he might have thought I was a bit tired, having not played on the Saturday. But I felt fine and was looking forward to finishing the game. The crowd gave me sympathetic applause as I trudged off and Ronnie ran on to replace me.

And the uncertain pattern of those early matches was maintained. I was picked for the next game against Aston Villa and scored a great goal from the edge of the box but named as substitute for the one after that against Wimbledon. That was par for the course for games against so-called physical sides. Usually it was either myself or Ray Houghton or both who were 'rested' in those games. On this occasion we went there, played five at the back, and beat them 2–1, so achieving the object of the exercise.

I was back for the following match against Manchester United, which was televised live from Anfield. That was one night I won't forget in a hurry – I managed to score a hat-trick and we beat United 4–0. People said I had grabbed the opportunity to prove something to Kenny but that thought never entered my head. It is always special to score against United but to notch three was fantastic and that was satisfaction enough. I was even more delighted the following weekend when we went to Everton and I managed to nick another couple in a 3–2 victory. We absolutely murdered them, taking a 3–0 lead, but then let them off the hook a bit.

It was another great start which seemed to set us up for the season. We won our first eight league games and dominated the First Division table and by the end of November we had won twelve and drawn two of our fourteen matches. There had been a few hiccups, though; I was sub for a game at Spurs, came on and scored and then in the next match against Luton Town I scored again, and this time I was taken off shortly after. But we were doing well and whatever changes Kenny made, unsettling to me personally or not, seemed to be justified by the results. Then we came to play Arsenal at the beginning of December. It was a crucial game as far as the league was concerned because, although the Gunners had not won as many matches as we had, they too were unbeaten in the league and chasing us hard in second place. It was a game anybody worth his salt would have loved to have played in and I was staggered yet again when the team was announced and I was not even on the bench. Two games earlier I had scored my eleventh goal in ten league starts to win the game at Coventry. But Kenny decided to play an ultra-defensive formation at Highbury, naming seven players who had experience in the centre of defence.

Quite honestly, the team got murdered. Our unbeaten league record was shattered by a 3–0 defeat. It was the first time the side had really lost when I had been left out and it sparked off a few questions from various people who were as much in the dark as I was about what was going on. I suppose it could be said that Arsenal at the time had a reputation for being physical and Kenny might have thought the game would not suit me. They played with three big players at the back in David O'Leary, Tony Adams and Steve Bould, and they could dish it out a bit. But there was a lot of criticism expressed that Liverpool should be above worrying about the opposition's strengths and that the manager should always pick his best team.

I have to say that none of that came from me or anybody closely connected with me. Whatever thoughts I had about it, I kept to myself. I never went banging on the manager's door or running to the press to complain. There was not a lot I could do if people wanted to put one and one together to make four. Whenever I was asked, all I said then was what I believe now, that it was the manager's job to pick the team and I accepted that. Anyway, the situation was taken out of his and my own hands in the next game after he brought me back for the return game against Sheffield United. I went over on my ankle and the resulting torn ligaments kept me on the sidelines for two months. I knew it would be difficult to get back when I was fit because the competition for first team places had been strengthened by the arrival of Jimmy Carter from Millwall for £800,000 and the evergreen David Speedie from Coventry for nearly £700,000.

But I was back in the squad as soon as I recovered and was handed the substitute's shirt in a 2–2 FA Cup draw against Brighton and again when we beat them in the replay 3–2 after extra-time. Our next game against Manchester United saw me taking another breather as Speedie celebrated his Liverpool debut with the goal that earned us a 1–1 draw. David was an infectious, fiercely competitive character who did really well in the short time he was at the club. To be fair, he wasn't at Anfield long but he gave everybody a lift. He was a good crack and great fun in the dressing-room. We may have been rivals for a first team shirt but there was no ill-feeling between us. I liked him and got on well with him. Later, it turned out we had more than competition for a first team shirt in common when we both found ourselves on the club's dispensable list.

David scored two more in his next game – one of three successive local 'derbies' against Everton. We had surrendered the top spot to Arsenal but got it back with a 3–1 victory over our neighbours. I was still finding it tough to get back in from the start, although I was substitute in that match and again when we struggled to a goalless draw against the Blues in the next – a fifth round FA Cup tie at Anfield. I went on and hit the post but it was not one of our better team performances. The replay came three days later at Goodison Park and this time I was named in the line-up. Little did anybody at the club know when Kenny read out the team names that it was the prelude to what was probably the most eventful three days in Anfield's chequered history.

The game started well for me. I scored after half an hour but Graeme Sharpe equalized a minute into the second half. Then I put us ahead again but Sharpy levelled for the second time almost immediately afterwards. It was a real thriller with first one side and then the other gaining the initiative, but an Ian Rush effort looked like winning it for us as the match headed towards injury time. That was when Tony Cottee popped up to square the match again and send it into extra-time. John Barnes edged us in front for the fourth time but Cottee's second equalizer meant another replay was necessary. It had been one hell of a game but the mood was a little subdued in our dressing room afterwards. Kenny didn't say much apart from expressing disappointment that we had lost the lead four times. Ronnie typically was less diplomatic, particularly having a go at our defence who really couldn't complain because we had given away some daft goals with schoolboy errors.

But that was it. No major rows, no bust-ups, no angry retaliation. The game was history. We were still in the Cup; we were still top of the league and the next match was at Luton Town on the following Saturday. That was the one we were fixing our sights on. There was a pattern for our visits to Kenilworth Road. We were due to have a little workout on the Friday morning and then leave earlier than usual in order to have a session on Luton's plastic pitch. Normally we would have a chat on the bus but this time Ronnie ordered us to wait in the dressing room.

In walked Kenny and without any warning or preamble he announced quite simply: 'I have handed in my resignation.' There was a deathly silence and everybody looked at him and then each other in stunned disbelief. I thought for a second he might suddenly burst out laughing and tell us how much he had us fooled. Kenny was a great wind-up merchant and nobody would have put it past him to say he was not travelling and then turn up at the hotel having driven down himself.

But any such thoughts soon disappeared. His manner was stiff and he was clearly very upset. 'I have decided I want to spend more time with my family,' he went on. Then he went around the dressing room shaking everybody's hand while we wished him all the best. We all trooped out, still in a state of shock, got on the bus and left for Luton. Apparently there had been a press conference arranged because, as we prepared to leave, the place was crawling with reporters, radio men and TV crews unaware of the reason for their presence .

We found out officially that Kenny had quit when it came over as a newsflash on the radio as we travelled south. I was as stunned and unprepared for what had happened as everyone else. And I was certainly taken by surprise when the newspapers latched on to the theory that not only was I the man responsible for the manager resigning, but they also put forward the even more ludicrous suggestion that a supposed feud between myself and my wife Sandra and Kenny and his wife Marina was at the bottom of it all.

As I have already said I was never very interested in what was written in the press but I had to take notice when reporters came to me with various wild stories which bore no resemblance whatsoever to the truth. The popular one was that Sandra had rowed with Marina because she was upset at me not being in the side. Of course she wasn't happy; she shared my frustrations, but the thought of her taking the matter up with the manager's wife was too preposterous for words. I could always tell Sandra something without it going any further. She never even saw Marina, never mind had a go at her. If she did see her she would treat her with the respect due to the manager's wife. But she would much rather keep out of the way.

The rumours grew more outrageous. Dalglish, taunted by the press about me coming back against Everton and scoring two goals, was supposed to have said, 'Right, that's it. Let Mrs Beardsley pick the team. I quit.' There was another report that I had gone in after the match, taken my boots off and thrown them at the manager. The papers also seemed to make an issue out of the fact that, although we lived two doors away from each other in Southport, there was not a lot of social contact between our two families. They had a right old free-for-all, each one outdoing the other in their flights of fantasy. It would have been laughable, were it not so serious and damaging.

It all started on the evening of Kenny's resignation. Sandra rang me in our hotel to tell me she was practically besieged by reporters. They were never off the phone or away from the front door. She sounded both desperate and angry and I felt deeply sorry for the situation she was in, especially as she knew less than anybody about why the manager had resigned. In order to escape she went round to Barry Venison's house to sit with his wife Julie. It was just ridiculous. She was actually forced out of our house and in later weeks she felt she couldn't attend matches at Anfield for fear of recriminations.

The truth was Sandra and Marina had always got on very well right from the night they met when I first went to talk to the Liverpool officials. We stayed in a hotel for five months but then we saw the house we liked near where the Dalglishes lived. Before I bought the place, I went to Kenny and asked if he had any problems with me living so close. He said straight away that he hadn't. 'If it's all right with you, it's fine by me,' he said.

What he was actually saying was, 'I am the manager, I can do as I want – you, as a player, have to watch what you are doing.' In the event he showered me with good advice ... about the price I should be paying and other matters. And he and Marina helped us to organize things when we moved in. To be honest, we never saw a lot of each other, but that's only normal. A manager's wife does not mix with the wives of players. Occasionally we might see each other in the back garden and exchange a few pleasantries but that was all and neither of us wanted any more. As for not popping round to each other's house for a daily cup of coffee, which is another thing the papers made an issue out of, it was just not the done thing. We got on with our lives and so did they.

If I had the chance to do it all again, I would definitely move into the same house. It was a lovely place to live and, apart from the obvious exception, nobody bothered us at all. The fact is Steve McMahon lived four doors the other way and nobody made a song and dance about his social calendar. Later, after I moved back to the North-East and put the house up for sale, Kenny offered his help in showing prospective buyers around and making sure everything was secure. That doesn't sound like the action of two people who were supposed to be at each other's throats!

Whatever reason Kenny had for quitting, it was certainly not down to me. Maybe after 24 continuous years in the game he wanted a break – and who could blame him for that? The timing of his departure, when we were in the Cup and top of the league, seemed to suggest the pressure on him was too fierce for him to go on. Any Liverpool manager is there to be shot at; you are not expected to fail. But not even his worst critic would suggest he had not been anything other than highly successful. After all, he had won three championships and two FA Cups.

I can quite honestly say I never made any trouble for him. I did go to see him a couple of times early on when he left me out but accepted his reasons. Later, when it happened I just didn't bother to request any explanations. I felt I should have been in the side but he knew that and I'm certain he would not have expected me to feel any other way. If I had been having a nightmare on the occasions I was left out, I might have understood. But I thought I was playing well and that's what made it all the more frustrating. It got to the stage where I could almost forecast the games I wouldn't be playing in. The significant aspect from my point of view is I have had no problem playing against the so-called physical sides since I left Anfield. I look forward to those games as much as all the others. I just love playing, full stop.

But it is all in the past. Kenny has come back with Blackburn Rovers and won his fourth title as a manager. He has got Liverpool out of his system and so have I. That is the way you have to operate in football. I would certainly play for him again if the circumstances arose. I have nothing but admiration for him and the way he lived his life. In many ways I tried to model myself on him – the manner in which he looks after himself and the sheer professional way he prepares for matches. I have hero-worshipped him ever since I was a kid in the crowd at Hampden Park. For me, there will never be another Kenny Dalglish.

8

LEAST SAID, SOUNESS MENDED

I have made it a policy never to look back in football. I have made decisions with the positive thought in my mind that at the time they were for the best. That is why, although it was absolutely right to sign for Liverpool when I did, it was equally correct to leave Anfield when I did. Not that I had a lot of choice. The fact is, looking back as I can now, my days as a Liverpool player were numbered from the day Graeme Souness returned to the club as manager.

His appointment came at the end of a season which started off with such bright optimism but, somewhere along the way, the normally well-oiled smooth-running Liverpool machine lost its direction. The resignation of Kenny Dalglish was a major setback but, during the next nine days, the team suffered a series of hammer blows which did serious damage to our hopes of landing at least one of the game's top honours for the fourth successive season.

Ronnie Moran took over as caretaker manager. He had made it known he didn't want to be considered as a permanent successor to Dalglish which I thought was a pity. I still believe Ronnie could have done the job at least for a couple of seasons, especially since his appointment would have continued an unbroken line of managers nominated from within the club. But mine was not to reason why. I had a job to do as a player and I desperately wanted to add to the prizes I had already picked up in the three years I had been at Anfield. Nobody could have assumed command in more difficult circumstances than Ronnie. Here was a club that always prided itself in being able to control its own destiny, suddenly being forced into doing something it hadn't done for over thirty years – which was put itself in the market for a manager.

Ronnie could in no way be blamed for what happened in the next three key games. Everything was up in the air and nobody really knew what was around the corner. We went to Luton and although Jan Molby knocked in a penalty to give us a half-time lead, we fell away badly in the second half and a goal from Kingsley Black and a couple from Ian Dowie gave Luton a well- deserved 3–1 victory. Then, having lost the toss for the choice of grounds, we went back to Goodison Park four days later for the second replay against Everton. This was another major disappointment. Dave Watson, a player who has developed a reputation for scoring important goals, got one early on and although we battered them after that, we couldn't score the all-important equalizer. The match was in complete contrast to the 4–4 draw a week earlier. This time nothing went in for us. They hung on and we went out of the Cup. I suppose it had to happen. After being ahead four times in the previous game, the first time we went behind in the tie, we couldn't do anything about it.

The next item on our very busy agenda was the six-pointer against our title rivals Arsenal. I suppose if the Gunners had to pick a time to play us they couldn't have envisaged a more appropriate day than that Sunday afternoon. They were on a roll and playing well. They had gone back to the top of the table a week earlier when we lost at Luton while they hammered Crystal Palace. Everybody at Anfield felt the world was falling apart around us. Even at their most generous, Arsenal in those days were always difficult to break down and always caused teams problems. This time David Seaman, their keeper, had a blinder, making save after save to deny us; and then Paul Merson hit what turned out to be the only goal of the match in the second half. It was a real sickener for all of us because it meant Arsenal went three points clear and we knew it was going to be difficult to pull them back.

Despite the result, Ronnie kept me in the side and I was like every other player who had a desperate urge to perform for him. We half-put things right with three successive wins culminating in a 7–1 thrashing of Derby County at the Baseball Ground which took us back to the top spot, and that old winning feeling seemed to be back. How wrong we were. Queen's Park Rangers brought us back to earth with a thud when they beat us 3–1 at Anfield and the title race was virtually sealed when Southampton's Matt Le Tissier made fools of us on 1 April, scoring the only goal at the Dell. Two days later Arsenal walloped Aston Villa 5–0 to go five points clear, and they never lost another league game after that.

Graeme Souness finally made his entrance on 16 April to end all the speculation about the job. Nobody would argue that he was the right choice with his previous record as a player at Liverpool; his experience in Italian football and his achievements as manager at Glasgow Rangers. He had said earlier that he did not want to become Liverpool manager but I learned to accept first hand that what Souness said and what he did were not always the same. At our first team meeting after his appointment he talked about his ambitions for Liverpool. He told us he had been a success wherever he had been, and he wanted more than anything to continue that at Anfield. It was soon clear that he did not like the accustomed Liverpool methods. Tried and tested traditions were not part of the Souness approach. He came in and changed a lot of things very quickly.

The team started off well under him with successive 3–0 home wins against Norwich City and Crystal Palace but we followed that with back-to-back away defeats at Chelsea and Nottingham Forest. I missed the latter match because he named me as substitute and I stayed on the bench. I was sub again for the final match of the season against Tottenham Hotspur at Anfield, coming on for the last twelve minutes. It was a memorable little contribution for two reasons. Firstly I finished up with a couple of stitches in a head cut after an accidental collision with my former Liverpool team-mate Paul Walsh, then playing for Spurs. Secondly, and more significantly, those twelve minutes were my last in a Liverpool shirt at Anfield.

The impression a lot of people got was that maybe Souness had had his card marked by Kenny Dalglish about me, especially after what happened in the later months of Kenny's management. Whether that's true or not, I'll never know but I find it difficult to believe. Kenny, to be fair to him, never left me out of games against sides with a reputation for playing football. I don't think he would have dropped me for a match against Spurs which is what Souness did. I have to admit I was disappointed, because I would have liked to have played for a full ninety minutes in my last game for Liverpool.

What would happen to my Liverpool career was on my mind during that summer. There had been speculation in the papers about various comings and goings, and I felt it was reasonable to find out exactly where I stood with the manager.

So I made an appointment to go and see him and ask about my situation. At the end of the season the team had played in a tournament in Singapore and one of the games was against the newly-crowned English champions Arsenal. We drew 1–1, but lost the match on penalties. I thought I played well in the game. Souness must have thought so too because when I went to see him he told me, 'You show me the commitment you demonstrated against Arsenal and you will be in my team at the start of the season.' His words gave me encouragement – but they turned out to be as false as my hopes that I still had a career with Liverpool.

I was optimistic as we resumed our pre-season preparation. Souness had warned us that it would be the hardest build-up we had ever had. And he was not wrong. It was not that we messed about in what was the normal training for a new season, but the policy in the past had been to bring us gradually to a peak condition for the big kick-off. That was not what Souness had in mind. On our first day back he pitched us straight into long runs around the training ground and by the end of the week the length of these had doubled. But he was the boss and everybody worked their socks off. I trained as hard as anybody and was always in the front three or four in my group. Then we went on a pre-season tour of Germany and Scandinavia. I didn't think it was a problem when I was taken off with about twenty minutes to go of the match in Germany. It was accepted that these games provided an opportunity for the manager to see as many players as possible. There had been a few notable changes in playing personnel, particularly with the arrival of Dean Saunders and Mark Wright, who cost over £5 million between them from Derby County. We moved on to Sweden and I was left out of the next game, coming on as sub for the last half-hour. That was also the pattern for the third match. Then we came to the fourth game against a Swedish team called Ludvika.

The game was in the evening and the pattern was that we would train on the pitch in the morning, leave our boots and the rest of the kit at the ground, go back to the hotel for a meal and an afternoon rest, and then return to the ground for the match. I got as far as having lunch and was just on my way to my room when Souness came to me and said, 'Peter, I want a word with you before you go for a rest. Would you wait over there?' I retreated to one side and after a while he walked over and announced, 'I've had an offer for you.' I asked him from which club and he told me that it was Everton. I asked him how much, to which he replied curtly, 'I am not prepared to tell you.'

He said there was a plane leaving the local airport at ten to five for Stockholm with a connection to London. He admitted it was a bit of a rush but explained that it was the way Howard Kendall wanted it. He said the Everton manager had requested that I be on the plane and he was going to have me picked up to meet him to discuss the move. Souness then made a point of telling me not to say a word to anybody about the deal because he wanted it kept quiet. He then turned away and I went up to my room. I was sharing with David Burrows who was getting ready for his rest when I walked in. Of course, I told him what had happened, there was no point in keeping it a secret from him because he would want to know why I wasn't going to my bed. I tried to phone my wife Sandra but she was out, so I packed my bags and told David I was going for a walk to have a think, and besides it was only fair to leave him to sleep before the match. I told him I would be back later to pick up my bag.

I then went to John Barnes' room and gave him the news

simply because Barnesy was my pal and I wouldn't want to leave without saying goodbye. Then I went for a stroll. As soon as I walked outside, the first person I saw was Mike Ellis, the football reporter from the *Sun* who was one of the group of pressmen who were covering the tour. You can imagine my surprise when he came up to me and said, 'So you're off to Everton then?' I just muttered, 'No, where did you hear that?', remembering that the manager had ordered me to keep the deal secret. Mike must have been surprised by my denial; it made me look especially foolish when he told me that Souness had just announced to the press what he had asked me to keep quiet about. I tried to find him to get some sort of explanation, but he had disappeared and I could not reach him. But I did find Ronnie and Roy to say cheerio. They gave me their best wishes and a little later I was off to the airport.

When I got to Stockholm I managed to contact Sandra and we had a chat about the move. What was on my mind was that Souness did not rate me as a player, and I was obviously not part of his plans for the club. She knew I was never one to hang around when I was not wanted. The good point of a move to Everton was that it was a great club and we didn't have to pull up stakes and move house or anything like that. My mind was in a bit of a whirl as the plane headed for Heathrow, but by the time it landed I was a lot clearer about what I was going to do. Brian Greenhoff, the Everton chief scout, was waiting at the airport and he drove me to the Bell House Hotel in Beaconsfield where Howard Kendall was waiting to talk to me. The first thing that struck me was the complete contrast in characters between the two managers. Compared to the rather frosty meeting with Souness, Howard was cheerful, kind and warm in his attitude towards me.

I politely declined his offer of a glass of champagne and

accepted a soft drink instead and then, with his opening salvo, he unknowingly made me aware of the underhand way Souness had handled things. 'This is a bit of a nuisance for me,' he commented. I told him I didn't understand what he meant, to which he replied, 'It would have been a lot easier for me if I could have seen you in Manchester tomorrow.' It turned out that when he made an offer for me, Souness had agreed but then told him he wanted me out straightaway. Which was a completely different story to that which I had been given in Sweden, when he told me it was Kendall who wanted me on the flight to meet in London.

I thought Souness' attitude was rather pathetic. I couldn't see any reason why I couldn't have stayed for one more night, watched the match, said my goodbyes to the players and staff and then caught the plane to Manchester the next day. He did the deal with such indecent haste that he didn't even allow me to pick up my boots which were back at the ground with the rest of the kit. The next time I saw them was a few weeks later when Barry Venison brought them back and gave them to me. Any reasonable man would surely have handled the situation with a little more feeling. Wouldn't it have been better too for Kendall, who had to miss two days' training to come south to see me?

Howard and I chatted until about one o'clock in the morning about the deal and what his plans were for Everton. He was so easy to talk to; what came across clearly was his love for the club and how determined he was to get things back to the days when he twice took them to the championship. The next day he drove me back to Southport and later I met him with Sandra. It took me about ten minutes to decide that I wanted to sign for Everton. Howard told me the fee was £1 million which was something Souness did not feel inclined to reveal to me. It was a lot of money, but I felt I could justify it and do a good job for Everton. There was one little extra thing which I felt I was justified in asking for. I had given good service to Liverpool and the move was not of my making. I certainly hadn't rattled any cages at Anfield and I felt an *ex gratia* payment was fair. I contacted Peter Robinson about it and he said he would have a word with Souness. Later, he came back to me to say Souness had approved my request.

I don't know whether he was frightened I might say no and be under his feet a little longer, but I was never inclined to do that. At the end of the day it was clear he didn't fancy me as a player. He's entitled to his opinion and he gets paid for making decisions like selling me. But what annoyed me was the way he went about it. I never caused him any trouble and he wanted me out of the door – and this after virtually promising me I would be in his side at the start of the following season. It was almost as if he regarded me as a trouble-maker who might have tainted the dressing room had I stayed any longer. I found out later he told Barnesy about the deal after I left Sweden but said he didn't think I would sign for Everton because I didn't have the bottle to switch clubs. Well, he was wrong about that, just as he was wrong about a few other things while he was in charge at Anfield.

There have been a few other players who switched to the other side of Stanley Park, but the likes of Steve McMahon, Kevin Sheedy, Alan Harper and Dave Watson were only young when they were at the rival clubs. There had, until then, been no transfer between the Liverpool clubs of a player for as much money and with as high a profile, although Gary Ablett followed me later for £750,000. Nevertheless, I was looking forward to the change. I didn't anticipate any problems with either set of supporters. I always had a great relationship with the Liverpool fans and I was hoping for the same at Everton.

I had achieved everything I had hoped for in the four years at Liverpool. It was like somebody handing me a key to unlock all of my football dreams. I had won two League Championship medals, experienced two FA Cup finals and won one, and played in three FA Charity Shields. It was a pity it all ended on something of a sour note, but I suppose every silver lining has a dark cloud – and Souness was my only problem. I have been fortunate enough to play for what I believe are the most knowledgeable football followers in the country in Liverpool and at Newcastle. And, having buried the anger of the way I was treated in the end, I turned my attentions to justifying the faith that Howard Kendall had shown in me.

After having experienced the pleasures of success it will always be one of the disappointments of my life that I was not able to help transfer some of that Liverpool glory across to Everton after my transfer on 5 August 1991. It was not just for myself, but more for Kendall and everybody at Goodison, in particular his number two Colin Harvey, another person who had Everton blue blood running through his veins. The club had been going through a lean spell since they won two championships in three years and maybe suffered, as close neighbours do, in comparison to what had been achieved by Liverpool. But there was an air of friendliness and camaraderie about the place which put a new player instantly at ease.

In all the time I was there Kendall treated me like a king. I didn't score until the seventh game against Sheffield United, but the goal didn't do us a lot of good. That was our fourth away league match of the season and we lost the lot – including a 3–1 defeat on my return to Anfield. You can imagine how desperate I was to perform well in that game. In spite of our indifferent start, the boss had us really wound-up, which I'll admit didn't take a lot of doing, and we really fancied our chances. The crowd were brilliant and they gave me a great reception. There was none of that 'Liverpool reject' stuff that you might have expected at most clubs. Merseyside fans are different ... even when I moved to Everton, I was surprised by the number of people who came to me and said, 'Peter, they might not want you at Liverpool...but you are welcome here.'

Anyway, it was a great occasion and not a little strange experiencing the whole thing from the other side of the tracks. Well, the honeymoon didn't last long. My former room-mate David Burrows scored a deflected goal straight from the kick-off – I think the goal was timed at 48 seconds – and we were fighting a losing battle after that, especially when Dean Saunders knocked in another after a quarter of an hour. We finished up losing 3–1 and were accorded the sympathy Merseyside winners love to dispense to the vanquished. A couple of disappointing home draws followed, so it was hardly the happiest of dressing rooms after that Sheffield United defeat dropped us down to 19th in the First Division table. I don't think I had ever been lower than that, even in the worst days at Newcastle. Fortunately, although we never figured as high as we should, that was the lowest we descended. I managed to score in the next four games, including the goal that ended our away drought at Manchester City, and then hit a hat-trick against good old Coventry, who always seem to come around for me just when I need them most.

But in spite of the problems on the pitch, Kendall, without being too easy-going because he could hand out a rollicking as fierce as the next man, kept a great rapport with everybody in the dressing room. If I made a bad pass in training, he was always there with a little aside like, 'Hey you, Beardsley, you don't become a good player overnight ... it takes a little work!' There was a tremendous team spirit without any loners. My big pal was Ian Snodin, another lad who always had a smile on his face in spite of some terrible luck with injuries.

You didn't have to look far for the real characters at Everton. There cannot be many people in the world like Neville Southall. His life is his football. I have never come across anyone who trains with such single-minded dedication. But he is a strange lad. On away trips he always commanded a section on the bus with two seats facing, where he stretched his feet out under the table and went out like a light. He could also be allocated the most luxurious bedroom and he would pull the mattress on to the floor and sleep on it. But what he was good at was his job. I would always put Peter Shilton up there as the best goalkeeper I have played with, but Nev wouldn't be a bad second. His handling, reflexes and positional sense were superb. He provides tremendous reassurance to any defence he plays behind.

I managed a one hundred per cent appearance record for Everton in that first full season and scored twenty league and cup goals, which was some consolation for the disappointment at not winning anything. Most of the time I played up front with the likes of Tony Cottee, Mike Newell and then Mo Johnston, who came to the club in November from Glasgow Rangers. I felt sorry for Mo. He had cost £1.5 million, and because of the big fee a lot was expected of him, but things never went the way he hoped or his effort and application deserved. He had a great attitude and always gave one hundred per cent effort but he did not have the best of luck either with injuries or maintaining his reputation as a goalscorer. He would be the first to admit that he did not put the ball in the net enough to appease his critics. The lad took a lot of stick, but I wish the people who had a go at him could have seen how hard he worked in training and how keen he was to do well.

He had a moment of glory in the return derby match against Liverpool just after Christmas. We had picked up a little to get ourselves into the top half of the table, and we were looking for revenge for that defeat earlier in the season at Anfield. Again we left ourselves with everything to do when Nicky Tanner scored for them before half-time, but Mo scored an equalizer after an hour and we battered Liverpool after that, but they hung on for a 1–1 draw.

I was not so fortunate with injuries in the second season at Everton. I missed a few games early on after pulling a hamstring and I was out for a spell later after another knock. But I still managed 39 appearances, which I was pleased with. When Kendall bought me one of the things he said attracted him was the fact that I did not miss many matches because of injury. Nobody likes to tempt fate but when I've read about the unfortunate accidents that happen to other players, I have to count myself lucky. I would certainly not have liked to have suffered in the same way as Alan Shearer, Paul Gascoigne and many others who have had long lay-offs through serious injury.

When you stop to consider all that, maybe it puts poor results into perspective. But that seemed no consolation for an even worse second season at Everton than my first. The only real personal highlight was when I scored the winner against Liverpool at Goodison, giving me a record which I think might be unique. There cannot be many players who have scored winners for both sides in Merseyside derbies. I remember the game well because it was the only time we beat Liverpool while I wore a blue shirt. Mark Wright scored first for them, but Mo Johnston maintained his good record against our neighbours by equalizing within a minute. It looked like heading for another draw when I got the opportunity I had been hoping for. There were six minutes left when I picked up the ball on the right and played a one-two with Gary Ablett. As it came back, I hit a shot low just inside Mike Hooper's right hand post.

As soon as I struck the ball I knew Mike was not going to stop it. It was in all the way and I was off on a celebratory jig. I ran from the edge of the box right around the pitch to the dug-out and did a high-five with my mate Snodin who had just been substituted. It was one of the most satisfying goals I ever scored and it was not without personal significance that it was against the Liverpool manager who had sold me. I didn't look at Souness' face when I ran across but I knew he wouldn't be too happy. The goal was enough pleasure and I didn't need to make any gestures to rub it in. To his credit Souness came over to me after the game, shook my hand and said to me, 'Well done, I'm pleased for you.' Actually, they were the first words he had spoken to me since I left him in that hotel in Sweden.

The Everton celebrations gave me some idea of what it would be like if we had really given the supporters something to cheer about. But the man I felt for most was Kendall because he deserved better for everything he put into the job. He never missed a day at the training ground although, I am certain that, had his other commitments allowed, he would have spent more time actually being involved in sessions. But nothing escaped his eagle eye as he watched out of his office window and in the canteen afterwards he would stroll across and make some comment about somebody's bad pass or great goal.

Kendall's knowledge of the game had to be experienced to be fully realized. He combined that with a burning desire to bring back the glory days. You could tell he was heartbroken by our poor results. He wanted the players to die for the club and I always felt we didn't give him the success his efforts warranted. He was always very professional and very thorough and had a wonderful relationship with his players. I never had a cross word with him all the time I was there, but that's not to say I wasn't on the wrong end of his tongue now and again. I think he had a special link with Everton supporters. They never got on his back, but there was no doubt he was under considerable pressure, even if most of it was self-imposed.

He spent quite a bit of money bringing in players like myself, Mo, Mark Ward, Barry Horne, Gary Ablett and Matt Jackson. We had a Polish international winger called Robert Warzycha who must go down as one of the most long-suffering footballers in the history of the game. I don't believe there can be anybody who was substituted more times during a season. By my reckoning he was taken off twenty times, including one spell of six games in succession! Yet I felt at times Robert was on a different wavelength to us, and I mean that in a complimentary sense. I thought he was too clever for the way we played. Andrei Kanchelskis has been a great success for Manchester United and Everton but I rated Robert just as highly, or maybe even higher than him.

Although there were times when we played a lot better than results indicated, our record was not a good one. We were the ones who had to hold up our hands and say as a team we did not do the business, but Kendall never pointed any fingers. He never let his inner feelings show and stood by every one of us without a word of public criticism. I could never complain about the way I was treated. Kendall gave me a completely free rein. All he said to me was, 'Go and be dangerous where you can.' That suited me down to the ground because I am the sort of off-the-cuff player who reacts to what he sees. People have often said that, in different circumstances, I should do certain things but I cannot be pigeon-holed like that.

I honestly don't know myself what I am going to do next with the ball. I am happy to say that on the occasions I try something and it comes off, it makes me look good and we might get something out of it – even if it happens only three times out of ten. When it doesn't, of course, I can look pretty stupid. I have been like that all my career. I take chances, but positive chances. Maybe that's why I have always been appreciated by the people who watch the game. The opinions of your team-mates count too, and it was nice when my Newcastle and England team-mate Rob Lee once said to me, 'Pedro, sometimes you have nightmare games because you try and do things differently. Anybody can pass a ball five yards but you try the difficult one and when it doesn't come off, it looks bad. But keep trying.'

Anyway, whatever had gone wrong in my two seasons at Everton, I was looking forward to putting it right in the following campaign. I shared Kendall's assertion that we weren't far away from being a good side. I certainly had no thoughts about moving although there had been speculation linking me with several clubs. We finished the season in style with a 5–2 success over Manchester City and the team was due to fly to Mauritius to play two matches in an end of season tour. I had other things on my mind because Sandra was well into her second pregnancy and the baby was due during the summer. I was hoping to be excused from the trip to look after her. But the manager said he wanted me to go because I was an attraction for the people organizing the tour and also he thought it was good for team spirit. He promised that if any complications developed with Sandra, he would get me back on the next plane.

After everything he had done for me, and especially because I felt I owed him something for what had been a disappointing season, I agreed to go. We played matches against Aston Villa and the Mauritian national side and it turned out to be an excellent trip, just what was needed to banish the blues. Everybody was very relaxed. Apart from the football, all there was to do was swimming, surfing and sunbathing – a real paradise of a place and I thoroughly enjoyed every second. When it was all over Kendall came to me and thanked me personally for going and for my attitude to the games. I found that rather strange because all I did was what was expected of me professionally. It was almost a thank-you for what I had done at the club. I just nodded and told him to forget it because the pleasure had been all mine.

Whatever the manager's motives were at the time, my own thoughts turned out to be quite prophetic. I was sitting at home towards the end of June when I suddenly got a telephone call. 'Hello Peter, it's the boss here. Can you pop in and see me tomorrow just for a chat,' I heard Kendall saying. We arranged a time at his office at Bellfield and when I called, I found him behind his desk looking relaxed and cheerful. 'Sit down, lad. How's your summer going?' he asked, smiling. We chatted amiably about the holiday and how Sandra was coping and then he dramatically changed the subject. 'We need a big man, what do you think?' he inquired. I said I thought it might be a good idea because it would give us another option.

Then he blurted out, 'I'm selling you.' At first it didn't sink in but when it did my expression must have spoken volumes about the way it had hit me. 'Who to?' I heard myself asking. 'Derby County – £1.2 million,' he added. There was a silent pause while we just looked at each other. He told me to think about it and that Arthur Cox would like to talk to me. He said that he didn't really want to sell me but he needed some money to buy players and this was something like a last throw of the dice. My first reaction was what a sly old devil Arthur was. We had spoken to each other on a regular basis all the time I was at Liverpool and then at Everton, and he never mentioned a word of it. In fact, he had phoned me about three weeks earlier, asking if he could have one of my England shirts just as a keepsake. He was somebody I would always go to for advice because he was as close a friend as I have ever had. But it just underlined the principles Arthur has always stood by. He would never try to coerce me into a move without first going through the proper procedure.

Having said all that, in spite of the undoubted attraction to renewing the professional association I had with him at Newcastle, I still did not feel inclined to drop out of what was going to be the only the second year of the FA Carling Premiership. I was certain I had a few years of top flight football left in me. I mentioned that to Kendall who then said he had also promised to keep Newcastle informed of any developments. He asked me to pop outside for a minute while he tried to contact Kevin Keegan. In the event, he finally got hold of Terry McDermott because Kevin was away on holiday. I found out later that Terry Mac had spoken to Kevin who said straightaway that he wanted to be involved.

I was unaware of Newcastle's interest when Arthur drove up to visit Sandra and myself at our home in Southport. In fact, the only other club I thought I might have joined at that time was United's North-East rivals Sunderland. Not many people know that Terry Butcher gave me a call and asked if I would be interested in joining them. I told him quite honestly that I would be prepared to talk to anybody who could agree a fee with Everton. He said he would get back to me, but he never did. Whether his directors had knocked it on the head I don't know, but that was as far as it went.

But deep down Arthur also knew he had tough competition if Kevin Keegan showed any interest. It was ironic that these two who shared such a mutual under-standing and admiration should be rivals to sign me. No doubt, because they too enjoyed a long-standing close relationship with regular contact, they both knew how they stood regarding me. But Arthur made a very persuasive case for me to sign. He likened the situation at Derby to the one at Newcastle when Kevin went there. He told me I could do a similar job at the Baseball Ground to the one Kevin had done on Tyneside. When I mentioned about dropping out of the big league, he said it would only be for a season because with me at Derby they would be sure to get promotion. His final words were that he wanted me to join them but the only other club he would be happy about me going to would be Newcastle.

A couple of days later Kendall rang up to confirm Newcastle's interest. There was none of the bad feeling that had accompanied my move from Liverpool. He sounded genuinely sorry that circumstances had dictated the steps he was about to take. I hoped that the players he would bring to the club would carry it to the success which had been out of reach while I had been there. The thing about Kendall was, not only did he want to win something for the fans, but he knew how they wanted the success to come. Everton fans have been nurtured on entertaining, stylish, exciting football. I am certain Joe Royle knows that too, being an ex-Evertonian himself. Joe had to scrap for the points that took Everton to safety in his first season as manager. But he is just as much a football purist as the next man, and I am certain in future seasons we will see my old club turning on the exhibition stuff their traditions demand.

Kendall drove a harder bargain with Newcastle. He told me the fee would be a little higher than he asked Derby for, because United were now a Premier League club. But they had agreed to pay it anyway and he had given Kevin Keegan permission to speak to me. I was very excited about that. I knew, all things being equal, I would be returning to Tyneside to join Kevin Keegan's fabulous Toon Army.

9

A TOON ARMY RECRUIT

Money for me has never been a green-eyed idol to be worshipped above all else. My moves from club to club have either been fortuitous or for the sake of furthering my ambitions to be successful. If I've made a few bob on the way, that has been a bonus. I didn't get into football to be rich – I did it to fulfil a boyhood dream to play on the game's great stages and I've been fortunate to realize those dreams. There are clubs I would never join even if they offered me a king's ransom. But I would never criticize other players who have an entirely different attitude. Good luck to those who have taken the money and moved on – after all, a footballer's career is a short one with many all too brief through injury.

Having said all that, there are limits! Money had to be a bad second to personal motive and pride when I eventually got around to discussing my second transfer to Newcastle. One thing is certain, I could have made an awful lot more if I had taken up Arthur Cox's offer to join Derby County in June 1993. More than I was getting at Everton, and a lot more than Kevin Keegan put on the table when we met at Wetherby to discuss the nuts and bolts of the move. Let's just say the difference was in excess of £1000 a week.

I had been waiting for Kevin's call since I was alerted by my Everton manager Howard Kendall that Newcastle were definitely interested. Sure enough, the phone rang and I found myself listening to a voice I hadn't heard since we parted company as team-mates the night of Keegan's epic finale as a player at Newcastle. He asked how I was and inquired after my wife Sandra's progress with her second pregnancy and then said, 'I know it's difficult to get about because of Sandra's condition but come and see us when you can.'

There had obviously been contact between Kevin and Arthur and he knew how much I had been offered by Derby and he told me, 'I don't want you backing yourself into a corner where you end up having to come to us. Sort out the Derby thing because we won't be able to match either their offer or even Everton's for that matter.' He could hardly be accused of being pushy. He made it clear he wanted to sign me and just left it to me to arrange a get-together. I arrived at Wetherby with Des Bremner, the former Aston Villa midfielder who now works with the PFA. He came along mainly as an observer and advisor if he was needed. We were early, getting there before Kevin, who walked through the door a few minutes later with Terry McDermott and immediately apologised for being late. I pointed out that he was in fact ahead of schedule and we had just got there a little early. He just quipped, 'All right then, Pedro, sorry we're early.' He was very relaxed and that put me at ease. It was more of a friendly chat than a transfer meeting. He put forward the deal and said, 'I'll understand if you feel we're not offering you enough and that you decide to go somewhere else but we obviously want you to come to us.'

I knew straightaway that there was no other club for me. We parted company without any final decision as I wanted to talk to Sandra before committing myself. I knew she would be behind me wherever I was going. I had a lot of respect for Keegan as a player but you could multiply that by a hundred when you measure the regard I have for him now as a man and a boss. I wanted to play for him. I knew he had pushed the boat out to spend so much money on somebody who was nearer 33 than 32. I knew there were doubters not only at Newcastle but also within football in general. A few eyebrows were raised when the deal was made public.

But I felt inspired by the challenge. I wanted to respond to the faith the boss was putting in me not only because of my own ambitions, but also because I felt that exciting times were just around the corner at Newcastle and I wanted to be part of them.

I rang him the next day and told him I would accept his 'measly pittance'. Actually, I was not so badly off and I would imagine I am probably still one of the highest paid players at the club. That doesn't bother me, nor did the fact that I was far and away from being the top earner at either Liverpool or Everton. Kevin sounded pleased and, demonstrating typical consideration for Sandra and the impending birth, told me to get up to Newcastle in my own time to complete the formalities. I had two other immediate responsibilities – to inform Howard Kendall at Everton and call Arthur Cox to tell him I would not be joining him at Derby. He appreciated my reasons and told me I was returning to a far better Newcastle than I had left because I was going to play for a great manager. 'Our relationship will never change, Peter,' he added.

It is somewhat ironic that our paths have since crossed again with Arthur joining the coaching staff at Newcastle. I couldn't resist a little dig when he arrived. 'Fancy seeing you here,' I said. 'It would have been charming if I had gone to

Derby and you came here and left me in the lurch.' He just chuckled and told me, 'If you had gone to Derby you might have been manager by now.'

Newcastle put out the welcome mat in some style when I came up to sign. I met the chairman Sir John Hall, who is the man responsible for providing the finance which has changed the fortunes of the club. Sir John is clearly ambitious and unwavering in his plans to turn Newcastle into one of the top clubs in Europe. The appointment of Keegan as manager has obviously turned out to be a master stroke, but the club has made giant improvements not only on the field but in every other area, not least in the ground itself which is now one of the finest in the country. The place is unrecognizable from the one I left to join Liverpool. It is now operating in the big league without the sense of inferiority that was always there before. Even after we won promotion with Keegan in the side, you always had the feeling that the directors were content just to be in the First Division. Not a lot of effort was made to have a crack at the major prizes. There was just no ambition.

Now the outlook is totally different. We have a side who can compete with the best, a ground which can be compared with the best, and plans for new training facilities which will be the best. The past may have been mediocre, but the present is very good and the future prospects of the club are excellent. It has taken a lot of foresight, ambition and money to get us into our present situation. When somebody like Sir John declares that Newcastle will be in the top six clubs in Europe by the turn of the century, you have to listen. You certainly would not back against a man who has achieved so much for a miner's son from Ashington.

At the end of the day it might not happen, but at least the effort is being made. The club is in for the top players; it is prepared to pay top dollar both in fees and wages. And now the rest of the country is talking about Newcastle in terms of being one of the top clubs in the country. As I have already said, I never look back but still it makes you wonder whether I would have gone to Liverpool and achieved so much success if the opportunity to do the same had been offered by staying at Newcastle.

Certainly I don't think there would have been the same willingness to sell as there was then. The only reason players leave Newcastle these days is if the manager believes it will be in the long term interest of the club for them to go. When I left, the club needed money to spend on a new stand and I was one of the most saleable assets. The difference today is that millions have been spent improving the facilities at St James' Park and at the same time Newcastle have acquired a reputation of being one of the country's top buying clubs. The sad thing is that it has taken so long to harness their horizons to the passion and loyalty of the supporters who have had to suffer all this time.

You could still sense the euphoria of the team's First Division Championship triumph in the build-up to the 1993/94 season. The place was buzzing. You looked around the dressing room and among the familiar faces of players like my former Liverpool team-mate Barry Venison, there were the new stars of the team, the ones who had earned the previous season's promotion triumph – Rob Lee, John Beresford, Paul Bracewell, Lee Clark, Steve Howey and a player whom I was looking forward very much to partnering up front, Andy Cole.

The pre-season preparation could not have gone better and could there be a more appropriate way to wind it all up than a return to Liverpool on the Monday night before the big kick-off? It was a well-deserved testimonial match for Ronnie Whelan and I was more than happy to be part of the tribute to such a great servant to Liverpool. Ronnie hadn't enjoyed the best of luck with injuries in his later years at Anfield, but he kept bouncing back to the extent that he regained his place in the Irish squad, albeit temporarily. I haven't come across many who had a better attitude to the game than Ronnie did.

For my own part I went back full of anticipation, and more than a little pride. I was returning as a member of my home town team which I felt at long last could stand alongside the best in the game. That for me meant Liverpool. In addition to that, I wanted to show their supporters I could still do a thing or two. Both sets of players chatted amicably in the tunnel before the game. As far as I was concerned it was not a match to be taken lightly, but at the same time it could be played in a true spirit of friendly competition because, after all, it was a testimonial. As we walked up the passage to the pitch I noticed Neil Ruddock who was making his first appearance at Anfield as a Liverpool player. I turned to him and wished him well for his future career at the club. 'You'll love it here,' I told him. 'It is a great place to play your football and I am certain the supporters will love you.' I was convinced what I was saying was true – and subsequent events have proved me right. He nodded and said thanks, and then we were out on the pitch.

How could I know that, within two minutes of the kick-off, that eagerly-awaited evening of nostalgia would become a nightmare of excruciating pain and mental anguish, courtesy of the aforementioned Mr Ruddock? We had barely kicked-off – I certainly hadn't even had a sniff of possession – when one of our central defenders, Kevin Scott, who was near the halfway line, played a long ball high into the Liverpool penalty area. Ruddock and I were alongside each other but I knew he was favourite to get to the ball first and decided to make only a half-hearted challenge, edging to one side to get clear. It was not even a genuine attempt to reach it. But Ruddock suddenly jerked his left elbow and smashed it flush into my face. I thought I had been trampled by the Household Cavalry. The pain was fierce and I knew immediately that something serious had happened. I was stretchered off and it was later discovered that I had a broken right cheekbone.

I had an operation to have a metal plate inserted in my face. The surgeon who did it had performed a similar operation on Kenny Dalglish a few years earlier, and he did a magnificent job on me. But that was the end of my hopes of starting the new season with Newcastle. While they went out to play against Tottenham Hotspur in front of a packed house at St. James' Park, I was lying in a bed at home in Southport nursing a sore head, a face that looked as though I had been ten rounds with Mike Tyson, and a sense of total anti-climax.

I am firmly convinced that Neil Ruddock used his elbow deliberately. I will never change my opinion about that and I don't care what anybody says. There was just no need to do what he did. He must have known that I offered no real threat for the ball; he was given a free header to clear it. I can only think the reason why he did it was that he was trying to demonstrate to Liverpool supporters that he was a hard man. It is an image he has since cultivated with some success. Even in that match, he followed up his challenge on me with a ferocious tackle on Rob Lee. I have felt the weight of some hard tackles in my time and been kicked up hill and down dale, yet I have never moaned or complained because you accept that as being part and parcel of the game. But in my opinion, Ruddock's action went beyond the bounds of competitive aggression. He was out of order and he put a fellow professional in hospital and out of football for six weeks. I was extremely fortunate that the damage was not any worse.

I have played against Ruddock since and even joined him in England training sessions. We don't speak about the incident. I don't see the point because I don't expect him to admit that he did it on purpose. The pity is that he is a brilliant defender with a lot of ability and a sweet left foot. He is also one of the most determined competitors in the game ... fine qualities that should not require him to overstep the mark. I resolved not to let him get away with it and instituted legal proceedings with a view to a claim for damages. My motives were more to get him to acknowledge publicly the wrong he had done, rather than to exact any financial compensation. However, after thinking carefully about it and seeking legal and personal advice, I decided to let the whole thing drop. I was told the legal bill could be as much as £40,000 which, had I lost, would have added insult to the injury. Paul Elliott has since found to his cost that such legal action is fraught with problems because there is a fine dividing line between success and failure, no matter how blatant a foul might seem to be. In that Anfield friendly the referee, a local man who had taken the game as a favour to Ronnie, hadn't even awarded a foul against Ruddock.

I swallowed my pride and avoided looking at myself in the mirror for a few weeks. I am no oil painting at the best of times and well aware that one of my often-used nicknames from rival supporters is 'Quasimodo' which doesn't bother me in the slightest. For a few weeks after getting that elbow, I think to call me that would have insulted Quasimodo! Since then Gary Mabbutt suffered a similar injury after a bang from John Fashanu and the PFA have used his picture to promote a very worthy campaign against the misuse of the elbow. But I have to say that Gary's features were no worse than mine. I believe these challenges are not only despicable, they are dangerous and could easily result in an opponent losing an eye. I am pleased that they have become less frequent and that referees and the football authorities are clamping down on the aggressors.

I was feeling very sorry for myself on that opening day of the season. I sent the boss a telegram, wishing him and the team all the best and saying how much I would have liked to have been involved. He rang me and told me to be patient and things would work out. If there was one consolation it was that, after about a fortnight, I was able to start jogging and get myself fit fairly quickly. But I felt so frustrated at missing out, especially when the team lost against Spurs and were then beaten in the second game at Coventry. The third game was against Manchester United at Old Trafford. I remember getting a call from Freddie Fletcher, one of the Newcastle directors, suggesting he pop around to see me. He was in a party of officials who had flown down to Manchester. It was a nice thought, but it was a little too far out of his way and anyway I was still far from a pretty sight.

Andy Cole's first Premiership goal earned the lads a point at United and that gave them a bit of a lift-off. But I was determined to play my part, even with the metal plate still in my face. I had managed to get a lot of training in, and I was pencilled in provisionally to play against Sheffield Wednesday in a Monday night match. But the boss decided it was maybe a little too soon and we decided to postpone my return until the game at Swindon Town the following Saturday. I was now chomping at the bit. I wouldn't let negative thoughts bother me as to what might happen if I got another bang, or I would never have come back. It was a chance both myself and the gaffer were prepared to take. We had in fact decided the morning after the Sheffield Wednesday game that I would play. The story put out in the papers was that it was a last minute decision but my mind was fixed all week on pulling on a black and white shirt in a league match for the first time for over six years. I was really up for it, and it was a moment that matched my debut for Liverpool or Everton. I had missed seven games but for me it was all about making up for lost time. We had a great start, leading by two goals and we really should have murdered Swindon. We hit the bar three times but they came back with a couple and we had to settle for a draw which was a bit disappointing.

My first home game was against Notts County in the first leg of the Coca-Cola Cup. It was an early first-hand experience of the phenomenal goalscoring power of Andy Cole, who scored a terrific hat-trick in our 4–1 win. The return leg in Nottingham was even better, one of two games that season where we knocked in seven goals and I managed to break my scoring duck when I got one of them. But I still played second fiddle to Coley, who helped himself to another hat-trick. We were playing well and winning matches, but then along came Les Ferdinand to remind us that life had its complications. Les came to St James' with Queen's Park Rangers and gave one of the best individual performances by a striker I have seen. He destroyed us almost single-handed and it was easy to see why the gaffer was eventually prepared to pay £6 million for him. He was magnificent that day, but I had seen it all before. The previous season he personally ravaged Everton at Goodison Park, scoring a hat-trick in a 5–3 win against us.

He is one of several players I believe will benefit from being at a bigger club – and I mean that as no disrespect to QPR. At Newcastle he will be given a bigger platform on which to parade his undoubted talents. The same applies to Matt Le Tissier although I know I won't be popular with Southampton supporters for suggesting it, because they know as well as anybody where they would be without him. He is capable of winning any match on his own as he proved when we went down to The Dell for our league match. We absolutely paralysed them but anybody who was there or saw the game on television would remember his two brilliant goals that won the game for the Saints. They were poor on the day, but Matt rescued them as he has on many occasions. Some nice people have said it about me but I have to admit that it applies to Matt even more – he never scores a bad goal. There cannot be a player who has had so many of his strikes included in Goal of the Month. Some of them are truly breathtaking.

Le Tissier is a class player, but I believe his international and personal ambitions have suffered because he is not playing in a successful team. With all due respect, he can stay at Southampton all his career, but if he does he will never win a league champions medal. They might win a cup one day because any team can be lucky enough to do that. I have been in a similar situation myself when I was at Newcastle the first time, the main difference being that Newcastle will always be considered a bigger club than Southampton. I made a decision to leave because I wanted to win things. Matt has got to make the decision about whether he wants personal honours or whether he wants to stay at The Dell. I know he loves the club and the supporters worship him, but surely they would have to be honest and recognize that a player of his talents should not miss out on the game's glittering prizes.

What was great from my own point of view was that I

never missed another game after I came back from injury. At the end of the season Newcastle were firmly established as one of the top teams in the country. We ended up in third place which was the team's highest finish for over fifty years. Most of all, we won friends throughout the length and breadth of the land because of the way we played the game. We became known as the entertainers and if it was a pleasure to watch, it was definitely a treat to be involved.

Of course, with so many people at the club whose careers had developed at Liverpool – Keegan, McDermott, Venison, myself – there were inevitable comparisons with the great Merseyside club but we didn't try to copy Liverpool. Theirs was a unique success which any club would be proud to emulate. The only similarity in training were the sessions with the ball and the enjoyment you got from the daily routine. But the boss wanted us to create our own image and I believe we did that. We had very good individuals who were able to blend into a team unit – players like Rob Lee who works so hard but has the added ability which enables him to create things out of nothing. Our aim was a simple one: to get forward in numbers as often as possible. Andy Cole was the focal point up front but there was myself, Rob, Scott Sellars, later Ruel Fox, Lee Clark, Steve Watson, and even the full-backs Barry Venison and John Beresford were all actively encouraged to play the ball in the final third of the field.

There were many other incidents that season. I picked up a rare booking after a challenge on that irrepressible character Vinnie Jones. I was annoyed at Vinnie because I felt it was his reaction more than the tackle that got me a yellow card. I'll admit I fouled him in making a genuine attempt to go for the ball but he certainly made a meal of it, moaning and gesticulating to the referee who felt obliged to take stronger action than he might otherwise have done. I thought Vinnie was out of order, especially when I remembered the number of times he had booted me in the past. These days enough referees are carrying out their responsibilities to interpret the letter of the law with excessive enthusiasm without players putting extra pressure on them by their antics. I have never tried to influence an official into booking an opponent and I have been kicked about as much as the next man. What satisfaction can there be in getting a player booked, maybe sent off, and possibly fined or suspended?

Halfway through the season I was made skipper of the side. I take the responsibilities of the role seriously, but regret the circumstances in which it happened when the boss took the armband from Barry after he and a couple of the lads broke a curfew. It was just one of those things which happen at a club but it underlined the no-nonsense disciplinary code laid down by Kevin Keegan. The manager has a simple philosophy – he treats his players as professionals and expects us to behave like them. And he will jump on anyone who breaks the rules, whether they are the least significant staff member or a high profile player. He proved that on a couple of other occasions with Andy Cole and Lee Clark.

We were due to play at Wimbledon in the Coca-Cola Cup which was obviously a big game for us. And we were as shocked as anybody when the boss told us before the match that Andy would not be involved. He had apparently told Keegan he was homesick and had gone off to stay somewhere in London. The boss was quite firm but fair about the situation, saying that while he was in his current state of mind, it was better that Andy didn't play. It was the sort of decision that another manager might not have had the courage to make, knowing the pressure on jobs these days. Leaving out your top scorer was a brave decision but I don't suppose he even thought twice about it. Later he got Andy to sort out the problem and although the media had a field day, within the club it was soon history and in less than a week everything was back to normal. It certainly didn't appear to have any lasting effect on Coley because he scored against Wimbledon in his first game back on the day I scored a hat-trick. After that I averaged almost a goal a game till the end of the season.

The Lee Clark incident was even more of a storm in a teacup, but again the gaffer acted instinctively in dealing with it. Clarky was upset about being substituted in a match and lost his temper as he came off. It was out of character for the lad and he regretted it straight away. He was on the carpet and had the riot act read to him, but everybody at the club was happy when it was all sorted out. I know what it's like to be taken off when I have felt I didn't deserve it. A player feels disappointed and frustrated, but maybe young Clarky learned on that occasion it is better to count to ten and keep your feelings in check.

Towards the end of the season Kevin Keegan underlined the complete change in outlook at the club when he spent £5 million to sign first Darren Peacock from Queen's Park Rangers and then Ruel Fox from Norwich City. They had contrasting debuts, Darren in a 3–0 trouncing of Foxy's team and Ruel in a 4–2 defeat at Wimbledon. But their arrival clearly showed the club meant business; that the promise of future success was not just idle chatter. It seems to be the way of things at the moment. If you want to compete, you have to spend the money. Success comes at a price and those who either cannot or will not pay for it will fall by the wayside.

The big disappointment was that we didn't win anything and we really fancied our chances in the two main cup competitions. Whether Cole would have made a difference or not at Wimbledon is hypothetical; what is fact is that I made a dreadful mistake which led to their first goal and almost certainly cost us the match. I went to clear the ball after a corner and mishit it straight to Andy Clarke who cracked it in. I had a hand in creating the chance for Scott Sellars to equalize but then we were beaten by a late winner. We were even more devastated to lose in the FA Cup to First Division Luton Town. We didn't play particularly well against them at home but managed to give ourselves another bite of the cherry by snatching a draw. But we let them off the hook in the replay at their place. I should have scored a couple of goals which would have made a difference.

The bonus was that we finished high enough in the league to qualify for Europe which was going to be something special for me because it would be my first experience of Continental cup competitions. Had it not been for the consequences of the Heysel tragedy, I would have had four successive years of it at Liverpool, including two European Cups. I had transformed many of my schoolboy dreams into reality and now, at long last, I was in line for an overdue date with Europe.

10

STRIKERS AND STRIKES

One of the first real lessons of my football education back in my early professional days at Carlisle was that you cannot win matches on your own – you need to be helped ... and you need to help. I learned that in many ways a striker is only as good as his striking partner. In the years since, I have played alongside the best in the domestic game and have been taught plenty by all of them. I have to admit that I am not the ideal forward to play up front with. Whereas I find it easy to gel with others, there are times when I can sympathize with anyone who has to link with me because I would concede quite readily that he has the more difficult job. To be effective, I have to do my own thing and any team-mate has to fit in with that. A prime example of this has been at Newcastle after Paul Kitson arrived. It was very difficult for Paul because he has found himself up front on his own a lot while I have been flitting about here, there and everywhere. That suited players like Gary Lineker, Andy Cole and, to a certain extent Ian Rush and John Aldridge, but it is different from what Paul has been used to. Basically I act as the linkman between the midfield and the forward player. I can operate in a 4–4–2 formation but I am more likely to drift about.

At Newcastle, the boss Kevin Keegan allows me a free hand. It was the same at Everton and Liverpool where both Howard Kendall and Kenny Dalglish allowed me plenty of freedom, and I'd like to think it worked out well. At Anfield I actually had a similar role to that which Kenny himself played so successfully throughout his career, scoring a lot of goals and linking up so well with the likes of Ian Rush. As a forward you naturally have to rely a lot on the service you receive but I like a foot in both camps because I want to be involved more than operating just as a front man. Maybe I err too much on that side because it means I don't support the striker as much as I should. When you're winning you can get away with it but if the team goes through a bad patch, people look for reasons. It didn't affect us so much in my first season back at Newcastle but in the following seasons, because I didn't score many goals, it obviously led to a few questions being asked.

Kevin knows my game better than anybody because he had first-hand experience of what I do best when we played alongside each other. When I look back on all the forwards I have partnered – and they include some of the best in the English game – I have got to put him up there at the top. When I came back home from Canada I was completely overawed by the prospect of being in the same side as one of the stars of world football. But it was only when you experienced what he was actually capable of, that you realized his reputation was well-founded. Not only did he score goals but he had the knack of being just where you needed him when you needed him. He was also the fittest man I have played with. He had so much energy, drive and commitment, as well as complete assurance on the ball. Between us that season we scored 47 goals and with Chris Waddle helping himself to 18, it totted up to 65 between the three of us.

After he left I played spasmodically with players like Tony Cunningham, George Reilly and Billy Whitehurst, none of whom might have had the charisma or talent of Keegan, but were genuine triers and I had a lot of time for them. Nobody could ever accuse them of giving less than one hundred per cent, either on the field or in training. It was just that they came at a time of anti-climax for the club when the pattern of play was not what the crowd wanted or were used to, and consequently they weren't particularly popular. Tony and Billy would run through a brick wall for the club; George was a different type but just as honest. After I moved to Liverpool I had to assume the responsibility of being a big fish in a very big pool. The fact that it was a record deal meant I was up there to be shot at. But life was certainly made easier by the fact that there were so good players around to cover up for the mistakes you made.

I have always felt you only get out of the game what you put in; if you cheat, you only end up cheating yourself. If young players want evidence of the rewards you derive from dedication and application, they only have to look at somebody like John Aldridge, who at 37 was still knocking in goals by the dozen for Tranmere Rovers last season. Aldo was a delight to partner and the older he got, the sharper he got. He had arrived from Oxford United a few months before me and maybe needed time to adjust to the Liverpool way but he came on by leaps and bounds as a player in the time we were together at Anfield. His asset was his finishing; he was lightning in the box. He was not the strongest on his left foot but compensated by the intelligent way he manoeuvred the ball on to his right. If you analysed his goals you would find 95 per cent came from his predominant foot but there was also a fair proportion that were headers. There was myself,

Barnesy, Ray Houghton and Steve McMahon who were the four prompters, and Aldo was always there on the end of what we created.

The pleasures of partnering John Aldridge multiplied considerably when Ian Rush came back to Anfield. When news of his return leaked out there was a tremendous buzz in the area but nobody looked forward more than myself to seeing him wearing a red shirt again. Looking back to when I arrived I had detected a note of disappointment about the place among supporters who were sorry he had gone to Italy in the first place. His return meant a few changes up front and we found ourselves getting switched around quite a bit, but I soon learned what made him so special. He has a tremendous appetite for work. It has always been there but I think it has become more obvious lately with him partnering young Robbie Fowler. The lad is learning his trade in the best school but it is plain to see that he is benefitting so much from Rush's industry. The wheel has turned a full circle because in the earlier days at Liverpool it was Dalglish who did a lot of the work for Rush.

The highest tribute I can pay to Rushie is that he is the best player I have ever worked with, apart from the gaffer, at closing people down and putting in more than his fair share of effort. He is a great kidder. He would appear to a defender that he wasn't interested in chasing the ball and would then suddenly pounce and put his opponent under all sorts of pressure. He was also the best I have seen at making diagonal runs across defenders. The timing of his forward surges was magnificent. I suppose that was a relic of the Dalglish days. Kenny could put the ball on a sixpence. Rushie knew when to go and the ball would be there for him. Between them they developed a great understanding which was still within the team when he came back. Rush is an incredibly unselfish player. He'll run all day as long as there is something on the end of it. He appreciates a ball delivered into the areas which enable him to punish defenders. It took me a while to tailor my game to exploit his tremendous assets. At first he was probably too quick for me but as the time went on I grew more accustomed to his pace and positioning and by the end of my time there I feel we had it just about perfect.

The fortunate thing is that at Liverpool you are allowed the time to get it right. At a lot of other clubs the pressure is on straight away to get success but there they preach patience and understanding. I benefited from that in my first few months at the club. That's why I believe critics among the Newcastle supporters have been too quick to judge Paul Kitson. Supporters will eventually see the best of him but the players and coaching staff all recognize what a fine player he is. He had a tough job, being the one handed the main responsibility for scoring after Andy Cole left, but he has stuck at it and never looked for the long grass. I just wish the rest of us had made more of a contribution in the final third of that season and maybe that would have taken the spotlight away from Paul a little.

My relationship with Gary Lineker was something special to me because we were playing for England and the partnership became very successful. Gary was well established on the international scene before I got involved and already building a reputation as a world class striker. He was still with Everton but shortly afterwards was transferred to Barcelona after playing on the losing side against Liverpool in the 1986 FA Cup final. I believe he became a better player for his time in Spain. One of the main reasons was his determination to make the best of his move which was underlined when he learned how to speak Spanish. It was significant that neither Mark Hughes in Spain nor Ian Rush in Italy enjoyed the same success as Lineker and I think the difficulties they had in learning the language had something to do with it. It certainly didn't help them. I know Rushie in particular regrets he couldn't converse in the native tongue when he was in Turin.

You could almost see the improvement in Lineker every time he came back with the England party. His touch and all-round ability and game came on remarkably in two years. Not that there was anything wrong with him before that. He was a superb player who got even better. You would have to give Terry Venables much of the credit for that and I am sure Gary would agree. As far as I was concerned he was a joy to be associated with. He always had an uncanny sense of positioning and the brilliant control needed to make the most of it. It was a different kind of relationship from the regular one I had with Aldo and then Rushie at Liverpool. My games with Lineker were one-offs that came every few months. But in many ways they were a lot easier than club matches because you could relax more. The amazing thing with Gary was that he very rarely trained with England. He always seemed to be injured. But he would turn up for the squad get-togethers, hang around while the rest of us worked our tails off and then steal the show when the game started.

Gary was the kind of striker who did all his damage in the opponents' penalty area and he didn't like it cluttered up with team-mates. He wanted to be on his own up there and the advantage from my point of view was that he was so good at what he liked doing, it took the pressure off people like me who were not so fortunate in enjoying the kind of scoring record he had for England. People were kind enough to praise my part in his success but I have to be honest and say some of the credit was not due. He scored 48 international goals of which I could claim a hand in about 15. There was a spell when his goals dried up, and that was when I came under the spotlight and there were one or two voices suggesting I should be making a bigger scoring contribution. That sort of thing happens when things start going wrong and you expect a bit of criticism. But the truth is we were not doing anything different from what we always did. Nothing changed, only our luck. We just didn't get the rub of the green. I was disappointed when Gary eventually called it a day. I later had an incredible association with a chap called Andy Cole but I am convinced that, had I played with Lineker at club level, we would have been just as successful.

I found another excellent finisher waiting for me when I moved to Everton. Tony Cottee was a pocket of scoring dynamite. He had two great feet and was another who could sniff out a goal opportunity and be in the right spot to take it. He had his ups and downs at Everton but kept bouncing back just when his critics were ready to write him off. I lost count of the number of times he came on as substitute and scored vital goals. It was the ideal way of telling the manager that he should not have been on the bench in the first place. He certainly had a case when you analyse his goals per games ratio which was not a lot worse than one in two. Maybe it was Howard Kendall's way of giving him a bit of a gee-up. If that was the case it certainly worked. Tony had a great knack of scoring important goals and he carried that on when he went back to West Ham. In his first season back, his efforts did an awful lot to get the Hammers out of relegation trouble. Mo Johnston came halfway through my first season at Goodison. I have already said what an unlucky player I thought he was. He was certainly a lot better than his record suggested.

Then of course there is Cole, who was already a hero at Newcastle before I went back having scored eleven goals in the short time he had been at the club towards the end of their promotion season. I know there were a few raised eyebrows when he was bought from Bristol City for £1.75 million but you won't find many who will admit they were wrong about him. To be fair when I signed, Keegan told me he thought I was the ideal man to play alongside him. I took it in and waited to find out for myself what kind of player he was. I didn't know a lot about him but I did recall playing against him once in the FA Charity Shield when he came on as substitute for Arsenal against Liverpool. I remember he had only been on the field a few minutes when he rattled a shot inches wide into the side-netting. It was a chance he created out of nothing. The boss was extremely confident that he would score goals at the highest level and he was certainly right about that. I believe the football world is literally at Andy's feet. He is still only 24 with possibly another five years before he reaches his peak. The mind boggles at the thought of how many he will have knocked in by then. His great assets are his pace, the speed of his feet and his sharpness around the box.

We had a tremendous mutual respect. Andy might not have been everybody's cup of tea but we got on well on and off the field and there was never a bad word between us in the eighteen months we played together. He was a bit of a loner but I would never criticize him for that because, like him, I am not the best social mixer either. The only real difference between us was that he is a single lad who might have been expected to put himself around a bit. But off the field he is a very quiet, even shy person. His best mate at Newcastle was Lee Clark. Their friendship went back to their days in the England Under-21 side. The three of us always used to sit together on the team coach and chat about this and that.

If he had a fault, it was in his approach to training. He would be the first to admit he was hardly the most dedicated in the world. Maybe he could have worked harder but he never tried to hide the fact that the only time he was really happy was when the sessions were over. We were incredibly successful in our one and only full season together. Remembering the time it took to get it right with experienced professionals like Aldridge and Rush, it was remarkable that we managed to hit it off so quickly, especially with me missing the first seven games of the season. We managed 65 goals between us, with Andy's share a club record 41.

His transfer to Manchester United was the biggest shock of the season as far as I was concerned. I heard about it when I reported for training on the Tuesday morning and at first I thought somebody was pulling my leg. The deal upset a lot of Newcastle supporters but again it demonstrated the courage of the manager in selling somebody who, in his previous season, had become the most successful striker in the history of Newcastle FC. It was a case of money talking. Seven million pounds is an awful lot of money, especially as we signed Keith Gillespie, who is going to be a fantastic player, as part of the deal. The gaffer was the first to recognize the fact that Andy was such a favourite with the fans. He listened to their views in an impromptu get-together with supporters at the training ground and explained to them why he had done it. It was a remarkable piece of public relations that not many managers would have carried out. But the fans ended up cheering him, as they did in the following match against Andy's new club Manchester United.

Andy might have been a hero but his popularity on Tyneside will never match that of Keegan and although the supporters chanted his name when Alex Ferguson's team ran out and again during the game, it didn't compare to the demonstration of loyalty towards the Newcastle manager. But I have no doubts that Coley still has a special place in the hearts of the Toon Army. You can see them walking around the City even now with Cole shirts on. They are proud to wear them, and why not – he was a great player for the club. He can certainly look forward to a special welcome when he plays at St James' Park.

I feel proud that I was part of the England squad when he got called up for his first cap in the absence of Alan Shearer. I know how much it meant to him to come on as substitute against Uruguay because he felt he had done enough to be in the squad earlier. It would have been a fairy-tale had he scored but he was unlucky with a header that came off the bar. One thing is certain – that will not be the only opportunity he gets to score a goal for England.

At the end of the day the Cole deal suited everybody. He was happy because he has gone to the biggest club in Britain, Manchester United were happy or they wouldn't have paid the money and Newcastle were happy because they made a profit of over £5 million in less than two years. Of course the expectation was that the money would be spent straight away on a replacement. I think the deal happened so quickly they didn't have the opportunity to line up anyone else. In the end the boss has decided to keep his own counsel and wait until the right player becomes available at the right price. He has refused to spend money just for the sake of it and surely people should respect him for that.

Of course, I hope to have the opportunity before my England career is finally over of working some more with Shearer; after all he was another product of Wallsend Boys'

Club. He looks a different class playing for Blackburn Rovers. But so far in the few games we've played together with England I haven't really operated in my natural position enough to get a proper sight of him. He has played up front on his own but I haven't been the link man in the way that I was with the others. Still, you don't need to be on the same pitch to realize how good he is. He scores goals either by hitting 25-yarders or poaching them inside the six yard box. He has also made plenty for his Rovers team-mates such as the talented Chris Sutton. They have clearly learned a lot already from playing under Kenny Dalglish. I also rate Teddy Sheringham very highly. I have played with him once for England in that Uruguay match and he looked very impressive but my opinion about him as a player has been formed more by training with him which I think is often a better yardstick.

I have often been asked the $64,000 question – who do I rate the highest among all the strikers I have partnered? The answer would have to be a toss-up between Kevin Keegan and Ian Rush. In terms of being a goal-scorer and working hard and unselfishly for your team-mates, which is something I particularly admire and would hopefully aspire to myself, I couldn't split them. The greatest honour I could have is to be mentioned in the same breath. I would like to think I retained their enthusiasm for the game. The boss played until he was 33; Rushie is still going strong at the same age and I hope I have a year or two left despite the fact I won't see 34 again. Football is something to be enjoyed, and I don't mean just the matches themselves. It should be a pleasure to come into training every day; I know it is for me and the boss and Rushie are the same. You have to enjoy the training to enjoy the matches.

Nominating my top strikers is one thing; remembering my

best goals is another. But it is another question I am constantly asked by supporters either at football talk-ins or when they turn up in their thousands as they have done at our daily training sessions at Maiden Castle in Durham. It is one of the great imponderables. Do you remember a goal because it was spectacular or because it was important? There are many reasons for choosing one in front of another. But I have tried to put together a list out of the 200 plus I have scored in first class football in this country. It was a difficult choice because I have enjoyed scoring every one and I hope I haven't scored the best one of my career yet.

Anyway, it would have to be a bit special to top the one which I still consider to be the best so far. It came during my first spell at Newcastle in that tremendous promotion season and sadly the only United supporters who witnessed it were those who made the long journey to Fratton Park, Portsmouth. The gaffer scored after a minute and my great moment came a couple of minutes before half time. Keegan chipped the ball to me down the left hand side. I had cut inside one defender and then gone outside another and then started coming along the bye-line towards the goal. The ball bounced invitingly for me to take on and go around the Portsmouth keeper Alan Knight without breaking my stride. I got to within about four yards of the goal and then feinted to shoot which threw another Pompey player who came diving in and missed the ball completely. The United fans were screaming, 'Put it in; put it in.' It must have seemed like an eternity to them but in the end all I had to do was tap the ball into an empty net.

For sheer importance and personal delight I would have to say that goal number two was the one I scored for England against Poland in a European Championship qualifying match. I had come on as substitute for Gary Lineker who had given us the lead and then got injured. I was about ten yards outside the corner of the 18-yard box when Lee Dixon played a ball through to me down the inside right channel. I just took a touch and noticed out of the corner of my eye David Platt making a great forward run. I also knew there was only one defender in front of me and in that split second I was faced with the choice of crossing to Platty or having a crack. Actually it was the Polish keeper who made my mind up for me because he obviously thought I would cross it and moved instinctively to his right to cover the angle. That opened the gap between himself and the left-hand post so I thought, 'Sod it, I'm going to have a go myself'. I just hit it right-footed and you could see the swerve on the ball as it rocketed into the top corner. The goal gave me an awful lot of satisfaction for several reasons, the main one being it sent a little message to the England manager Graham Taylor who didn't think I was good enough to start the game in the first place. The BBC must have thought it was good because they included it in the opening credits for *Grandstand* every Saturday.

The third one would have to be the left-footed half volley I scored for Liverpool in my second Merseyside derby game against Everton. The ball had been crossed in from the left. Steve McMahon and John Barnes had worked a one-two before it was played in. John Aldridge had gone to sweep it in but the ball hit his heel and spun into the air and as it came down I kind of ran around it and hit it as it dropped. It shot in off the underside of the bar – right in front of the Kop, which made it even more special.

I would also have to include the one I scored against Norwich City two seasons ago among my favourites. It was similar to the England one against Poland. I was out on the right touch line and again I saw the keeper move and you could tell he thought I was going to cross the ball. You could almost sense him thinking, 'Well, there's no way he'll shoot from there.' And I just loved the expression of surprise on his face as he tried to get back across his goal to save it. I knew as soon as I hit it that it was in the net. A couple of weeks before the Norwich game we played Arsenal at St James' Park and I enjoyed the goal I scored to win the match in the last minute. Barry Venison had played a nice ball to me and I just turned and hit a shot from 25 yards which went from right to left into the bottom corner. The timing of that goal, as well as the shot itself, made it one I won't forget it in a hurry.

For the same reason, the sense of occasion made the goal I scored which won the Championship for Liverpool in my first season at Anfield one that will always stand out in my memory. It was not the most spectacular of strikes but it was the one which clinched my first Title winners' medal and that made it for me. All right, we looked odds on to win the Championship because we were streets ahead with five or six games to go. But it was my first honour and it was my goal that earned it.

I'll always remember the 4–4 draw against Everton not because it turned out to be Kenny Dalglish's farewell match at Liverpool but because I scored two of the goals, the second one being one of my particular favourites. The ball was placed to me square when I was about 40 yards from goal. I started running with it, side-stepping a challenge from Martin Keown before hitting a left foot shot that absolutely flew into the corner past Neville Southall.

Scoring at Wembley is always a special thrill and that's why I would have to include the winner for Liverpool against Arsenal in the 1989 FA Charity Shield. Barry Venison put over a centre from the right and it missed everybody before reaching me at the back post. It bounced up rather awkwardly and actually hit me on the hip but as John Lukic, the Arsenal keeper, came out, I just dinked it over him on the half volley. Again, being the only goal of the game, it meant a lot to me. Winning is important and I have been lucky enough throughout my career to score a lot of deciding goals. I managed to do just that in our match at Tottenham in the 1993/94 season. It was an eventful game, although not quite as eventful as the visit of Spurs at the end of the following season when we drew 3–3 and both sides finished with ten men, having had Pavel Srnicek and Colin Calderwood both sent off. I scored first at White Hart Lane but Nicky Barmby equalized from the penalty spot. When I missed an absolute sitter I thought our chance of winning had gone. Then we got a free-kick in the last minute. Andy Cole took it quickly and played it short to me near the left wing. I thought I had nothing to lose and decided to go for goal. There were three Spurs players barring the way, Dean Austin, Vinny Samways and Calderwood but in the end they seemed to get in each other's way and by the time they were able to get in a tackle I was in the box so they couldn't really commit themselves in case they gave away a penalty. I just cut inside and whacked the ball into the roof of the net. I was especially pleased because that miss earlier might have cost us the game.

Another I enjoyed was one I scored against Aston Villa. I had the ball moving between my feet going towards goal with Gary Charles and Paul McGrath moving in to tackle. They seemed to fall over themselves and that gave me the chance to tuck a shot low into the corner past Mark Bosnich. Maybe they would be disappointed with their defending but if the chance comes I'll always do my best to take it. I would also have to include the goal at Crystal Palace that maintained our

A proud moment as my England boss Bobby Robson hands over the championship medal. The dressing room ceremony was less formal.

Captain of England … exchanging pennants with Israeli skipper Malmilian before the friendly international in Tel Aviv in February 1988.

A Highland Fling with 'Choccy' McClair … we drew that game against United 3–3 in April 1988 but beat them to the title.

Liverpool memories ... the tragedy of Hillsborough remembered in the tributes that linked the two clubs on opposite sides of Stanley Park.

Graeme Souness is welcomed as manager by Ronnie Moran but his arrival was the beginning of the end for me at Anfield.

A mess of legs as Wimbledon's Lawrie Sanchez and Dennis Wise attempt a tackle and John Barnes gets in on the act.

Euro disappointment in Germany in 1988. Ronald Koeman is beaten but so were England, by Holland 3–1 in Dusseldorf.

Fun and games with Gary and Gazza during preparation for Italia '90 at Bisham Abbey.

A World Cup nail-biter ... in action against Cameroon in Naples in the 1990 quarter-finals. England won in extra-time with two penalties.

My best England performance ... challenging Matthaus and Buchwald for the ball in the World Cup semi-final against Germany in 1990. We lost on penalties.

All change on Merseyside and a spell in action for Everton in 1992 but sadly for me and the blues boss Howard Kendall (below), my two years at Goodison Park did not produce the success both of us hoped for.

Hats off on the day I returned to Newcastle. Keegan wanted me but the chairman Sir John Hall wasn't too sure.

A soldier in the Toon Army shows his face – the passion of Tyneside in black and white.

Graham Taylor wrote me a letter thanking me for my contribution for England but I made a comeback (below) after his departure as manager, winning my 50th cap against Denmark on 9 March 1994. We won 1–0.

A tip from Terry ... I'm hooked on England but the new England coach tells me about the one that got away during training.

Scoring the second goal for England in our 5–0 demolition of Greece in a friendly international at the end of the 1993/94 season.

Physio Derek Wright takes one look and its a case of turning the other broken cheek on the opening day against Leicester in August 1994.

Less than two months later and I'm fit and raring to go between Blackburn's Mark Atkins and Tim Sherwood at St James' Park in our 1–1 draw.

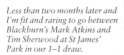

Together with Andy Cole, who broke scoring records when he was at Newcastle, and transfer records when he made his shock move to Manchester United.

UEFA Cup frustration as the Athletic Bilbao keeper makes another save in the 1–0 defeat in Spain which ended our hopes of European glory.

My pride and joy ... with my wife Sandra and children Drew and Stacey.

My friend Bruce Grobbelaar shows he still has what it takes with his save for Southampton. Team-mate Matt Le Tissier takes a back seat.

Lining up a red. The style may not be quite Steve Davis but who cares? Snooker is always a great way to relax.

In pensive mood ... remembering maybe the disappointment at missing out on Europe and losing in the FA Cup quarter-finals. Still, there is always a next time.

one hundred per cent start to the 1994/95 season. We had won our first six games but the record looked likely to go when we were being held to a draw with time running out. I played in midfield that day alongside Steve Watson. Again it was a last minute affair. Ruel Fox played the ball to Watto who touched it on to me and then made an angle, inviting the return pass. I shaped to shoot but instead cut inside the defender and lashed in a left-foot shot that flew past Nigel Martyn with Watto still screaming, 'Pass, pass!'

As I have said the goals that make the occasion are always the memorable ones but you never forget those where the occasion is made for something special. For that reason I have left until last but certainly not least, my goal which marked Kevin Keegan's final league game against Brighton back in 1984. As it happened the gaffer gave me a bad pass, which he readily admitted to later, and it looked like it would be cleared by Eric Young. But I got in one of my famous slide tackles and whipped the ball away from under his feet, falling over in the process. But I managed to pick myself up and chipped a shot over the head of the formidable figure of Joe Corrigan from twenty yards.

I suppose I could have picked out a few more and no doubt there will be people who will remind me of some I haven't mentioned – like those which have completed the eight hat-tricks I have managed throughout my career. I have a collection of match balls which I hope is not complete yet. One in particular I treasure came from a live television game for Liverpool against Manchester United. I was disappointed because at the end of the game the ball was booted into the Kop and one of the Liverpool supporters took it home. I made an appeal in the local papers and on radio to get it back and the chap returned it to me which was really nice.

I also managed one at Everton and so far have hit three at Newcastle; the first against Manchester City; the second against Sunderland which gave me a special treat and then in my first season back against Wimbledon. That gave me a lot of satisfaction, especially coming three days after we had lost to them in the Coca-Cola Cup. They were cock-a-hoop after that, making noises about us being a soft touch, but we buried them. My ambition now is to score four in a game. It is a tall order but the way we play our football at Newcastle, anything is possible.

11

ROBSON'S CHOICE

Terry Venables cost me a hundred pounds when he brought me back out of the international wilderness but it was a price I was happy to pay – although I have to say there was a little 'insider dealing' involved which might have influenced the outcome of a couple of bets I had with Kevin Keegan and Terry McDermott when I rejoined Newcastle. The ink was dry on the contract; all the handshaking was done and the photographs taken when the boss and Terry got me in a quiet corner and told me, 'Pedro, we're going to get you back in the England side.' I would never argue with Kevin, especially when he was ganging-up with his sidekick, but I thought for once he was shooting for the moon. I was 33 at the time and, to all intents and purposes, on the international scrapheap. So I just said, 'I don't think so, gaffer.' Straightaway he said, 'I'll have a friendly £50 bet with you,' and Terry chimed in, 'And so will I.' The wagers were struck and I walked away thinking there couldn't be many easier ways to win a hundred pounds!

It was not without significance that Keegan made such an issue about England. He knew how much playing for my country meant to me and he also knew my disappointment and frustration that my chances of pulling on that famous white shirt had apparently gone when I was just one cap short of that magical half century. I still believed I was capable of performing on the world stage. In fact, I considered the only changes in my ability, temperament and physical condition from the day I won my very first cap had been for the better. And why not? Since that January evening in Cairo back in 1986, I'd had four years at Liverpool and two at Everton. I had played with and against some of the top players in the game and had to be a improved player for it. I did not consider age as any disadvantage. There's a lot of truth in the old saying, 'You're as young or as old as you feel', and my bones and joints showed no signs of beginning to creak.

The big football event of 1986 was of course the World Cup in Mexico. At the turn of the year I hadn't even had a sniff of an England call-up. There had been media pressure on Bobby Robson to give me a chance but I discounted it. I dared not hope too much and anyway I was more concerned with the frustrations of club football at Newcastle. We lost in the third round of the Milk Cup to Oxford United, a team who we did the double over in the league. That was nothing to the disappointment of going out of the FA Cup in the third round to Brighton who were only an average Second Division side and one we should have had few problems with. Nevertheless, that 2–0 defeat by the Seagulls certainly had fortunate repercussions for me.

Robson had to name a squad to play against Egypt on 29 January. It was a strange date to fix a friendly international match because it clashed with dates of FA Cup fourth round replays, something which, as fate would have it, didn't concern me. Under the circumstances, with many of his regulars missing and the game representing an opportunity for the England manager to look at possible fringe players for his World Cup squad, I would have been disappointed not to have been given a chance. It was still one of the biggest thrills of my career when the squad was announced and the name of P Beardsley was included.

We were asked to assemble on the Saturday evening at a hotel in Luton. I drove down from the North-East, stopping at Woodall Services on the M1 for a sandwich on the way. Bobby Robson was waiting to greet me, shaking my hand warmly and saying, 'It's nice to have you with us, Peter. Just relax and enjoy yourself.' To be honest I was a bag of nerves.

Times have changed. I think the young footballer of today is a far more assured and confident person than he was even little more than a decade ago. It amazes me to see them today either in club football or at international get-togethers. They are completely uninhibited and without a care in the world. But I was knocked over by the sheer importance of it all. You were met, allocated a room – I shared with Kenny Sansom – and generally cosseted and made to feel something special. I loved every second of it.

Kenny, who was with Arsenal, was the perfect room-mate for taking away all the pressures. He had been on the international scene for a few years and knew the ropes inside out. He marked my card on a few things but it was his sense of humour I'll always remember. He was a laugh a minute, cracking jokes and doing irreverent impressions of some of the powers that be. His particular party piece was a take-off of Norman Wisdom that had the lads in stitches. All that helped to break the ice, but I didn't have to get on a plane the next day to feel my head was in the clouds.

You could hardly have picked a better trip to get the taste of football with an international flavour. On the first day in Egypt we had a trip to the Valley of the Kings and visited the

Pyramids and the Sphinx. There were the usual camel rides which I declined. But all this was a good laugh before we got down to the serious business. Bobby named his team – Shilton; Stevens, Wright, Fenwick, Sansom; Steven, Wilkins, Cowans, Wallace; Hateley, Lineker. Danny Wallace won his first, and, as it turned out, his last cap while Gordon Cowans was recalled after an absence of three years. I found myself chosen as one of the substitutes, which I expected and was not unhappy about. I was involved and that was all that mattered. I just sat on the bench, waiting and wondering whether the fairy-tale would be completed. Then came the magic moment. There were about 25 minutes to go when Bobby turned to me and said, 'Right Peter, I think it's time you had a go.' We were leading 3–0 through Trevor Steven, Wallace and an own goal when I went on, ironically as a substitute for Gary Lineker. My great thrill came when I rolled a square ball to Cowans and he hit a screamer from about 25 yards. We won 4–0 and as we walked off I thought to myself, I could really get to like playing for England.

A month later we were scheduled to return to the Middle East for another friendly against Israel. This time a few more established players were available and I wondered if I would get another chance. I was in good scoring form for Newcastle. There had been a bit of a fixture break because we were out of the FA Cup but in our last league game before the squad was announced I had collected both goals in a 2–1 win at Nottingham Forest. I was delighted when Robson called me up again and looked forward to repeating the euphoria of the Egyptian experience. The England boss made it an even more memorable trip when he called us together after our final training session and named his line-up – Shilton; Stevens, Martin, Butcher, Sansom; Hoddle, Robson, Wilkins, Waddle;

Dixon, Beardsley. My heart was pounding. The rest of the lads either shook my hand or patted me on the back and wished me luck.

Bobby then held a press conference and confirmed the team to the reporters who always travelled with us. Of course, they wanted to interview me and I just told them how delighted I was, how much I was looking forward to starting my first England match and how I hoped I would not let anybody down. Gary Lineker was unavailable because of injury so the striking partnership between Kerry Dixon and myself was something of an experiment but it provided both of us with an opportunity to stake a claim for consideration in the World Cup squad with the finals in Mexico barely four months away. I was desperate to do well but we could not have got off to a worse start. After eight minutes an Israel defender relieved our pressure from a corner with a massive boot down the field where a team-mate got clear of Alvin Martin and buried the ball in the net.

Bobby was responsible for granting me the greatest honour of my life when he made me skipper of England. It was only for one match, a friendly against Israel in Tel Aviv on 17 February 1988 and I have to be honest and say there were circumstances that prevailed to make it happen, but I still regard it as the highlight of my career. The gaffer made a few changes for the game but Bryan Robson was picked to play and would of course have worn the armband but he pulled a thigh muscle the day before the game and had to drop out. Of course, there was a lot of speculation and discussion about who would take over as captain and I was astonished when he told me, 'Peter, the job's yours. You might as well be captain because you do everything else – you carry the skip, you carry the balls …' He made a joke of it really but I still couldn't sleep the night before the game and the occasion – leading the team out, the exchanging of pennants and all the other pre-match activity – was something I will never forget. There was also a bit of leg-pulling from my team-mates about sorting out the bonuses and requesting permission to have a few drinks on the evening before the game. But it was a great occasion for me. We drew 0–0 but the result took second place to what it all meant. It's certainly something I will be able to tell my grandchildren.

That game was when I learned first-hand about the competitive qualities of Bryan Robson who in my opinion has to be one of the finest footballers ever to pull on an England shirt. He is not only a great player but also a tremendous leader, who provides immeasurable inspiration to the people around him. He had a magnificent match which turned the game in our favour. He displayed nerves of steel by knocking in an equalizer from the penalty spot and then crowned an incredible individual performance by scoring the winner late on. On the face of it we might have been expected to beat Israel with a little more in hand. That, anyway, was the general verdict of the media and the manager took a bit of stick in the papers the next day. Because of that, although I thought I had done reasonably well, I was worried whether I would get another opportunity. The competition for World Cup places was hotting up. I was a bit of a latecomer and really I had been selected only when Robson had been unable to exercise all his options. I had to wonder whether I would be so lucky if everybody was available.

The next England game was a tough one against Russia in Tbilisi and again luck was on my side when it came round. My fears were unfounded when I was included in the squad. Dixon was unavailable because his club Chelsea were involved in the Full Members' Cup Final at Wembley on the Sunday before the game. However, Lineker was back and Tony Woodcock and Mark Hateley were also involved. I joined up with the party fully expecting the closest I would get to playing would be as one of the substitutes. Opportunity knocks in football in different ways and sometimes it beckons as a result of the misfortune of others. But, whatever the circumstances, a player has to make the most of what comes his way and chances fell like manna from heaven on that trip. First of all, Woodcock turned up at Luton hobbling and clearly in great pain. It turned out he had gout of all things. Of course, nobody was going to let him get away without a few leg pulls but in all seriousness he was really struggling. It was decided to take him to Russia in the hope it would clear up before the match. As it turned out it didn't.

Then on the Monday, Hateley arrived in Tbilisi with a thigh strain which he had picked up playing for AC Milan the previous day. The physio worked on him continually but he was forced to pull out. That left myself and Gary Lineker as the two recognized front men although Robson had Chris Waddle available. In the event he named all three of us but the odds were stacked against England. Russia had developed into one of the top sides in Europe and were fancied to do well in Mexico. Not many teams went there and came away with a victory. The boss was quite open about his intentions when he announced the side. He said it was one of his last opportunities to experiment before he finalized the names of the players who would be going to the World Cup. The Russian match would help him to make up his mind about people.

It was the first time I shared a striking role with Lineker and I am certain that what we did influenced Robson when he was forced to reconsider his attacking alternatives at a later date. I thought I did well personally and the highlight came when I set up the only goal of the game for my pal 'Waddler'. It was Chris who started the move with a ball knocked down the right for me to chase. To be fair, the big Russian defender who came across to cut the pass off looked odds-on to get there and clear it. I dived in with my favourite slide tackle, nicked the ball and raced clear into the Russian penalty area. Lineker made a run for the near post but I noticed Waddler coming in behind him. So, instead of rolling it for Gary, I put extra pace on the pass across the goal. Gary left it, either because he had spotted Chris or had been given a call, and my old Newcastle team-mate took a touch and lashed the ball into the roof of the net. We had a bit of luck when the sweeper Chivadze missed a penalty for Russia but we deserved our victory.

That made it three wins out of three for me in an England shirt and for the first time I felt I had a real hope of gate-crashing the World Cup party. I was unaware at that time of the problems that were to interrupt my international career. The next England game was the following month against Scotland at Wembley but, because of postponements due to bad weather earlier in the year, there was a bit of a backlog of club fixtures which had to be cleared up before the end of April. Newcastle crammed in seven matches including two in London, at Chelsea on the Saturday and the famous 8–1 slaughter at West Ham the following Monday, two days before the Scotland international. Because of these games I was not included in the original squad, but I was pleasantly surprised when Robson invited me to join up with the party the day before the match. He had advised me that I wouldn't be required to play but it was an opportunity to maintain my link with the team.

At the back of my mind was the notion that he had positive intentions towards me and this thought was strengthened when a chap turned up at the training quarters and measured all the players for a World Cup suit. By this time I was getting rather excited until it was pointed out that although 30 lads were getting measured, there would only be 22 going to Mexico. The consolation for the unlucky ones was that they would at least be given the suit. I wondered whether that would make up for the disappointment of not being on the plane and I hoped I wouldn't have to find out. As it happened, after our workout on the morning of the Scotland match Bobby asked me if I fancied being one of the substitutes and I didn't need any further persuading. I didn't get on but I still enjoyed the occasion, especially with England beating the old enemy 2–1 with goals from Terry Butcher and Glenn Hoddle against a second half penalty from my future Liverpool boss Graeme Souness.

We played the two remaining games of our league programme and then I settled back to wait with increasing trepidation for the announcement of the Mexico squad which was due early in May. There was no advance notice; no inside information. Obviously Willie McFaul, as the Newcastle manager, would have been told privately but he kept it quiet and, because the season was over, there was no need for contact between us. Then the day dawned and I got a call from the local evening paper in Newcastle to tell me I was in. I managed to stay cool and express my delight but inside I was bouncing. I was on my way to Mexico with a squad of players who were ready to carry the hopes of millions of English fans back home. I was happy to be going but realistic enough to believe it could only possibly be as a standby player. I didn't expect to kick a ball.

Such thoughts were not allowed to dampen my enthusiasm or pleasure as we climbed aboard the jumbo jet that was to take us on the first stage of our Mexican adventure, which was a period of altitude training in Colorado Springs. It was a magnificent place. We used the facilities at a US Air Force Academy and they did not skimp on the hospitality. We were well looked after but the preparation was no picnic. It was hot and I had never experienced training at altitude before. Breathing was difficult, especially after doing some of the hard running that was geared to preparing us for the conditions we would experience in Mexico. We played a game against Korea in Colorado and beat them comfortably 4–1 but then faced a stiffer test against Mexico themselves at the Los Angeles Coliseum. I was picked but still harboured no illusions about what Bobby Robson probably regarded as his best team. The four-man Everton contingent, made up of Gary Lineker, Peter Reid, Gary Stevens and Trevor Steven had arrived late after losing in the FA Cup Final to Liverpool a week earlier and weren't really considered, although Trevor did eventually come on for Ray Wilkins.

It was an unforgettable game for two reasons ... I scored my first England goal and it was the start of the injury problems that would eventually cost Bryan Robson his World Cup place and force a team re-shuffle which was to present me with my big chance. The Coliseum was familiar territory for me. I played there a few times when I was with Vancouver Whitecaps and I was determined to create an impression. Mexico had gone 17 games without losing but we shook them when Mark Hateley scored with two great headers from crosses provided first of all by Chris Waddle and then by yours truly. I was enjoying the game and I was about to start liking it even more. Glenn Hoddle knocked a perfectly-placed free-kick over the Mexican defence and all I had to do was chest it down and thump it. The Mexican keeper Larios obligingly opened his legs and the ball shot through them into the net. We won 3–0 which amply consoled me for the jarring whack I got in the face from Mexican defender Manzo's elbow.

Robbo had to go off twenty minutes from the end with a recurrence of the shoulder dislocation problem which had made it touch and go whether he would make the World Cup finals. Of course, there were a few voices raised in hindsight later suggesting he should not have been risked but you would never have got any of the players to agree with that. Even injured he was a source of strength to the rest of us. Our final warm-up game was in the even more familiar surroundings of Vancouver although our game against Canada was switched from the Whitecaps ground to another local stadium because Bobby didn't want us to play on astroturf. I was on the bench because the boss wanted to look at what he anticipated would be his number one strikeforce of Hateley and Lineker. He had a special word with me, telling me I was unlucky to be left out after the way I played against Mexico. I did manage to get on under unfortunate circumstances for the last twenty minutes when Gary had to come off with a badly sprained wrist after a nasty fall. The reception I got from the local supporters was one of the best I have ever had. It was really something. Again it was a Hateley goal which won us the game and set us up nicely for the real action.

By this time I had a new nickname which had been coined by Terry Butcher. He christened me 'Ceefax' because he said I was full of useless information. It came about because I was an avid studier of any itinerary that we were given. Professional footballers are by nature a lazy bunch who never have to worry about travelling or accommodation arrangements. It is all done for them by club secretaries or other administrators. They just turn up and are ushered here, there and everywhere. But I make it my business to know the times of planes and buses and the names of hotels along with phone numbers. It is just a habit of mine. I also liked to work out things like flight schedules. I remember on the plane from Vancouver back to Los Angeles, the pilot announced the flight duration as normal and when we landed I happened to remark to the boss who was in the next seat that he had been spot on. Bobby was tickled to death. 'You're a rare bird, Peter. I can't believe you took the trouble to work it out.'

I have a bit of a thing about flying anyway. Because I was once told the most dangerous periods are the first and last ninety seconds of any flight, I always check my watch so I know when to relax. Not that I did much of that after we changed planes at Los Angeles and headed for Monterrey in Mexico. Without a shadow of doubt it was the most terrifying flight I have ever been on. Almost as soon as we got off the ground, the aircraft started bouncing about like a cork on the ocean and it was like that for the whole of the three hours we were on board. What made it worse was that I was trying to help Lineker with his food because his arm was strapped up. It would have been comical if we hadn't been beside ourselves with terror. I have never been so glad to walk down a gangway and plant my feet on the ground.

We soon struck up a great relationship with the locals in Monterrey. Their particular favourites had to be Sansom and Hoddle who not only taught them a few words of English but also had them spouting cockney rhyming slang. A coffee was a 'Bill Roffey' and tea was 'Bertie Mee.' It all helped to create the right atmosphere and they wanted us to win the group because that would have meant us staying in Monterrey for the later stages of the tournament. As it happened, by the time we had played two matches, we were just desperate to stay in the tournament with our prospects of getting past the group stage looking extremely slim. I was one of the subs for the opening game against Portugal. Both Bryan Robson and Gary Lineker had been declared fit which gave everybody a lift, although Gary had to play with his arm in a plaster cast. We had the chances to win the game but it was Portugal who scored with a quarter of an hour to go. The boss immediately put me on for Waddle and replaced Robbo with Steve Hodge but we were unable to alter the scoreline.

We licked our wounds and Bobby did his best to lift the team's morale. Our next opponents were Morocco and we all felt the game represented an opportunity to get our disastrous start out of our system and go on from there. If anything it was even more of a tragedy. Bryan Robson got carried off after his shoulder went again and Ray Wilkins got sent off for venting his frustration at one of the many strange decisions by throwing the ball at the feet of the Paraguayan referee. It was an untypical rush of blood and Ray apologised profusely to the lads later but under the circumstances we were relieved to manage a goalless draw. Had the Moroccans chosen to be a little more positive that might have been difficult but they were ecstatic about the result. You would think they had won the Cup judging from their reaction at the end. Not losing against England was one of the great achievements of their football lives. I viewed the whole match from the substitutes' bench and afterwards contemplated a premature return to England.

We had a major inquest into the defeat and planned our tactics for the crucial third game against Poland. Bobby had written all the possible permutations on a board; where we would go if we won or what might happen if we drew. He went on and on and then, almost as an afterthought, finished by saying, 'Of course if we lose, we'll be going home.' He didn't mean to be funny but his remark brought the place down. The meeting was at a local monastery and we finished the day by having a barbecue and a game of cricket. By the time it was over, our spirits had been lifted and we were ready to give it our best shot. The boss obviously had to make changes with Robbo injured and Ray suspended. For the first time since the Russian friendly I found myself partnering Lineker up front.

The game couldn't have gone better had I written the script. We won 3–0 thanks to Gary's great hat-trick; I played my part in the second and generally our partnership worked a treat. Afterwards the other players and officials were very complimentary. Mark Hateley, who had been gutted at being left out and even made his feelings known to the boss, was among the first to come up and congratulate me on my performance which was nice. The press lads, obviously influenced by the fact they would be staying out a bit longer, were equally happy. That made a change because the team had been given so much 'stick' after the first two games that the boss had banned all the papers. It was the players who hadn't performed but it was Robson who got hammered. And he took it on the chin without a word of criticism for the team. Things were different after the Poland win. We had reached the next stage of the tournament and only Paraguay stood between us and a place in the quarter-finals. The mood of the whole party was one of expectant optimism.

We had a couple of scary moments early on against Paraguay but then Gary put us in front. Then, while he was having treatment for an injury, we won a corner. Normally he would take up a position standing next to the keeper so I took it upon myself to do exactly that. Glenn Hoddle took the kick, and Alvin Martin challenged for the ball which landed at Terry Butcher's feet. He half-volleyed a shot which hit the keeper on the chest and dropped invitingly at my feet and I just side-footed it in. The goal made the whole Mexico experience worthwhile. To score in the World Cup was what my dreams had been made of. Lineker recovered to round the day off with the third goal and we were in the last eight and getting more confident by the minute. It was all coming together at the right time.

Four days later we were back in Mexico City's Aztec Stadium to play Argentina in front of a packed 114,580 crowd. A few people had expressed concern that the game had been handed to a Tunisian referee but none of us could know just how well founded that anxiety would be. The boss got us in the dressing room before the game and told us to keep our discipline, to pass and move and above all to go out and enjoy the occasion. The atmosphere was absolutely unbelievable. I certainly had not experienced anything like it before or since. We all know how the game turned on Diego Maradona's disgraceful handball but that incident would never have happened had I been a little luckier with a first half shot that hit the side-netting and was inches away from opening the scoring. But I'll never know how Maradona got away with his famous 'Hand of God.' It was blatant. His second goal was a marvellous example of his undoubted skill but the predominant word to describe the Argentinian's performance was more likely to be 'cheat'. John Barnes came on along with Chris Waddle for the last fifteen minutes and helped to transform the game, crossing for Gary Lineker to pull one back. We had them rocking at the end but it was all to no avail.

It was a rotten way to go out because we felt we were as

good if not better than Argentina and they went on to beat West Germany in the final. We had been given the option of staying on but by the time Maradona was lifting the famous trophy, I was back at home on Tyneside and looking forward to enjoying what was left of my summer break. Thankfully, our performances in Mexico took the sting out of any criticism of the manager. Bobby Robson was handed the job of guiding England towards the European Championship finals in Germany two years later and after that the 1990 World Cup in Italy, and nobody was happier than me about that. I think that decision was justified certainly by the way we qualified for the European Championship, dropping only one point in a group which also included Yugoslavia, Northern Ireland and Turkey. The highlights were our 8–0 trouncing of the Turks at Wembley and a 4–1 win over the Yugoslavs in Belgrade.

We had hopes of doing well in the finals but to be honest we were nothing short of a disaster in Germany, losing all three of our group matches. Jack Charlton had done well since taking over as manager of the Republic of Ireland and we knew we were in for a tough opening game in Stuttgart. Ray Houghton, who has made a habit of scoring important goals for Ireland, put them ahead early on and we were always chasing the game after that. To be fair, they kept our clear-cut chances to a minimum but it was a closely fought match and I don't think we deserved to lose, although the Irish supporters who celebrated long into the night might find it hard to agree with me. Our next game was against Holland and although we lost 3–1, thanks to a Marco Van Basten hat-trick, I felt we played really well. Bryan Robson, the great indestructible following an operation to cure his shoulder problem, scored an equalizer for us and had another marvellous game for

England. Although Van Basten came back with two more, I still say we deserved something out of the game.

The last match against Russia was purely academic. We were out anyway. Bobby decided to make a few changes. He called myself, John Barnes and Gary Lineker in for a chat and explained the reasons for his team selection. He stuck with Gary, although he was struggling with what was diagnosed later as hepatitis. But Bobby told me he was leaving me out because he thought I looked tired, and he told Barnesy, 'Buck up, son, because you are playing bad.' The phrase stuck because back at Liverpool whenever I asked him how he was getting on, Barnesy would smile and say, 'I'm just playing bad, Pete.' We lost 3–1 to Russia and the press had their knives out for the boss again. Looking back, it had to be our results in Germany which eventually cost him his job but I think, as things turned out, the Football Association might just have been a little premature in getting rid of him.

All the players had enormous respect for Bobby but we all knew we had let him down. Again we hadn't performed to the best of our ability. We were all desperate to put things right in the qualifying games for the 1990 World Cup although it wouldn't be easy in a group which also included Poland, Sweden and Albania. We started indifferently with a goalless draw at home to Sweden but we played well enough to win the game without enjoying a lot of luck in front of goal. The trip to Tirana deep behind what was then the Iron Curtain was an experience. Our hotel was besieged by hundreds of locals who would not leave until Chris Waddle and myself had thrown them souvenirs. We had a comfortable 2–0 win. I was sub for the game but came on for Waddle near the end. The return match at Wembley the following month was even more emphatic. Lineker scored early on and I managed to add a second before the interval. We were all over them in the second period and it was a bit of a Geordie takeover. I made it three; Chrissy Waddle scored a fourth and Gazza made it five two minutes from the end.

There was no disguising Robson's delight in our dressing room when it was all over. I think he had a special regard for Chris and myself because we hailed from his neck of the woods in the North-East. But there was little doubt that Paul Gascoigne brought a twinkle to his eye. He was the first to spot the international potential of Gazza and that foresight was to be well rewarded.

Our hopes of qualifying for the finals flourished with a 3–0 win over Poland at Wembley and we finally clinched it with two goalless draws in Stockholm and Chorzow. We finished second in our group behind Sweden with the creditable record of three wins and three draws with ten goals scored for none against. Bobby typically thanked us for our efforts but to a man we felt we owed him something and perhaps reaching the finals went some way to repaying that debt. Sadly it was too late to stop him going. Speculation about his future had been rife and the FA didn't do a lot to kill it. In the end he announced he would see the World Cup out and then be on his way. That seemed to suit the powers that be but I felt they should have waited until the outcome of the World Cup before deciding what to do. It would have been a ludicrous situation if we won the trophy, as we very nearly did, and the manager was rewarded with what amounted to the sack.

12

ENGLAND REVISITED

There was almost a siege mentality within the England camp regarding the welfare of the manager. Sure, we all felt the basic urge to play well for our country but we felt the way Bobby Robson was being treated by his FA bosses and certain sections of the media was unjustified and, as players, we had to shoulder some of the blame. The least we could do was try to give him a good send-off in the World Cup in Italy. It was this motivation, added to our own personal pride, that really put us in the mood in the build-up to facing the Republic of Ireland in the opening group match in Cagliari. The gaffer had already kept a promise he made to me when I was invited to attend the England squad reunions towards the end of the season. I was still recovering from a stress fracture of the leg which had forced me to miss the last two months of Liverpool's season but he told me, 'Prove your fitness, Peter, and you'll be in my squad.' I still had doubts about whether I would be selected against Jack Charlton's team. After all I had missed the warm-up games against Czechoslovakia, Denmark and Uruguay and my only international experience of any note since playing against Brazil in March was when I came on as a sub in Tunisia nine days earlier.

What persuaded the boss to risk me was my performance in a friendly against a local side a week before the Irish game. We were leading 5–0 at half-time without any contribution from me and during the interval Bobby came to me and said, 'Come on Peter, score me a goal.' I obliged with a hat-trick in the second half; we won 9–0 and as a result a couple of days before the first game he told me I was in the team for the crucial opener. That man Lineker gave us the lead after eight minutes and I felt we were holding the lead comfortably. To try and tighten things up, the boss took me off and brought on Steve McMahon after 69 minutes. Sadly the switch rebounded on us with tragic consequences. 'Macca' was only on the field three minutes when he lost the ball on the edge of our penalty area, allowing Kevin Sheedy the chance to grab a shock equalizer. We were absolutely gutted because we felt we had thrown victory away. To be fair, the boss came to me later and apologised. 'It was my mistake, Peter. If I'd left you on we might have won.'

Our next opponents were Holland, one of the pre-tournament favourites, who had been held to a shock draw by Egypt in their first game. Bobby decided to leave me out which was disappointing, but if it was the price for beating the Dutch I was happy to pay it. I was still not fully in my stride for the tournament and this was certainly a factor that he was forced to consider. We battered Holland – stars and all – but were robbed when a Stuart Pearce 'goal' was disallowed by the Yugoslav referee. Pearce smashed in a free-kick that left Hans Van Breukelen groping but, to everybody's amazement, the official ruled the kick was indirect. It certainly came as a relief to the Dutch keeper who had made a valiant but unsuccessful attempt to stop the shot. The game finished goalless which meant we had to get something from our final group match against Egypt or face an early exit.

Again I didn't manage to make the starting line-up but I was one of the subs. It was a dour struggle but we got through thanks to a Mark Wright header from a free-kick taken by Gazza, who was rapidly becoming one of the stars of the tournament. I remember he took the kick from a position just in front of the bench and I jumped on him in delight when the goal went in. I eventually got on the field when Steve Bull went off six minutes from the end to earn myself another cap, but reaching the second round gave me much more reason to celebrate.

Our three group matches had all been in Cagliari but as top qualifiers we were required to switch to Bologna to challenge Belgium for a place in the quarter-finals. Bobby again saw fit to leave me out, explaining that he felt maybe I needed a couple more games to get me match fit but there wasn't enough time to arrange anything. I accepted the situation and was content to be involved as one of the subs. I sat and shared with him the sheer anguish of watching the Belgium game stretch goalless towards the end of ninety minutes and then into extra-time. We carried some luck, especially when the Belgians twice hit the woodwork. The result could have gone either way but fortune favoured us for once when David Platt pivoted to score a brilliant goal from a Gazza free-kick in the final minute of extra-time. We all danced about, hugging each other unashamedly. Bobby had had his bad times but now it seemed his luck was beginning to change with a vengeance.

It was on to Naples and a confrontation with the surprise team of the tournament, Cameroon. Platty, who had come on as sub to win the Belgian match, deserved to be in from the start this time. Bringing him in for Steve McMahon was the only change and he duly celebrated by giving us a half-time lead with a superbly-taken goal. Then John Barnes got injured just before half-time which forced the boss into deciding who to put on in his place. The four subs – myself, Macca, Steve Bull and Trevor Steven – spent the interval period warming-up in the gym at the back of the dressing room, wondering who would get the nod. In view of the match situation and the need to keep things tight, I thought McMahon was favourite. Bobby might have even decided to give Bully a go and gamble on another goal. I certainly didn't fancy my chances and was truly gobsmacked when he popped his head around the gym door and announced: 'Peter, you're going on.'

My feeling of surprise rapidly changed to one of anxiety when, within eighteen minutes of the second half, Cameroon equalized from the penalty spot. It got worse four minutes later when they took the lead. I thought, what a nightmare. Fortunately, the Mexican referee awarded us a penalty which Lineker despatched with unflappable coolness eight minutes from the end of ninety minutes. Then, after the game had gone into extra-time, he repeated the dose again from the spot. We were in the semi-finals of the World Cup and you would have struggled to find a more relieved man in the city of Napoli that evening than me.

It was north to Turin for the clash of the tournament against our old rivals West Germany. The big question everybody was asking concerned Robson's team selection. Come the morning of the game, nobody in the squad knew what was in the boss' mind. We prepared at Torino's training establishment and then he ended all the guessing and speculation by naming his line-up – Shilton; Parker, Butcher, Wright, Walker, Pearce; Platt, Gascoigne, Waddle; Lineker, Beardsley. My delight was in complete contrast to the feelings of the unlucky ones. Steve McMahon, in particular, was naturally devastated. This was the biggest game of my life and I was determined not to let down myself, my country, the supporters at the game and the millions back home. And, if I say it myself, I don't think I did.

A lot of people said whoever won the match would win the World Cup. The way the tournament works, you don't have a lot of anticipation time – as soon as one game is over and you're lucky enough to be still involved, you're on top of the next one with whatever travelling may be involved. I found out on the morning of the Germany game that I would be playing. The burning topic was whether Barnesy, who had had to come off at half-time in the quarter-final match against Cameroon, would be fit enough to resume. I knew if he could have made it, he would have played, but such are the fortunes of football. For the second time in successive matches, my chance came when his disappeared. Because the decision was delayed until the last possible moment, I didn't have time to get really nervous. Bobby Robson was obviously desperate for John to play but when he knew he wasn't going to, he came to me and told me I was in. There were one or two of the rest of the lads who were a little upset, as I would have been had I not been selected, but I was determined not to let him down and I don't think I did. The pleasing thing for me is I don't think, as good as he is, Barnesy would have done any better.

For the game itself, I was marked by Guido Buchwald. He kicked me and I kicked him back. Brehme scored for the Germans after an hour with a deflected free-kick and Lineker equalized with a memorable effort ten minutes from the end to send the game into our third successive extra-time. It was still deadlocked after 120 minutes and so we headed for that dramatic penalty finale. During the brief break we discussed frantically who would take the kicks and that was when a fateful decision was made. Gazza had been due to take one but a tragic booking had meant he would miss the final through suspension and he felt, under the circumstances, somebody else should take his. Chris Waddle, who had not been on the original penalty list, volunteered to stand in for his mate.

The five players nominated were myself, Lineker, Platt, Pearce and Waddle. Bobby, visibly shaking and beside himself with anxiety, suddenly came up to me and whispered, 'There are 55 million people watching this at home son, don't let me down.' Talk about pressure! Gary turned round to the boss in protest. 'Hey, there's no need for that gaffer. He'll do his best and nobody can ask any more.' But I felt good. In fact, from the moment I was chosen to take one of the penalties I knew I would score. I had played so well in the game and I had an unshakeable confidence in my ability to knock it in.

The teams matched each other goal for goal. Lineker took the first one and scored for the second time in the game; I went second and made it count and so did Platty who came after me. It was 3–3 but then tragedy struck for Stuart whose shot was saved by Illgner in the German goal. Thon made it 4–3 for them and then it was down to Waddle to keep us in the World Cup. No player should be subjected to an ordeal like that and my pal buried his face in his hands after he put the ball over the top. We trudged off absolutely shattered, mentally and physically. Gazza was in tears and he wasn't the only one. Buchwald came looking for me to swap shirts. I obliged him, although it was usually something I declined to do.

At the end of it all, I felt we could all hold our heads up, most of all Bobby Robson. We deserved more than we got, a fact acknowledged by the German coach, the great Franz Beckenbauer. He admitted after the game they were fortunate to be in the final. We had certainly been involved in the tournament's most memorable game. The final turned out to be the biggest anti-climax of all-time, a drab, scrappy, colourless encounter in which Germany's opponents Argentina had clearly set out their stall to take the game to penalties and fully deserved to be beaten within sight of extra-time. In the end Germany's semi-final scorer Brehme foiled the South Americans with a late penalty.

All that was left for us was to share in the carnival atmosphere that marked the third place play-off game against the host country Italy in Bari. There were Mexican waves and singing and dancing and, although we lost 2–1, the result took second place to the occasion. Both teams did a lap of honour at the end and were cheered off the field. It was an appropriate finale to Peter Shilton's illustrious international career and a nice way for Bobby Robson to say goodbye. He was so close to bringing the World Cup back to England and certainly proved himself a tough act to follow. What he has achieved since winning championships at PSV Eindhoven, Sporting Lisbon and now Porto has underlined that language is no barrier to his skills as a coach. I was especially sorry to see him go because we had a special relationship. From the day he first picked me, he never left me out of any of the squads in which I was fit enough to be included. I was proud to be associated with Bobby but now I looked forward to playing under the man appointed to be his successor, Graham Taylor.

I was pleased to be included in his first squad for a friendly against Hungary at Wembley. You always wonder what will happen with a new man at the helm. He would obviously have his own ideas and it would be a question of whether your style or even face fitted. The way he started and the actual get-together was excellent. He was friendly and warm and outlined his plans and intentions and everything was fine. I was one of the substitutes because he gave Steve Bull a chance alongside Gary Lineker which was fair enough. Gary, as usual, scored the goal that won the match and later in the game Taylor brought Chris Waddle on for Bully. I stayed on the bench. The big priority was qualification for the 1992 European Championships and we had some familiar hurdles to negotiate in order to get to Sweden, with the Republic of Ireland, Poland and Turkey in our group.

The first qualifier was against Poland and that meant a six-day preparation. I thought Taylor was brilliant. He met us all on the Thursday and in the evening opened a few bottles of champagne, which was a nice touch. He also had lots of little leisure activities arranged which helped the new boys to settle in and get to know everybody. He brought in Steve Harrison to help him with the coaching and it was all fresh and enjoyable and had plenty of variety. In the evenings we had daft little games which gave us all a laugh. The object was to find out who was the worst at whatever we did and I remember once that doubtful honour fell to me. The boss handed a bottle of wine to each member of the winning team and then produced the biggest melon I had ever seen and presented it me saying, 'Beardsley you were an absolute nightmare.'

We couldn't have been in a better frame of mind for the match. I was again one of the substitutes, hoping this time I might get on which I eventually did when the boss made a double substitution early in the second half. Gary Lineker, who had given us a first half lead from the penalty spot and then got injured was replaced, alongside Steve Bull, by myself and Chris Waddle. My great moment came in the dying seconds. Lee Dixon played a ball for me to chase down the inside-right channel and as I kept going forward I noticed

David Platt had made a great run down the middle. He was on his own and nine times out of ten I would have laid the ball to him but it was another of those situations where the opposition keeper made my mind up by anticipating wrongly. He moved to cover the pass and left enough of a gap for me to crack the ball past him.

The goal kept me in the squad for the next Euro game against Ireland in Dublin. For the first time I started a match under Taylor because Waddle, who had been named in the original line-up, was a bit off colour and dropped out at the last minute. It was a bit of a rush job because the game was in the afternoon and there wasn't a lot of time to rearrange the preparation. It was just a case of trying to slot in and make the best of it. Under the circumstances we did very well. Platty put us ahead and although Tony Cascarino rescued a point for the Republic, they would have to admit we were the better team and were unlucky not to win the game. I also started in the return match at Wembley the following March. In fact on the Monday morning before the game the boss asked three players, myself, John Barnes and Lineker to travel in the car with him from the hotel to the training ground instead of going on the bus with the rest of the lads. He told us we would all be playing and went through a few things he wanted from us. It was very rare for any England manager to give players the nod so early and I was delighted. But the match was not such a happy occasion. Like the first game it ended 1–1 with Niall Quinn equalizing a Lee Dixon opener but maybe on that occasion we didn't play well and were a little fortunate to get a point.

I was as disappointed as the rest – and even more so when I was apparently made one of the scapegoats by being left out of the squad for the following European qualifier in Turkey. It was a decision that confirmed a nagging doubt about my prospects under Taylor. England won 1–0 through Dennis Wise's first England goal. But the team performance was nothing special and maybe for that reason I was back on the scene three weeks later for an end of season tournament against Russia and Argentina at Wembley. I was named as one of the substitutes for the game and won my 49th cap when I went on for Ian Wright with twenty minutes to go. We won the game 3–1 but it was the last football I kicked for England under Taylor. Four days later I stayed on the bench when we drew 2–2 with the Argentinians but I really got the message when, without a word of warning or explanation, I was omitted for a four-match summer tour of Australasia and the Far East. I suppose his team selection was justified because England won all four matches but I was really choked about being ignored.

I have to think, when it came down to it, that it was the way he wanted to play that left me redundant. Taylor liked the long ball which obviously didn't suit my game. The system would have favoured a bigger man but England didn't have one. He played Steve Bull up there. He was brave and strong but he wasn't the biggest of players. Niall Quinn has proved his effectiveness playing as a target man in the Irish side but he is more than that. He has a superb touch for a tall man. Unfortunately England didn't have anyone of his size and skill. There was talk of him bringing in Mark Hateley but he never got round to doing that. Even when the manager included me in his first five or six squads, I suspected I didn't have much of an England future under him. I had a feeling my 50th cap would always be out of my reach. I didn't really want to win it as a sub. I would have liked to have won it in the grand manner by coming on from the start but, barring the kind of serious injuries you would never wish on a fellow professional, I just could not see that happening.

The crunch came when we flew to Moscow in April 1992 to play the CIS which was then the modern equivalent of what used to be the USSR. The party was 40-strong because we had two matches – a B-international on the Tuesday and the main game the following night. Taylor was scheduled to conduct a press conference as soon as we landed on the Monday but just as we were about to get off the plane, he named the teams to the players and I found myself in the B-team.

I couldn't believe it and would have had a word about it if he hadn't gone straight to talk to the press. I had played in a B-match before against Wales a year earlier but that was after I was coming back from injury and easing my way back into the international picture and he was doing me a favour. I remember after the game Lawrie McMenemy, his assistant who was in charge of the side, came to me and said, 'Well done, Peter, your class showed through.' I was happy with that although I knew it was far from what I was capable of. He also said I would be in the next squad, which I was, for the return European Championship game against the Republic.

If he had mentioned to me at Luton before we left what he intended to do I would have said, 'No thanks, I'd rather not.' I don't think I had let him or England down when I had played and I thought I deserved better. Anyway I decided to wait until after the game to speak to him. We led early on through an Alan Smith goal. I thought I did all right but at half-time he switched me to the right wing and then with six minutes to go he pulled me off and put on Graeme Le Saux. That made things even worse. I was really hurt by that because I didn't think I played badly although I had missed a chance just before I was substituted. I went to see the manager the next day and told him that I didn't think I had to prove myself by playing in the B-team and if that was all there was for me, I didn't want it.

He has said subsequently that I told him I didn't want to play for England at all which was not the case. He wrote me a letter thanking me for my services and apparently acknowledging that my international career was over. Let's just say our wires got crossed somewhere along the line. It was the last thing on my mind to refuse to play for England. I was always proud to pull on the shirt and that has never changed to this day. He could not have expressed himself better in the letter. He referred to the fact that I had 49 caps which was one short of the figure that entitles you to an allowance of two tickets for every Wembley international and assured me the tickets would still be available for me. He also sent Sandra some flowers.

There will be some people I suppose who would reckon I was a bit of a prima donna for not wanting to play in the B-team. I certainly would not want to create that impression because I have never felt too big for my boots. The game is too important to me for that. I felt it was something of a slap in the face, after being involved for over six years, to be demoted like that, especially when I was convinced I still had a contribution to make. Graham later rang me up and asked me, 'If I picked you for my squad, would you come?' Of course I said it would be an honour. I have always thought that. He could have named me in every squad he chose and never given me a single game and I would have accepted that because I loved being involved. In the end it was just sad the way things worked out.

I had made a contribution in the run-up to the European Championships in Sweden and nobody could argue with Taylor's results in the qualifiers. England finished top of their group, winning three and drawing three of their six matches and I was as disappointed as any supporter when we failed to qualify for the semi-finals. There is no doubt that as manager he suffered through the loss of key players like Paul Gascoigne and later Alan Shearer through injury. He was also unfortunate in that established players like Peter Shilton and Terry Butcher had retired before he took over and Bryan Robson half retired. Then there was Gary Lineker's farewell and the manner of his going, which I don't think was handled very well. Gary had announced his intention to retire after the European Championships but England still had a chance of getting through to the later stages when they faced Sweden in the final group game. David Platt scored an early goal but the Swedes equalized and then Gary was pulled off after 64 minutes and replaced by Alan Smith. As we all know Tomas Brolin scored the winner for the host nation and one of the most notable post-war international careers had come to an ignoble end.

I won only four caps under Graham Taylor. Doubtless had he stayed on as England manager, I would still be one short of my half century. His downfall, especially when England were robbed of a place in the World Cup finals in America by Ronald Koeman in that unforgettable match in Holland, turned out to be my gain. I wanted us to qualify as much as the next man but if we had, the chances are he might still be in the job and I would have been out in the cold.

To be fair, he was subjected to the kind of scurrilous abuse in the papers that nobody should have to put up with, no matter how poor the results were. The pressures of the job were bad enough without all that. It was just his professional opinion I disagreed with. But I would never allow my personal feelings to cloud my support for the England team. I had a lot of friends in the squad and felt desperately sorry they didn't go to America. Certainly England's absence took the edge off the tournament as far as I was concerned.

I suppose it was inevitable that our World Cup failure would cost the England manager his job but to be honest the whole question of who would take over was of little more than passing interest. There were my bets with my Newcastle boss and Terry Mac but I thought it was nothing more than flannel on their part. I hadn't kicked a ball for the full England side for over two years during which time bright young prospects like Alan Shearer, Teddy Sheringham, Les Ferdinand, Stan Collymore, Chris Sutton and Andy Cole were fast emerging. I felt I could still compete but a return to the international scene seemed more fanciful than fact.

I did think the eventual appointment of Terry Venables as the new-style 'coach' would not damage my chances. His idea of football was to get it down and play which was certainly more my style than his predecessor. But I still wasn't holding my breath. The timing of his first squad for a friendly against Denmark at Wembley could hardly have been better. I was playing out of my skin for Newcastle, scoring goals and establishing a formidable striking partnership with Coley. I hadn't worked with Terry before and he obviously had made a few inquiries. I didn't know at the time but Terry had been quizzing Kevin and one or two others like Bryan Robson whom he had appointed to his back-room staff along with the likes of Don Howe. The gaffer revealed later that he had told Venables I was playing well but let him draw his own conclusions. It seemed there were a few people whose opinions led to Venables making his decision.

Anyway on the Monday morning before he announced his first squad, the boss called me over during training and told me I was in the squad and that I'd better have the hundred pounds ready to pay him and Terry. I was obviously delighted and, in spite of all speculation, pleasantly surprised. I still wasn't certain whether I would be playing but when we met up at Bisham Abbey, Venables told me straightaway that I would be in the team which was terrific. He even said, 'You'll be happy to get that 50th cap at long last.' Don Howe was great as well. We always got on well when he worked with Bobby Robson and it was like turning the clock back. He just said, 'Welcome back Peter, you've worked hard to get here.' The fact that he was involved made it a lot easier for me and I also welcomed the opportunity to work with Bryan Robson again.

There were a few new faces but Gazza was there and so was Platty, Paul Parker, Tony Adams, Gary Pallister and Graeme Le Saux and they were joined by players like Alan Shearer, Paul Ince and Darren Anderton. It promised to be a tough game because, although they missed out on the World Cup finals, Denmark were European champions. We managed to beat them 1–0 with a goal from David Platt. Of course, when I got back to Newcastle, the gaffer and his pal were standing there with their hands out. I greased their palms with the money they had won and was happy to do so; I would have forked out a bit more than a hundred pounds to get my England place back. Keegan couldn't resist a huge grin. 'When I make promises Pedro, I keep them,' he chortled.

It was a good way for Venables to start. His brief was to assemble a side good enough for the European Championships in 1996 and do better than we have the last couple of times we've reached the final stages. Obviously he didn't have the worry of qualifying because the tournament was held in England but it was still awkward because, while our rivals would have been sharpened up by battling their way through the groups, England had to develop a competitive edge through a programme of friendly matches. There is inevitable pressure on the coach to keep winning but, as he has said in the press, the main priority is for England to get it right on the night and if that means losing the odd friendly on the way, that is of secondary importance.

Not that anybody wants to lose and I think the results since Terry took over underline that. Our next games came in quick succession at the end of the season against Greece and then Norway. The England coach demonstrated he was not averse to calling up what many would regard as the golden oldies when he gave Arsenal's Steve Bould and Aston Villa's Kevin Richardson their first caps. With myself and Tony Adams involved as well as the younger lads, there was quite a mixture of ages in the team but it proved altogether too strong for the Greeks, who had after all qualified for the World Cup finals in America by finishing unbeaten winners of a group which included Russia and Hungary. We beat them 5–0 and I managed to get my name on the list of goalscorers along with Anderton, Shearer and two from Platt. We found it tougher against Norway. The match ended goalless but I was happy with my performance.

Venables was very understanding when I missed out on the first international of the season against Romania because of my broken cheekbone. He rang me at home to ask how I was and assured me that I would be back in the squad when I recovered, which was a lovely gesture. And he was as good as his word. But there was a triple celebration at Newcastle when he not only included me in the squad for a friendly against Nigeria but he chose my United team-mates Steve Howey and Rob Lee as well. I had played in the same England side with former Newcastle players such as Waddle and Gazza but it must have been a long time since three current United players started an England match. It was another indication of how the team had progressed under Kevin Keegan. Steve and my old pal Neil Ruddock played really well at the centre of defence but poor Rob had to go off early on after injuring his arm. I thought we played well without managing the comfortable victory we deserved.

Then it was back to Dublin to cross swords again with Jack Charlton and his Irish battlers. It turned out to be one of the most regrettable nights of a season during which the game's image has taken something of a battering. There was nothing in the build-up to indicate the disgraceful scenes which brought the game to an untimely end. The Dublin people, as usual, were very friendly. The squad had six days together before the game and our spirits and confidence were high. There didn't seem any sign of trouble until David Kelly put the Republic in front and then all hell let loose with hooligans raining anything they could lay their hands on down onto the people below them. It was really frightening and the referee had no alternative but to take us off the field. We thought and hoped the police would sort it out. As it happened we had played badly as a team; I was having a nightmare and the break gave Venables the opportunity to sort a few things out.

It was clear the troublemakers were out to stop the game which, unfortunately, is what they did. Alan Shearer popped his head out after about ten minutes to see what was happening and he came back straightaway and said it was chaotic and there was no chance of us getting back on. Everybody felt sick about what had happened. There was also frustration on our part because we wanted the opportunity to improve on what had been a poor opening spell. The only consolation was that the Football Association informed us later that we would be awarded our caps as usual but it still could not remove the memory of what had been a black night for football.

We finished the season with a poor performance against Uruguay, who held us to a goalless draw which seemed to be what they came for. The next day the papers had a bit of a go at players like myself and John Barnes, suggesting that we may be past our sell-by dates. It won't be the first time I have taken stick and lived to prove the critics wrong. I suppose we were easy targets on a night when everybody felt frustrated at not being able to break down the South Americans. Barnesy, who has demonstrated a lot of character in the past when supporters have had a go at him during Wembley games, suffered more than me which was terribly unfair. To me, he is still at the peak of his form. He has had a tremendous season with Liverpool and would always be in my England team, although Terry Venables obviously disagreed when he left him out of the squad for Euro '96. Barnesy has so much to offer, especially in bringing along the younger players like Jamie Redknapp, Nicky Barmby and Robbie Fowler.

The boss – even though his title was 'coach' he still merits the description – was brilliant after the game, thanking the players for their efforts and offering the same 'see you around' farewell without giving any hint about whether you would be back for the next game. In fact, Venables has been superb all down the line with me. He is always cheerful but with a serious edge when it comes to the business of winning matches but as a coach he is very innovative and full of enthusiasm. Always when we get together he has a special word here and there, praising my attitude in training and inquiring about the way we do things at Newcastle. I have enormous respect for the man. If he turned around tomorrow and said, 'Enough's enough, thanks very much', I would accept that and walk away happy. He has awarded me England caps I never thought I would get. There are some good younger players knocking at the England door and I had no problem when he picked one of them in preference to me for Euro '96. That's not to say I wouldn't loved to have been involved in the European Championships. But all good things come to an end sometime and Terry had to do what he feels is best for him.

I hope that doesn't sound as though I am trying to talk myself out of a few more caps. Far from it. I find it easier to play for England in many ways. The pace of international matches is a lot slower than the Premiership because of the way continental sides approach the game. The physical side doesn't worry me so I would be disappointed if I was not capable of performing for England for the next three years. I don't expect to but I could if given the opportunity. At the moment I feel I am covering as much ground as anybody and probably more than I used to. I feel so much better and sharper in everything I do. Every cap I am awarded is a bonus because I was resigned to stopping at 49 and I am making the most of my new lease of life.

I believe Graham Taylor was wrong to consign me prematurely to the international rubbish tip. And there were one or two others who could also have made his life as England manager a little easier had he given us the opportunity. It wasn't without significance that another of his rejects, Chris Waddle, played well enough for Sheffield Wednesday following his move from Marseilles to win the Footballer of the Year award in 1993 and he has been in top form in the two years since. They say football is all about opinions. In my humble one, Graham Taylor's were wrong.

I was really delighted and a little surprised to be included in the squad for the Umbro Trophy tournament at the end of the season. If I was honest, I would have to say I didn't think I would be picked and that's what I told people when they asked what I thought my chances were. But I appreciate that Terry Venables still believed I was worth my place.

13

A DOUBLE MISS

Last season was one that promised so much and, in the end, delivered a double disappointment. Missing out on the league title was a real sickener, but that setback was compounded when I was omitted from the England squad of 22 for the European Championships.

On assessing the two, there is absolutely no doubt about which affected me the most – the fact that, as skipper of Newcastle United, I did not experience the pleasure and honour of lifting the Championship trophy. As a Geordie myself it would have been special, and to suggest that forfeiting the title to Manchester United was a nightmare would be a masterpiece of understatement. But I have to say that, as one of the players responsible, the buck stopped with me and the rest of my team-mates. We only had ourselves to blame. In the position the team were in at the beginning of the year – twelve points clear with less than a third of the season left – we should have gone on and won the Premiership title. If you ask me why we didn't, then the answer has to be that too many of us lost our form around the same time. After Christmas, five or six of us just did not maintain our early season consistency, and that was too many for the rest of the team to carry.

Quite unfairly in my opinion, some supporters and sections of the media criticised the signing and contribution of Colombian international Faustino Asprilla who joined us in February from Italian club Parma. We had noticed what a good player he was from watching Italian football on Channel 4. In my opinion, since his arrival at St James' Park he has enhanced that reputation. 'Tino' is a quality player who will prove his worth to the club and our supporters in the future. I suppose it was just as well that he couldn't understand English when he arrived so the criticism, whether verbal or written, didn't register with him. A lot was made of the fact that our team pattern was altered and I was forced to play on the right side of midfield to accommodate him. That wasn't Tino's fault, it was just down to me because I didn't play well in that wide position. In fact, I never have.

I had a three-month spell from January to early April when I played poorly, but I wasn't the only one. The goals had dried up from our attack, while our midfielders were not getting up fast enough to support the front men. So there were a number of players who were not really giving Tino the help he deserved.

You can't hide the fact that we did lose too many matches in the latter third of the season, but that was no fault of Tino. There are things about his play that will live long in my memory – the way he set up Les for the first goal in that seven-goal thriller against Liverpool at Anfield in April for example, and the fabulous finish that gave us a 3–2 lead which we lost in the dying minutes. And another new player to the team could not be faulted. David Batty, who had come to us from Blackburn Rovers, was probably our most consistent player in those final weeks of the season.

As far as England is concerned I respected Terry Venables'

decision to drop me from the Euro '96 squad but obviously I wasn't overjoyed about it. We had finished training on the Saturday in Hong Kong on our two-match tour of the Far East when Terry came over and informed me of his intention to leave me out of the final squad of twenty-two players. 'I said I would have a word as soon as I made the decision,' he told me, and then went on to explain why he preferred Nicky Barmby, whom he considered had 'passed the test' in the 3–0 win over China. I understood that, the only problem I had was that I never got a test and said as much to him. Terry accepted my view and, to be fair, mentioned what I had said in the press conference later. Nicky did very well in that China game, scoring two goals after having been out of the England first team for a while, and I knew that because the next game against Hong Kong was not a recognised international, I would not get the opportunity to prove myself again and that my European Championship hopes had gone. I asked for a special meeting with the press because I didn't want to come back and face a lot of hassle with different reporters and television people chasing me for my views. I wanted it done there and then so I could come back and spend time with my family which is what is important to me now.

I am convinced that, whatever happened during the summer, it would have been the end of my England career anyway. There is no way I could have gone on and become involved in the 1998 World Cup campaign. No matter that the new England manager is Glenn Hoddle; the former Spurs midfield supremo and Chelsea manager would be looking to blood a new generation of younger players and wouldn't pick me.

I will always be grateful to Terry Venables for giving me a couple more years and ten more caps with England when it seemed I was destined for the international scrapheap. It was brave of him to do that. When I heard he was giving up the job as coach I regarded it as a major blow for our standing worldwide. I don't fully understand the reasons behind his decision but if it was, as has been suggested in some quarters, that he couldn't rely on the support of certain members of the international committee, then it's very disappointing in view of what he's done since being in charge of the England team. Terry has turned the whole place around from the turmoil it was in when he took over. I suppose not having to qualify for Euro '96 helped, but I believe if he stayed on as England manager for the World Cup, he would get us through to the later stages.

Having been involved with the England set-up for some time now and judging by the wealth of young talent there is available, I can safely predict that the national side has a great future. I am convinced that Glenn Hoddle could not be taking over at a better time.

As for the build-up to England's first Euro '96 match against Switzerland, Terry certainly did not deserve all the aggravation that spoiled it somewhat. I'm referring, of course, to the alleged incident on that Cathay Pacific flight back from Hong Kong prior to the European Championships. I don't want to talk about that now because enough has been said, and I haven't spoken about it to anyone since. Terry had a meeting with the squad on arriving back home and apparently decided that the players should take collective responsibility for the damage incurred on the flight. I was not present and had nothing to do with that, and neither did the other four players who were left out of the final twenty-two – Rob Lee, Ugo Ehiogu, Dennis Wise and Jason Wilcox.

But back to the beginning of the 1995/96 season. Things

could not have started better for Newcastle Football Club. Even before a ball was kicked there was a tidal wave of optimism sweeping Tyneside after the summer arrivals of Les Ferdinand from QPR, David Ginola from Paris St Germain, Warren Barton from Wimbledon and Shaka Hislop from First Division Reading. The players were just as excited as the supporters. When I looked around the dressing room and saw just how many top class players we had at the club now and compared it to the situation during my first spell at Newcastle, I could only marvel at the giant strides the club had made in the past three years. The gaffer, Kevin Keegan, had certainly pushed the boat out in a big way. I did have an inkling about Warren's signing because the business was being conducted while he had been with me in the England squad for the Umbro Cup the previous summer. Being a Londoner he was more than a little inquisitive of what life would be like for him in the North-East. That was understandable. Before any player makes such a move he wants to know as much as possible about what he is letting himself in for. I told him he would have no problems and the deal went through in between two England games. He signed on the Monday and later that evening my brother Ronnie actually drove the pair of us down from Tyneside to rejoin the England squad preparing for the game against Sweden at Elland Road, Leeds.

Two days later the boss got out the cheque book again and Les Ferdinand arrived. I was delighted the club had again demonstrated its ambition by attracting one of the most sought after players in the country. Les could have gone anywhere but the package that was offered, with the prospect of success as well as financial security, persuaded him to join Warren in the great Newcastle adventure. The fact that later in the season he was voted Player of the Year by his fellow professionals proved that he made a wise choice although, like the rest of us, he too would have been distraught that the award was all he had to show for his efforts during the season. I had no doubts that Les would join a long line of successful strikers at Newcastle. The supporters had been looking for someone to fill the void left when Andy Cole went to Manchester United and Les was the perfect solution.

One person who I know was extra happy about him coming was our defender Steve Howey who now had his most feared opponent as a team-mate! I knew Les from the odd occasion we had been in the England squad together but had seen enough of him wearing a Queens Park Rangers shirt to appreciate what he was capable of. There had been criticism of his appearance record, but he has certainly answered that, missing only one league game last season and desperately unlucky to do that. It has been a pleasure to play alongside him.

The same can certainly be said for David Ginola who has been an instant hit with the Geordie crowd. I remember him playing for Paris St Germain in the European Champions Cup and, from what could be picked up watching televised highlights of the match, he looked an outstanding player. But I don't think even I was prepared for the kind of individual flair I witnessed from David in a pre-season friendly against non-League outfit, Rushden and Diamonds. David was to face much bigger examinations of his skill but this was the perfect game for him to come in and demonstrate to the few hundred Newcastle supporters who had made the trip what he was capable of. David is a likeable character with a great sense of humour. He could not speak a lot of English when he first came, but now he can exchange Geordie expressions with the best of us. He has clearly enjoyed his first season with the club in spite of the odd problem with referees.

David is more than just a clever, highly skilful player, he is also an honest one who is prepared to take the knocks and retaliate by using his talent to outgun an opponent. He certainly did not deserve the kind of rough justice that was dispensed, for instance, by referee Gerald Ashby who handled our Coca-Cola Cup quarter-final at Arsenal in January 1995. I have always been an admirer of Gerald, but even he will admit that he didn't have the best of games that night. Just over a week before the tie, David had run Arsenal ragged in a league match at St James' Park, and the Gunners were obviously determined it wasn't going to happen again. Nothing wrong with that as long as they were fair about it, but they weren't, and Mr Ashby not only failed to give the Frenchman any protection but he actually sent him off after David reacted to yet another foul by full-back Lee Dixon, who had been fouling him all night. That followed his first yellow card for allegedly diving after a tackle by Nigel Winterburn that should have earned the Arsenal defender an early bath. The referee apologised later but the damage had been done by then and we lost David for three matches. I remember putting my hand on his shoulder as he walked off, but there wasn't much I could say to him to ease his anguish.

You could almost taste the excitement and anticipation when the Newcastle team ran out on to the field for the opening match of the 1995/96 season against Coventry City. St James' Park was packed to the rafters, creating the sort of atmosphere which I wouldn't hesitate to say cannot be matched on any other league ground in the country. The four new summer signings made their debuts; the crowd got their first real whiff of the exciting artistry of Ginola and the pace, strength and finishing power of Ferdinand, and we won comfortably 3–0. Rob Lee scored the opener and although

City made us wait I knocked in a penalty and Les crowned his debut with the third goal which was a great start for him. Anybody in the game will tell you it can be difficult to develop an instant rapport with so many newcomers in a team, but that was never a problem for us at Newcastle. The whole team seemed to gell from that very first game, instantly exhibiting the entertaining, positive and skilful football that was to become our trademark throughout the season.

If we were flying after Coventry we were in orbit by the end of August after winning our first four matches. We went to Burnden Park during the week and beat Bolton easily 3–1 with two more from Les, one scored after a great run from the halfway line, and another from Rob Lee. The following Sunday we faced Sheffield Wednesday at Hillsborough and, if anything, were even more comfortable winners that day. Ginola scored his first goal, a cracker from wide out on the left, and I got the other. Then we came up against our North-East neighbours Middlesbrough and beat them 1–0 with yet another courtesy of Ferdinand. It was all going so well and, to cap it all, Terry Venables included me in the squad for the first international of the new season against Colombia. I was ecstatic. But, like I said, a wise man always learns to expect the unexpected and my early season euphoria suddenly turned flat within the space of a couple of days.

I was training with the England squad at Bisham Abbey when I suddenly felt a twinge in my left knee as it gave way slightly. The physio had a quick look and we decided the best thing would be not to risk any more work. So, in order to give me a chance of playing at Southampton the following Saturday, I came straight back to Newcastle. The injury turned out to be a lot worse than we had first suspected. I had a test before the Southampton game and the knee was nowhere near being right, so I had to pull out of the game. It turned out to be a miserable day all round at The Dell. I had to watch from the bench in helpless frustration as we dropped our first points, losing 1–0 after playing well and having enough chances to win the match. It was a major setback for the team, but I had the added anxiety of wondering whether my early season injury jinx had struck again.

It didn't seem so when I managed to recover enough to play the following week against Manchester City. I hadn't done any training at all and certainly did not expect to figure against City when I turned up for treatment at our Durham training ground on the morning of the match. Afterwards I started lashing the ball about in the gym without any problems and I suddenly thought to myself, 'Hey, I could play here.' Kevin Keegan came up to me and asked me what I thought and I told him I felt all right. He just said, 'If you're fit enough, you're playing.' It was a big shock to the press lads but to be honest it was just as much a surprise to me. The boss even had to despatch somebody to Durham to pick up my boots only an hour or two before the kick-off. But we managed to rid ourselves of the Southampton hangover with another emphatic 3–1 victory. Les scored his sixth goal in as many games and I weighed in with the other, my third of the season.

The gaffer took the precaution of resting me for the following game, a Coca-Cola Cup first round first leg tie at Bristol City, which he used to give a match to the likes of Ruel Fox, Scott Sellars and Marc Hottiger, all fine players who were to leave the club that season. They wanted first team football but weren't getting it, so their frustration was understandable. It was some measure of the all round strength at the club, emphasised by the fact that throughout the season others such as Warren Barton, Faustino Asprilla, John

Beresford, Lee Clark and either Shaka Hislop or Pavel Srnicek were left out of the first team and Paul Kitson hardly had a look in, that the manager felt he could let three good players go. Foxy was the first to leave in October 1995. I wasn't so surprised at him going, especially considering the £4.2 million transfer fee. He wasn't in the team at the start of the season and only got selected at Southampton when I was injured. When he left for Spurs it was for twice the money the boss paid to Norwich City for him some twenty months before, so it had to be good business.

Back on the pitch, my knee began troubling me again. It was later diagnosed that my temporary respite had been because a piece of floating bone had moved around to the back of the knee and had become less affected by any movement. Anyway, I went for a scan on the Friday before we were due to play Chelsea and the decision was to undertake immediate exploratory surgery.

The club physio Derek Wright followed me home where I packed a bag, then took me to the hospital in Washington that evening and watched while the specialist Rob Gregory performed the operation. I was back out the next morning before anybody had realised what had happened. I even went to the match the following day and had the pleasure of seeing Les score the two goals that won us the game against Chelsea. He was on the mark again when we trounced Everton at Goodison Park the following weekend and scored another in the return Coca-Cola win over Bristol City. It was a bit of a shock to everyone when, after being picked for the England squad for a game in Norway along with Rob Lee, John Beresford and Steve Howey, Les wasn't even on the substitutes' bench in Oslo. There was speculation that the writing might have been on the wall for him internationally, but he has come back since and proved that wrong by being chosen for the Euro '96 squad.

Unfortunately, my injury kept me out of the Norwegian trip. But Rob Gregory had promised when he did the operation that I would be fit again within three weeks. It was an astonishing recovery, but now my problem was a familiar one about whether I could get back into a side which had never stopped winning. Fortunately, the boss found a place for me against Queens Park Rangers at Loftus Road and we won 3–2 with two goals from Keith Gillespie and, inevitably, another from our free-scoring No.9. We were lording it at the top of the league and, although we were doing well as a team unit, Les was the focal point of our attacks and he couldn't have done his job any better. The next team to be shot down in flames was Wimbledon, this time destroyed by a Ferdinand hat-trick. It was still early days but it was difficult to contain the enthusiasm and optimism of everybody who had anything to do with the club. The cynics were quick to point out that we had yet to confront any of our so-called title rivals – that the November period, during which we were due to face Liverpool, Blackburn Rovers, Aston Villa and Leeds United would establish whether our title challenge was real or just a sham.

Well, November came and went and we were still on course with a one hundred per cent home record, although I would be the first to admit they were some of the first really hard games we had that season. Liverpool would have been disappointed that they didn't get anything out of their visit to St James', although we started well and scored an early goal through that man Ferdinand again. Ian Rush equalised and we were under a lot of pressure after that but goals win matches and we snatched it near the end when substitute Steve Watson scored after David James could only parry a shot from

Rob Lee. We went on from there to beat Blackburn 1–0 and draw 1–1 at Villa, where I gave what I thought was my worst performance since I returned to Newcastle. I was absolutely shocking that day. It was just one of those games when nothing went right and the more I tried, the worse I got. Fortunately, the rest of the lads improved after a poor first half and we fully deserved a point.

I managed to be chosen as one of the substitutes for the England game against Switzerland in November without managing to get on. Marc Hottiger and I kept a long standing promise to each other when we swapped shirts; he had come to me as soon as the fixture was arranged and told me that was what he wanted. My fortunes changed against Portugal in December when I got on as a substitute for Les Ferdinand. It was only for 15 minutes but I enjoyed being involved in what was a fast, exciting game which ended 1–1 with Forest's Steve Stone scoring our goal. I have to say that the Portuguese impressed me a lot. They were very attack-minded and were probably the most positive team to play us while I was involved under Terry.

On the club front we scrambled a 2–1 home victory over Leeds United after going one down, and that enabled us to stretch our lead even further at the top of the Premiership. I thought it was a significant result because this was the type of game we used to lose. I remember particularly a tremendous individual performance from Rob Lee who fully deserved to be singled out afterwards by Kevin Keegan. The manager said he felt that on current form Rob was the best player in the country in any position. High praise indeed, but nobody in our dressing room would have disagreed with that. Rob's drive and energy in the midfield engine room was one of the main reasons behind our success in the first half of the season.

We were in an even better situation than the year before when we let a good advantage slip. I honestly felt that this time we were better equipped as a team to hold on to it. All we had to do was keeping winning games, especially because our main rivals seemed to be beating each other at the time.

I was on a real high on the field – while off it things couldn't have gone any better either, especially when, at the beginning December, I was given an early Christmas present by no less a person than Her Majesty The Queen. I had been awarded an MBE in the Birthday Honours and now it was time to attend Buckingham Palace for the investiture. We had drawn 3–3 at Wimbledon on the Sunday and I flew back that evening before driving back down to London the following day with Sandra and the two children and staying that evening in a hotel close enough to the Palace to walk there on the Tuesday. In fact, security demanded we did get in a taxi at the gates before being driven the short distance to the entrance. It was a great thrill to actually meet the Queen herself, although my daughter Stacey could not share the pleasure because she slept through the whole thing! But the Queen was very knowledgeable, even to the point of remembering I had cancelled two previous appointments at the Palace because of match commitments. She mentioned she was pleased I had managed to get a day off at last and also congratulated me on the way the team was playing at the time. She had certainly done her homework. That wasn't the only surprise because when I came out I recognised one of the policemen who was on duty outside the Palace as one of the lads who used to go to school with me back in Newcastle. It was a wonderful occasion, the memory of which I shall treasure for ever.

But, as ever, the celebrations were followed by a hangover. Defeat number two came at Chelsea the following Saturday when we got what we deserved for a poor performance, our worst of the season up to that point. What upset me even more was the behaviour of Chelsea's Mark Hughes during the game. He committed a serious tackle on Rob Lee and later had a whack at Darren Peacock and never heard so much as a whisper from the referee. In my opinion, he got away with it. I have rarely had a go at a player after a match, but I felt I had to say something on that occasion as Rob was very lucky not to be seriously injured. Okay, so Hughes has been the same sort of player all his career. You hear him complaining about his treatment from referees but when you get somewhere in the region of forty to fifty disciplinary points a season, the officials can't all be wrong and this time he didn't even get a yellow card when he was lucky to stay on the field. We all recognise there has to be a physical side to the game, but there is a difference between being hard and committing dangerous fouls. 'Sparky' has been a great, highly competitive player whom I have known since our days at Manchester United together, and I've always got on well with him. But on that day against Chelsea, I felt he overstepped the mark and I told him so.

After that game, we maintained our home form with victories against Everton and Nottingham Forest but that was the prelude to our rock-bottom performance against Manchester United at Old Trafford. I suppose, on reflection, it would be fair to say that it was the two defeats against United that cost us the title but there was no doubt that in that first game two days after Christmas, they must have thought they were getting a sackful of late presents. It was a big game for us and we had looked forward to it for so long but we just didn't perform on the night, it was as simple as that. They played well but had the confidence of an early goal from Andy

Cole. It was a bit ironic because 'Coley' has picked up an army of critics since he left us for Manchester. It was said that he'd lost his scoring touch, but the way he buried that shot into the back of the net after four minutes was straight out of the repertoire of goals he used to stick in regularly when he was at Newcastle. I know it sounds strange but in a perverse way I was pleased for Andy. He needed a break – I just wish it had been against another team! Having seen the contrast in his fortunes since he moved, I can offer no other reason other than he has had a marathon run of bad luck. He's had the same opportunities that he would gobble up without thinking at Newcastle, but while playing for United the ball has not gone in for him. It would not surprise me if Andy's magic touch returned next season and he won the Golden Boot award. Anyway, his goal that night was something to remember and it set his team up, whereas we just did not compete. It was no great surprise when Roy Keane struck the second. United were head and shoulders above us and fully deserved to win.

It was a setback for Newcastle, but we bounced back immediately. When I latched on to a Darren Peacock flick on to score my one hundredth league goal for the club against Bolton on 20 January to give us a 2–1 lead, that win took us twelve points clear at the top and we looked on course for a belated championship title. It was a special occasion for me because I joined an exclusive list of players to have hit the century mark on Tyneside.

When we reflect on the nuts and bolts of that season, it must be said that we let ourselves down badly away from home. We took only one point from a possible fifteen between February and March, and being beaten at home for the first and only time in the season by the eventual champions only made things worse. The old saying 'goals win matches' couldn't have been more true in that match against Manchester United. We felt it was only a matter of time before we would score because, for the first 45 minutes, we murdered them in every other facet of the game. But we didn't keep it going and Eric Cantona ghosted in at the far post to score the only goal of the match in the second half. You have to wonder where United would have been without the Frenchman. He was absolutely magnificent, especially in the second half of the season when he scored some crucial goals, and he certainly deserved his award as Footballer of the Year.

We experienced similar misfortune in the other two key games during the latter stages of that season, at Liverpool and Blackburn Rovers, when we played well enough to win but lost both in the last few minutes. People have hailed the Anfield match in April as the game of the season and rushed out afterwards to buy videos of it. It was an exciting game to play in but when you have lost 4–3 at the death you feel sick and devastated and you don't need any reminders of it.

In between those games I scored both goals when we bounced back to beat Queens Park Rangers 2–1. There had been a tactical switch during the game when I moved inside from out wide on the right and Rob Lee was substituted. The media wanted to interview me after the match about whether I had been forced into that wide role, but I declined to make any comment. I had no wish to put any further pressure on Kevin Keegan, whose decision that day should have been applauded because it helped to win us the game.

Like I said, the season was destined to end in crushing disappointment and the writing was on the wall even before the showdown on the last Sunday of the season when we faced Tottenham and Manchester United went to Middlesbrough. I didn't fancy United to lose no matter what we did, and sure enough they won that match and with it the Championship. United have had a fantastic run under Alex Ferguson and you can't take anything away from them. They will be a threat to any title challengers in the seasons to come with their fabulous squad of young players. But that 1995/96 season is now history, and Newcastle Football Club have the future to think about. We have established ourselves as one of the top teams in the country and hopefully next season we will be even better prepared for success. I would imagine there will be few dressing room changes, so we all know what to expect.

Personally, I intend to keep playing for Newcastle as long as Kevin Keegan wants me. Once he tells me to step aside that will be it – he is straight enough to do that and I would be honest enough to accept his decision. But I don't think there is a problem at the moment and, barring injury, I can't see the end coming for at least two years. That's at least how long I feel I can keep going at the highest level and if possible I would like to continue beyond that. I have no idea what's around the corner, or even whether Newcastle will be my last club. Much would depend on whether I get the opportunity to go on the staff or else just decide to call it a day. It is more than likely that Tyneside will be my last port of call. But if, for instance, the boss told me next season that I'm not good enough to carry on without offering me the chance to change the direction of my career, I would consider looking to play on elsewhere.

All things being equal, my hope is to stay with Newcastle in the Premier League as long as possible. There are things we can do together, not the least of which is winning that elusive Championship title. After all, there is still room in my trophy cabinet for a few more medals...

WHAT THE
MANAGERS SAY ...

Peter Beardsley has played under some of the top managers in the game at club and international level. Here they tell us how they rate him, from Bob Moncur, the first one to sign him as a professional, to Terry Venables, the former England boss who explains his influence on the younger members of the England squad.

BOB MONCUR gave Peter his first professional contract when he signed him for Carlisle United as an eighteen-year-old youth.

I had been constantly been badgered by Brian Watson, who worked for me as a part-time scout, to take this kid who played for Wallsend Boys' Club. We had him across for a few training sessions and he certainly impressed me. I had heard he had been to a couple of other clubs who were not prepared to take him on because at his age he would have had to go on a full-time professional wage which, if I remember rightly, was a minimum of £45 a week. I was over my budget myself but I went to the chairman and asked him, because I felt the lad was something special, could I go over my quota and sign him? It was still touch and go whether I got the go-ahead but then he had such an outstanding game in a friendly against a local side in Newcastle that I knew I had to sign him and fortunately the chairman agreed to back me. I played in the game myself and the fact he could get on the end of some of my passes really convinced me about his ability.

I remember in some of the five-a-side games we had at the time, he used to be absolutely brilliant. One day he took the mickey so much out of a goalkeeper we had called Tony Harrison that Tony lost his temper. Peter feinted to shoot and the lad dived first of all one way; then he picked himself up and Peter sent him the other way. He was leaping about all over the place before Peter just knocked the ball past him. The rest of the lads were in stitches but Tony was clearly not amused. It was one incident that stuck out in my mind and showed just what skill he had as a kid. I was loath to stick him in the first team so early but his performances in the reserves demanded it and I had to give him his opportunity. In fact my wife Camille, who had always taken a keen interest in Peter and watched him a lot, was the one who urged me to give him a go. I thought, 'What have I got to lose?' and stuck him in against Blackburn Rovers.

I used to love watching him play and some of the goals he scored used to have the hair on the back of my neck standing on end. I remember one in particular when he dummied the keeper and squeezed the ball in from a tight, narrow angle. From where I sat I didn't know whether it was in or not but he turned to me as soon as he hit it with his arm in the air and a broad smile on his face. He didn't even see the ball hit the back of the net. He knew it was a goal before it crossed the line. What he has done in the game since those days has not surprised me at all. You could see he had so much time and pace and class. With all due respect to the Carlisle side which wasn't bad, he was on a different level. He just had that extra talent that marks some players out as something apart from the rest.

I had gone to Hearts when I had a phone call from him to tell me he had the chance to play for Vancouver. I told him I thought it would be the wrong move and that he would be taking a backward step because I always thought if he waited for a year or eighteen months the big boys would be in to sign him. But he was impatient. He was about to be married and the money was good. I thought going to Canada would cost him a couple of years. In the end playing for Johnny Giles probably did him no harm but had he not gone, I have no doubts he would have wound up at a top club sooner than he did. I have watched his career closely since. I remember Arthur Cox, who was at Newcastle, phoning to ask about him. I just said, 'Do yourself a favour; go and sign him. He will be the answer to your prayers.'

Later, when I ran a squash club on Tyneside, Peter used to come across regularly and I helped to negotiate a lucrative boot deal for him. He asked me to get involved with him more but I could see then he was destined for bigger things and I didn't want Newcastle supporters to think I played a part in him leaving the club. Peter was always going to be a star and I will always be proud of the part I played in getting him started in the game. I saw him recently at Newcastle and he is still doing the things he did for me as a kid. He must be one of the hardest men in the game to tackle. He is a difficult man to kick – even at my best he was too quick for me. He has looked after himself and is reaping the benefit of that now. Basically he is still a kid at heart.

JOHNNY GILES was manager of Vancouver Whitecaps when he stunned the football world by splashing out £275,000 for Peter Beardsley. He recalls the game that convinced him he was worth the money.

I had taken over as coach at the Whitecaps around Christmas time and I was going over to Canada until the following March when the season started over there. In the meantime I appointed Peter Lorimer as player-coach and asked him to have a scout round to see if there were any decent players. One lad he had been tipped off about was playing in a match against Carlisle but when he went to the game it was Peter Beardsley who caught his eye. He saw him again and gave me very good reports on him. Later the Vancouver team came over to Bisham Abbey for pre-season training and as it happened, that Saturday we were there Carlisle were playing Brentford which was only just down the road. I thought it was too good an opportunity to miss to go and see Peter for myself.

I was certainly impressed enough to suggest to Tony Waiters, the club's general manager, to have a go for him. He asked how much he should bid and I replied, 'Whatever it takes.' We struck the deal and I thought it was a fair bit of money for an American club, especially when no British team appeared to be making a move for him. I liked him because of his attitude. Being honest, he didn't play out of his skin when I first saw him but he was very enthusiastic and you could see he definitely had something. I think his three years in Canada were good for him. He developed as a player. At first he tried difficult things, nine out of ten of which maybe did not come off. I tried to teach him to be a little more simple and he became a better player for it.

I have not been surprised about what he has achieved because he was always capable of doing fantastic things. He always had a great touch; a lightning turn of pace and his attitude and professionalism have always been first-rate. I used to tell him to be patient and use the time he had away from the English football scene to encourage his skills. I have seen a fair bit of him since and enjoyed watching him play. He is a lad with a rare talent and I will remember my association with him with a lot of pleasure.

RON ATKINSON was manager of Manchester United when he signed Beardsley on a six months probationary period with an option to buy him from Vancouver at the end of it. But he decided not to take it up. Atkinson remembers at the time he had an embarrassment of riches at Old Trafford and for that reason, Beardsley was a player he let slip through his fingers.

It would have cost Manchester United £500,000 to sign Peter from Vancouver and although I thought he was a very talented player, I felt at the time we had others at the club – lads like Mark Hughes were coming through – who could do just as good a job. Peter was unfortunate because he was the right player at the wrong time. That was a very good Manchester United side and it was difficult for anybody to break into it. I had seen him play well for Vancouver and thought he was worth a chance back in England, but in the end things didn't work out for him and I decided to let him go back. That doesn't mean I have been surprised by what he has done since. He is the type of lad who is always capable of returning to haunt you, but I have to say that what I did was what I thought was best for Manchester United. In the end, it didn't stop Peter becoming a success in the game, and I am very glad about that.

ARTHUR COX, the man Peter regards as the biggest influence on his life, stepped in to sign him from Vancouver and bring him back for his first spell at his hometown club Newcastle. But that was almost three years too late. Cox wanted him first before he decided to continue his career on the other side of the Atlantic.

I tried to sign him from Carlisle for Newcastle but we didn't have enough money because Johnny Giles and Tony Waiters topped anything we could afford. I first saw him when I was manager at Chesterfield. He played two or three times against us for Carlisle and I remember once we went up there and won 6–2, but he caught my eye because he was their one true class player. His performances stuck in my mind. When I first joined Newcastle as manager, the priority was to stop the team going down so, in that environment, it might not have been the right time to bring him in. Nevertheless I tried without success but all we could offer was half the fee that took him to Vancouver. All the while he was in Canada, Peter Kirkley and Brian Watson, his pals from his junior days, kept in touch with him and when Kevin Keegan came and lit the place up I felt he was just the player to come and do a job. It was a bonus when Manchester United failed to pick him up. Still, I would have had him sooner or later. As it worked out I sold Imre Varadi, who had done extremely well for us for £115,000, and I got Peter for £125,000, so all in all it cost us £5,000. And we had a year to pay it as well ... £60,000 deposit and the rest in twelve months. We got promotion before the second instalment was paid. When he told me how much he wanted, it took all of my control not to grab him by the hand and say, 'That's a bargain'. Instead, I had to say that it was a large sum, which persuaded Vancouver to let us pay the money over a year.

I remember when I first spoke to him, he was in a kiosk at the airport and we arranged to meet the following afternoon. 'Peter, by the way,' I said, 'we have not discussed a contract.' All he replied was, 'You'll look after me, boss.' I had never met him face to face or talked to him before that so there was an immediate bond between the two of us. He was so appreciative of everything but he was never as appreciative of me as I was of him as a player and a person. I remember after I put him on as substitute against Blackburn I had both Kevin and Terry coming to me and saying, 'Where did you get him from, he's absolutely brilliant.' He had their respect from day one. I was the first to recommend him to Bobby Robson, long before he eventually selected him. Kevin carried the team in the promotion season but Peter was not far behind. I used to put my arm around him and point to the empty terraces and say, 'Make sure they have something to talk about when they get to work on Monday.'

I sat back and watched him and Chris Waddle mature as players. Even today when he picks the ball up, I still arch forward on the seat because I know he is liable to do something special. There aren't many in the game like that.

Today, he is still the hardest-working player in the Newcastle team … and he's 35 years of age! I encouraged him to play to win as well as to entertain. After I had been gone from Newcastle a couple of years I took a call from Kenny Dalglish. It was typically short. He said, 'Arthur, what about Peter Beardsley?' My answer was short. 'Sign him. Pay whatever they are asking.' And that was it.

Halfway through his second season at Everton when I was in charge at Derby, I rang Howard Kendall and asked him if Peter was available. He said no but asked me to come back at the end of the season. I waited and just before Everton left on a tour of Mauritius, Howard, as good as his word, came back to me and said, 'Your timing is perfect; you've read the script, what's the score?' I asked him how much he wanted and he replied, 'In excess of a million pounds.' I told him, 'I'll give you a million and fifty.' He told me it wasn't enough so I said, 'All right, I'll give you a million and a quarter.' He said he would come back to me. Later he rang and said, 'That's done,' but added that he had an obligation to inform Newcastle of the situation. I knew that would make life difficult for me. I spoke to Peter and agreed a contract, but deep down I resigned myself to losing him to Newcastle. Fortunately, as things worked out, we're working together again. He still has a few years in front of him, and will play as long as he wants to. He is one of the nicest superstars that football has ever produced.

WILLIE McFAUL succeeded Jack Charlton as manager at Newcastle, taking over in a caretaker capacity with hopes of landing the job on a more permanent basis. He believes Peter Beardsley helped him to succeed in his aim but also suggests

ironically the eventual sale of the player to Liverpool was one of the factors which led to his downfall.

I have no doubts that Peter's contribution helped to get me appointed. When you have a change of manager, the spotlight is always on how the players react to the new boy. Thanks to Peter and the rest of the lads, we got off to a fabulous start and after ten weeks on probation I was given the job. I made one or two changes and tried to go back to the kind of football that had won us promotion under Arthur Cox. I appreciated Peter's ability and the fact that he was prepared to sign a new contract for me. It was a demonstration of his confidence in my ability as a manager and it also weighed heavily in the minds of the club directors when they made their decision. I spent a long time trying to get him to put pen to paper and he agreed on a new two and a half year deal. It was a feather in my cap at the time.

Some managers are wary of having star players around because they may feel they take too much credit. But Newcastle supporters need somebody to hang their hat on and Peter was always a great crowd-pleaser. The sad thing was that Newcastle couldn't keep him. When he signed his deal he hoped I would be able to bring in quality players to line up alongside him. That didn't happen. I tried to but my hands were tied. He had a great enthusiasm and keenness for the game, and his attitude to training and the way he looked after himself were always going to stand him in great stead. He took his knocks but he was always a great healer. I have always felt he had the capacity to keep playing until he was well into his thirties, and what he has done since and is doing now does not surprise me at all. I regretted having to let him go but a player of his stature deserves to be part of a side that wins things. I only wish we could have given him that vehicle of success when he was at Newcastle the first time.

KENNY DALGLISH paid a record £1.9 million to take Beardsley from Newcastle to Liverpool and insists he got his money's worth.

Peter was worth every penny. He did a magnificent job in the four years he was at Liverpool. He claims he had a bad time when he first went there but he never once let the club down. Sometimes it takes players longer to adjust than others. Peter became a very important member of an excellent team. He moved to Anfield to be successful and that's what happened. He was without question a terrific asset to the club. He is a wonderful professional with an outstanding attitude to the game, and he has proved since he moved to Newcastle that he is playing as well as ever. It was a pleasure to be associated with him.

HOWARD KENDALL was in charge at Everton when he paid their Merseyside neighbours Liverpool £1 million to take Peter Beardsley to Goodison Park. He thought it was money down the drain because of the player's age but remarkably he ended up making a profit.

I knew he had been in and out of the side, first with Kenny Dalglish and then Graeme Souness, and I just thought it was an opportunity to get a player who would give us a lift. He was an extremely gifted individual and I knew the crowd would take to him. They have done that wherever he has been. I knew he would create a buzz. The fact he was tremendously fit, a great trainer and always wanted to play was another factor. I also knew he would be great for the kids at the club. When I asked the chairman for the money to buy him, I told him it would cost us £1 million and we would probably have to write the money off because he would have no resale value. In the end we made a handsome profit, and there aren't many players in their thirties you could say that about. He was a smashing player for the club and I only sold him because we had a disappointing season and I wanted to try and do something different. I wanted to sell him to Derby because they were not in the Premier League ... and so there was less chance of him coming back to put one over us! He has done even better than I thought he would, and he could be playing top-level football for some time to come.

BOBBY ROBSON *was the England manager who gave Beardsley his first international cap and picked him for every one of his squads after that, except when he was injured. His favourite description of Beardsley was: 'He was my little gem.' Robson explains why:*

A gem is a priceless commodity and as far as I was concerned, Peter was priceless. He was so accomplished as a player. If you are small and you want to be a success in world football, you have to be very clever. He was little and he was very clever. He had twinkle-feet. They moved like lightning when he was on the ball. He could shuffle the ball from one foot to another. He could feint and double feint and go past people in a way that would make you think, 'How on earth did he do that?' He was also a prodigious worker. He was the first to run and the last. If ever you wanted him to work back for you from a forward position, he would do that without complaining. He was a tremendously fit player with an enormous burst of speed over short distances. He had an eye for a great pass and made it without any problems. And he scored goals – but unlike Gary Lineker, who was deadly in the six yard box, Peter got his from outside the penalty area.

I went to the World Cup in 1986 with him and left out Trevor Francis. I had to make some difficult choices – Trevor had been in the England team for a long, long time and I took Peter instead of him. That might have been a risk but it demonstrated the confidence I had in the lad. Trevor had a bit of a go in the papers a couple of days later but, maybe now as a manager, he sees things differently. I suppose now he would chop his players' heads off if they went bleating to the press about anything but he did the very same thing. Peter established himself as a vital member of my England team. His workrate was phenomenal, he knitted things together and he could operate from midfield into the attack. When things broke down, he would be the first back into midfield to help pressurize the opposition to win the ball back again. He and Lineker worked superbly together. They were a great foil for each other. When you think that England's two recognized strikers were hardly the biggest players in the world, it just shows what talent they had. All our goals had to be football goals, created on the ground.

I remember the game against Poland in Mexico. I had to have a drastic rethink about the team. I had to give it a lot of thought. It was our last chance and I came up with the right formula on the right day and Peter was part of it. He played a major part in keeping England in the World Cup. And it was the same in Italy four years later. When I brought him on for the second half against Cameroon, it was because I was looking for a little reliability and I felt he was the player to provide it. Then he had a marvellous match against Germany in the semi-final as part of a performance that was probably the best by any England side since the World Cup Final in '66. He had missed the latter part of his season with Liverpool and I felt he was fresh and coming into his game.

We won the Fair Play award to which Peter made a great contribution, and in the end I felt he and the rest of the team could feel proud of their efforts. We showed the rest of the world that you can be successful at the very highest level without being cynical. He was one of the players who made it a pleasure for me to be the manager of England. He was first out of the coach, picking up the heaviest bag or the bucket of water. He had no airs and the only graces he demonstrated were on the football pitch.

GRAHAM TAYLOR, who took over from Robson, gave Beardsley only four caps and, to all intents and purposes, ended his international career. But Taylor insists that his decision to leave the player out of his international squad was taken in good faith because he had been given to understand Peter had retired from international football. Later, this proved to be a misunderstanding.

The first thing I remember about Peter Beardsley on the international scene was how enthusiastic and helpful he was in every situation. Many people have said this before – Peter would never walk past the skip without offering to give a hand with the kit. Here he was, an internationally acclaimed player but never too proud to muck in with the mundane jobs. There are not many who would do that. That was off the field – on it I think he is a marvellous, highly talented individual with a superb touch and deceptive swerve that enabled him to leave opponents standing. As a club manager I had seen many players who could score goals for fun but were never going to be the answer at international level. I remember after Italia '90, I wanted to satisfy myself relatively early about whether Steve Bull could do a job for England and for that reason I put Peter on the substitute's bench for the first couple of games.

I think when I look back in my working with him, because he was such a pleasant lad to work with and not liable to explosive reaction, I maybe took him for granted. I don't talk about regrets but look for reasons how things could have gone differently and I am sure I would have handled his situation in another way as his club manager. I took on board an established international player and, if I made a mistake, it was in not recognizing the fact that, in spite of his experience, he was someone who needed to be talked to. He needed his confidence feeding. If that had happened, perhaps he would have been in the squad a lot longer.

As far as the matches against the CIS were concerned, I was faced with a horrific scenario whereby Manchester United and Leeds were going for the title; Liverpool were still in the FA Cup and Sheffield Wednesday and Arsenal had important games coming up. I therefore announced a squad which not only encompassed both the full and B-international matches but also had to include a list of provisional players. I remember getting a lot of criticism for doing so but it meant that I had to name something like fifty players to cover all eventualities. As it happened, twelve of them withdrew and it was a situation where, right up to leaving for Moscow, I didn't know who was going to be on the plane. I wish everybody had been like Peter. He was in the squad and was not a problem.

When we got out there, I put him in the B-side but, having done so, maybe I should have given him assurances about being in the squad for the European Championships in Sweden. The truth is I hadn't done that for anybody and I just left it. He was not at his best in the B-game and came to see me the next morning which was the day of the senior game and led me to understand he wanted to retire from international football. If it had been a club situation, I might have told him to go away and think about it but, after all that had happened, what he did knocked me out of my stride. After all, it was only hours before an England international.

When we got back I dropped him a note saying how sorry I was I couldn't get him his 50th cap. In hindsight I can understand how it all happened but, under different circumstances, maybe it wouldn't have. As it was I didn't get any reaction to my note. I wish Peter had said then it was all a misunderstanding, because he would certainly have been part of my plans for Sweden which by that time I was well and focused on. Later, I was openly criticized for not selecting him but I was not in a position to say why because Peter had asked me to say nothing to the press of what had happened – and I kept my word despite the criticism. After the Championships, my assistant Lawrie McMenemy defended my non-selection of Peter in a TV programme and gave the reasons for the decision.

On Thursday 10 September 1992, I telephoned Peter as a result of things I had been reading in the press. He explained that he was only referring to the B-team and had not meant that he wanted to retire completely from international football. He confirmed he would be available for future selection. Again we agreed to keep the conversation between ourselves and that he would keep on playing and I would take it from there. By that time Sweden was behind us and I was then looking ahead to the 1994 World Cup. I just felt Peter's performances with Everton, when I was looking to build a new England team with the likes of Alan Shearer, Ian Wright, David Platt, Paul Ince and Paul Gascoigne, did not justify his selection. Later, after he moved to Newcastle, he broke his cheekbone which ruled him out of an early international against Poland.

There is absolutely no question in my mind that, playing the way he has in the last two seasons, he was worthy of a place in the international squad and I would certainly have chosen him had I still been in charge. It would have been my pleasure to award him his 50th cap. Looking back, I regret the misunderstanding as much as he does. In a club situation, I'm sure it would not have happened.

KEVIN KEEGAN played alongside Peter Beardsley when both enjoyed a successful first spell at St James' Park. When Keegan returned to repeat as manager the promotion feat he helped to achieve as a player, he wanted a footballer with skill, presence and reliability to help him establish Newcastle in the top sphere of the game. And he had no doubts who it would be.

Peter was nearer his 32nd birthday than his 31st when I gave Everton £1.35 million to bring him back to Newcastle. And when you add together his talent and his example I think he has been the buy of the century. There is not another player on earth of that age for whom I would have paid that sort of money. The chairman Sir John Hall and all the other directors did not want me to sign him which was partly my fault because my policy was to buy players who I thought would always have a resaleable value. 'Pedro' certainly did not come into that category and I knew I was writing that money off. But sometimes you buy a car because you want to feel safe driving it; you might purchase an antique as an investment but a computer could be out of date in a couple of years. With Pedro we were investing in his ability to influence the youngsters and older players at the club at the same time as his ability and longevity. He can show players how to train much better than I can tell them.

And he hasn't changed either in his outlook or dedication in over a decade. I remember when he came as a player in his first spell at Newcastle, the manager Arthur Cox had mentioned Peter to me but, to be honest, although I respected Arthur's judgement, I wasn't over-excited by the lad's pedigree ... a spell at Carlisle; exile in Vancouver; rejected by Manchester United. And he was coming to Newcastle to help us win promotion. It seemed highly unlikely – but it didn't take me long to realize that Arthur had unearthed a diamond. I remember it as if it were yesterday. After about twenty minutes of our first training session together I went over to Arthur and asked, 'Where on earth did you find him?' I only had to watch Peter for five minutes. His exuberance and skill, the things he did with the ball, stood out a mile. It was a tremendous mixture. Nearly every day as a manager I see young lads and even older players who have one thing or the other, but rarely both. When you do, it is something special.

I enjoyed that promotion season at Newcastle. I had played in better sides, nobody would argue with that, but we always felt we had to score three goals to win a game. If myself, Peter and Chrissy Waddle could each knock one in, I was happy about our chances of getting something out of a game. We were good going forward but not too clever at the back. Fortunately, just like Arthur had predicted he would, Peter came in and gave us that extra momentum. You don't forget players like that. I brought him back to Newcastle because I knew what I was getting. A lot of the time when you sign players, you are shooting in the dark. You try and find out about them by asking other people's opinion. But I didn't have to do that with Peter.

I had spoken to Howard Kendall at Everton on numerous occasions and asked to be contacted if he ever thought of selling him. He kept his promise to do that. I didn't know that Arthur Cox at Derby was also in the race, but it was only because I happened to be at Newcastle and not another club that Peter chose to return. His link-up with Andy Cole was superb. I knew Andy was special but I knew Pedro had an extraordinary talent and when you put those two things together you are bound to get something remarkable. One of the biggest problems I had with him at first was trying to persuade him that life was not just about making goals for Andy. I knew there were occasions when he could have helped himself, but he was unselfish and derived as much pleasure out of Andy getting all the credit. When he finally got the message he really started scoring some spectacular goals.

He has been unlucky enough to pick up an injury at the start of both seasons he has been back, but his love for the game has seen him return to action sooner than many others who have had similar problems. He even asked to play in the reserves at the end of the season because he wanted to keep himself in shape for England. I had to tell him I would not risk him. He will play for Newcastle as long as he wants to. Don't forget, Peter Beardsley has not started to move back yet. He is still operating in the front line and hasn't started to think about occupying a less involved role in the team. That has to come and maybe it will be my job to tell him, 'Maybe you will be able to make a better contribution dropping further back.' That need not be for another two or three years yet if he wants it – and I think he will. I got off the playing bus when I saw a nice stop coming up. Peter is not even looking out of the bus window yet.

TERRY VENABLES took over as England coach in succession to Graham Taylor and reintroduced Beardsley as part of his first squad, awarding him the 50th cap he thought had passed him by. He subsequently left Peter out of the England squad for Euro '96 in preference to Nick Barmby.

Peter made it easy for me to select him for my first squad because of the way he started at Newcastle. I wanted him around for two reasons. Firstly, because he was a very good player and, secondly, because of the influence he had on the younger lads coming into the squad. I wanted them to look at Peter and how he conducted and applied himself and realize that was what you had to do to give yourself a chance. He was a pleasure to work with as a coach. He did the right thing all the time.

Whenever he played for me, he did not let himself or England down. Euro '96 proved a near miss for him, but I had to make room for some younger players in the squad. Having said that, I was delighted to be able to restore him to the England side when I first took over and take him past the 50-cap mark.

CAREER
HIGHLIGHTS

1961   Born 18 January to father Sammy and mother Catherine in Newcastle-upon-Tyne. Older brothers George and Ronnie, and younger sister Sandra.

1972   Joins Wallsend Boys' Club (wins first game 17–2!) and Longbenton Youth Club.

1975   Plays for South Northumberland Boys.

1977   Plays for his first men's team, his brothers' pub side, The Fusilier.

1978   Unsuccessful trials with Gillingham and Cambridge United.

1979   Signs for Carlisle United. Debut for reserve team at home to Wrexham (scores hat-trick) on 18 August. Debut for first team at home to Blackburn on 21 August (result 1–1.) First goal against Chester.

1981   Marries Sandra Devlin on 22 April, leaving for Vancouver Whitecaps the following week for fee of £275,000, still Carlisle's record sale.

1981/82 Plays under managership of Johnny Giles. Loaned back to Carlisle for NASL close season, playing 19 League matches (plus three as substitute) and scoring four goals as Carlisle finish runners-up in (the old) 3rd Division and gain promotion. Scores for Vancouver in friendly against Manchester United after 13 seconds (after United kicked off!). A second goal in the 3–0 win persuades United boss Ron Atkinson to pay £250,000 for him.

1982/83 Plays 78 minutes for United at Old Trafford in League Cup-tie versus Bournemouth, before being replaced by Norman Whiteside. Twice named as substitute in League matches without coming onto the field, and returns to Vancouver.

1983/84 Joins Newcastle United for £150,000. First match is a 1–1 draw at Barnsley. Newcastle win promotion to (the old) 1st Division, aided by Peter's 20 goals in 35 League appearances.

1984/85 Scores 17 goals in 38 League matches as Newcastle finish 14th, Jack Charlton having replaced Arthur Cox as manager.

1985/86 Another mid-table position for Newcastle as Peter hits 19 League goals under yet another manager, Jack Charlton's resignation allowing Willie McFaul to take over the hot seat. Newcastle crash 1–8 at West Ham, Peter's heaviest defeat in top-class soccer, and he concedes the final three goals himself as he dons the goalkeeper's jersey, the Magpies having lost two keepers through injury. Celebrates 200th League appearance, against West

Brom on 11 January. International recognition at last! First cap in Cairo as substitute for Gary Lineker as England beat Egypt 4–0. He goes on to make nine appearances for England, scoring against Mexico in a warm-up match for the World Cup. He misses only one of the World Cup matches in Mexico (against Morocco), and scores against Paraguay, before England go down to Argentina and Maradona's infamous 'Hand of God'.

1986/87   Disillusioned with Newcastle's apparent lack of ambition at the time, he is reluctant to sign another contract, and Liverpool buy him in July for £1.9 million. Six more England caps. Peter finally plays at Wembley for the first time in his 10th appearance for his country as England beat Northern Ireland 3–0 in a European Championship Group match.

1987/88   Peter struggles early on with Liverpool, not finding his form until the midway stage of the season. Liverpool equal Leeds United's record for unbeaten games since the beginning of the season, and Peter's winning goal against Spurs at Anfield clinches the title. In the Cup Final, though, Liverpool's 'Double' aspirations are thwarted by Wimbledon, as Peter has a controversial 'goal' disallowed, and Dave Beasant saves John Aldridge's penalty. For England, Peter wins a further eleven caps, and scores four times in a friendly against Aylesbury United. The season ends in disappointment as England lose all three games in the European Championship Finals in West Germany, Peter playing on the losing side against Eire and Holland.

1988/89 Scores 100th League goal, against Southampton at
The Dell on 24 September. For the second season
running, Liverpool almost win the 'Double',
triumphing over neighbours Everton in the Cup
Final, but losing a tense title-decider to rivals
Arsenal in the dying seconds of their final match.
Peter's disappointment is alleviated the next day as
wife Sandra gives birth to their first child Drew. The
previous month, Peter is briefly involved in the
Hillsborough Disaster, Liverpool's Cup semi-final
against Nottingham Forest being abandoned after
six minutes after fans are crushed to death on the
terracing. In winning eight more England caps,
Peter captains his country for the first time against
Israel and scores twice in a 5–0 win against Albania
at Wembley, his only international goals that
season. Turns down a move to Marseilles for £3.6
million, and the French club sign former Newcastle
colleague Chris Waddle.

1989/90 Peter scores the winning goal in the Charity Shield
at Wembley against Arsenal, and wins another
League title medal. Further Cup glory is denied by
Crystal Palace who upset the Reds 4–3 in a
dramatic semi-final, despite Liverpool having won
an earlier League clash 9–0! It's World Cup year,
and after an unconvincing start, England only fail
to reach the Final after losing to West Germany in a
penalty shoot-out. Eleven appearances (but no
goals) bring his caps total to 45.

1990/91 Liverpool finish second in the League, and lose a
marathon Cup-tie to Everton. Kenny Dalglish

resigns as manager, and some newspapers suggest that Peter was responsible for the decision. Ronnie Moran takes over as caretaker manager before Graeme Souness arrives from Rangers to take permanent charge. Under new England manager Graham Taylor, Peter only makes four more appearances (two as sub.). His last minute goal against Poland in a European Championship game at Wembley, despite being spectacular, fails to impress the new England boss. He now has 49 caps.

1991/92   In a cloak-and-dagger arrangement during a pre-season tour of Sweden, Graeme Souness sells Peter to Everton for £1 million. Peter plays in every League match, scoring 15 goals, plus four in the Cup. However, his international career seems to be over.

1992/93   Another mediocre season for Everton, although Peter manages another 10 League goals, including the winner in a 'derby' against Liverpool, accomplishing the rare feat of scoring winning goals for both sides in Merseyside confrontations. Daughter Stacey born 26 June.

1993/94   In the close season, Derby County try to buy him for £1.2 million, but Kevin Keegan offers £1.4 million and Peter is on his way back to Tyneside. He returns to Anfield for a testimonial match, where his cheekbone is broken by a flailing elbow from new Reds' signing Neil Ruddock. Misses the start of the season, but still scores 21 goals in 35 League appearances as Newcastle finish third in the Premiership and qualify for Europe. New England boss Terry Venables recalls Peter, who wins his 50th cap against Denmark.

1994/95 Peter plays in Europe (the UEFA Cup) for the first time. Ends the season with 15 goals from 44 appearances as Newcastle finish sixth in Premiership. Wins his 57th cap against Sweden in the Umbro tournament at Elland Road. Receives an MBE in the Queen's Honours list.

1995/96 Wins his 58th and 59th caps when he comes on as substitute against Portugal and China. Scores his 100th league goal for Newcastle against Bolton Wanderers. Makes 40 appearances and scores 11 goals as Newcastle United finish runners-up to Manchester United in the Premiership.

Summary (up to end of 1995/96 season)

	League		League Cup		FA Cup	
	Apps	*Goals*	*Apps*	*Goals*	*Apps*	*Goals*
Carlisle	102	22	6	0	15	7
Newcastle	147	61	10	3	6	2
Liverpool	131	46	14	1	25	11
Everton	81	25	8	5	4	1
Newcastle	104	42	6	3	15	5
TOTALS	565	196	44	12	65	26

England   59 caps (incl 14 as substitute)   9 goals

Honours

League Division 1   1987/88, 1989/90

FA Cup   1988 (runners-up), 1989

INDEX